Coláiste Oideachais Mhuire Gan Smal

Luimneach

LANGUAGE AND LITERACY

LANGUAGE AND LITERACY: THE SELECTED WRITINGS OF KENNETH S. GOODMAN

Volume II
Reading, Language and the Classroom Teacher

Edited by
Frederick V. Gollasch

Routledge & Kegan Paul
London, Boston, Melbourne and Henley

First published in 1982
by Routledge & Kegan Paul Ltd
39 Store Street,
London WC1E 7DD,
9 Park Street,
Boston, Mass. 02108, USA,
296 Beaconsfield Parade, Middle Park,
Melbourne, 3206, Australia, and
Broadway House,
Newtown Road,
Henley-on-Thames,
Oxon RG9 1EN
Printed in Great Britain by
The Thetford Press, Norfolk

Library of Congress Cataloging in Publication Data (Revised)

Goodman, Kenneth S.
Language and literacy.
Bibliography: p.
Includes index.
Contents: v. 1. Process, theory, research -
v. 2. Reading, language, and the classroom teacher.
1. Reading, Psychology of. 2 Psycholinguistics.
I. Title.
BF456.R2G63   401'.9   81-11848

ISBN 0-7100-0875-9 (v. 1)
ISBN 0-7100-9005-6 (v. 2)

CONTENTS

FOREWORD

In the early 1960s, as a doctoral student at UCLA, I became
interested in looking at reading. My interest grew from two
sources. One was my concern as a graduate student to familiarize myself as fully as possible with research and theory relating
to reading. The other was my curiosity about the implications
of the explosion of activity in the field of linguistics for education.

The more I read the more convinced I became that linguistics
had to have the key to some of the unanswered questions in
reading. As I pushed that idea I also realized that there were
many significant questions linguistics generates about reading
that had not even been asked before.

But an extensive survey of the literature in reading and
linguistics showed only a handful of writings in this field. That
left me with a dilemma. Either I was moving down a blind alley
others had already abandoned or I was out at the frontier of
the field. Events of the next few years made clear that the latter was the case. One can not now pick up a text or journal
dealing with reading without finding applications of linguistics.
I started with a few key assumptions:

Reading is language.
Readers are users of language.
Linguistic concepts and methods can explain reading.
Nothing readers do is accidental. It all results from
interaction with text.

As my work progressed, I came to realize that reading is a
psycholinguistic process, one in which thought and language
interact. I realized that readers seek meaning, that as they
read they are engaging in comprehending, constructing meaning through interaction with print.

The vehicle I chose to examine reading was simple: have
subjects read orally whole, real, language texts they hadn't
seen before and then analyze what they did as they read.
What readers did was produce miscues; not everything matched
what was expected; some of the responses were unexpected.
But the unexpected responses showed the reader at work.
Through these miscues we could see reading in process.

The analysis of these miscues led to my conclusion that reading could be characterized as a 'psycholinguistic guessing
game.' The reader makes minimal use of cues, engages in

vii

tentative information processing, predicts; samples, confirms or disconfirms and reprocesses or corrects when necessary. The reader is actively seeking to make sense of written language.

These concepts are the core of the theory of reading that I've developed. This reading theory and the model that represents it have been continuously developed in interaction with the analysis of miscues of real readers reading different texts. The model is a macro model, that is, it attempts to deal with the whole of the reading process.

As linguists, psycholinguists, and cognitive psychologists began to turn their attention to reading, they brought to some of the phenomena of reading new terminology which has been applied by others to my theory. It has been characterized as an analysis-by-synthesis view, an inside-out view, and a top-down view. None of these are terms that I have used myself. While each, depending on whose definition you use, has some applicability, none captures the essential meaning - seeking, interactive essence of the theory.

I was, and have remained through all my work, an educationist and a teacher educator. This volume focuses mainly on theory and research. But the reader should understand that my constant motivation has been to understand reading and other language processes in order to contribute to the improvement of teaching and learning.

That may explain why I can not be satisfied with limited research designs or perspectives with leaps from laboratory experiments to methods and materials. It may explain my insistence on a reality base for assertions about reading and learning to read.

A primary motivation for bringing this volume together is to make my work more accessible to the field. Perhaps because my work has been widely quoted in recent years, many references and treatments of my ideas are now being based on secondary sources rather than my own statements. It's hoped that greater accessibility will make it possible for readers themselves to check out representations and characterizations of my beliefs and convictions.

Publication, like all language activity, involves risk-taking. Every author must wonder, as I have, whether some day he or she will regret having made public statements he or she no longer believes. But it is only through public interchange of ideas that growth in any field or in the individuals involved takes place. In my own case, the response to my published work has done a great deal to shape and encourage it. As I read through the work published here, there were certainly times when I encountered statements I would no longer make in the same way today. Usually that was due to development and refinement of my position. Sometimes, however, an early exploration has given way to a view that is quite different. Just for example:

1 My early uncertainty about the need to go from print to sound in reading has given way to a deep conviction that reading and listening are parallel processes with no necessary recoding.

2 My early belief that dialect divergence contributes barriers to reading comprehension has been disproven by my own research.

3 It has taken me a long time to purge fully from my view of reading the preoccupation with words which I feel still pervades the field.

Fred Gollasch was of inestimable help to me in selecting these articles. He brought an outside perspective that we hope has made it possible to avoid overlap and to make the delicate decisions of which works are sufficiently obsolete that they might cause confusion if included.

A colleague recently shared with me a statement from William James cited by Abraham Kaplan, which in some sense seems to parallel closely some of the reactions to my work over the years. At the risk of seeming immodest, I offer it here:

The three classic stages of a theory's career. First a new theory is attacked as absurd; then it is admitted to be true, but obvious and insignificant; finally it is seen as so important that its adversaries claim that they themselves discovered it.

Kenneth S. Goodman
Tucson, Arizona
February, 1979

ACKNOWLEDGMENTS

The Introduction, Reading: A Conversation with Kenneth Goodman, was first published by Scott, Foresman in 1976. Copyright © 1976 Scott, Foresman and Company.

Chapter 1, The Search Called Reading, first appeared in Helen Robinson (ed.), 'Coordinating Reading Instruction,' Scott, Foresman, 1971. Reprinted by permission.

Chapter 2, Reading: You Can Get Back to Kansas Anytime You're Ready, Dorothy, first appeared in 'English Journal,' November 1974. Copyright © 1974 by the National Council of Teachers of English. Reprinted by permission.

Chapter 3, The Language Children Bring to School: How to Build on It, first appeared in 'The Grade Teacher,' March 1969, pp. 135-42.

Chapter 4, Reading: The Key Is in Children's Language, first appeared in 'The Reading Teacher,' vol. 25, March 1972, pp. 505-8. Reprinted by permission of the International Reading Association.

Chapter 5, Effective Teachers of Reading Know Language and Children, first appeared in 'Elementary English,' September 1974. Copyright © 1974 by the National Council of Teachers of English. Reprinted by permission.

Chapter 6, Children's Language and Experience: A Place to Begin, first appeared in Helen Robinson (ed.), 'Coordinating Reading Instruction,' Scott, Foresman, 1971. Reprinted by permission.

Chapter 7, Strategies for Increasing Comprehension in Reading, first appeared in Robinson, 'Improving Reading in the Intermediate Years,' Scott, Foresman, 1973, pp. 59-71. Reprinted by permission.

Chapter 8, Comprehension-centered Reading Instruction, first appeared in 'Proceedings of the 1970 Claremont Reading Conference.' Reprinted by permission.

xii   *Acknowledgments*

Chapter 9, Orthography in a Theory of Reading Instruction, first appeared in 'Elementary English,' December 1972. Copyright © 1972 by the National Council of Teachers of English. Reprinted by permission.

Chapter 10, Kenneth S. Goodman and Olive Niles, Behind the Eye: What Happens in Reading, first appeared in 'Reading: Process and Program,' National Council of Teachers of English, 1970. Copyright © 1970 by the National Council of Teachers of English. Reprinted by permission.

Chapter 11, Kenneth S. Goodman, Yetta M. Goodman and Carolyn L. Burke, Language in Teacher Education, first appeared in 'Journal of Research and Development in Education,' vol. 7, no. 1, Fall 1973, pp. 66-71. Reprinted by permission.

Chapter 12, Linguistic Insights Which Teachers May Apply, first appeared in 'Education,' vol. 88, no. 4, April-May 1968. Copyright © 1968 The Bobbs-Merrill Company. Reprinted by permission.

Chapter 13, Linguistics in a Relevant Curriculum, first appeared in 'Education,' April-May 1969, pp. 303-7. Reprinted by permission of the Bobbs-Merrill Company and Project Innovation.

Chapter 14, Let's Dump the Uptight Model in English, first appeared in 'Elementary School Journal,' October 1969.

Chapter 15, Words and Morphemes in Reading, first appeared in Kenneth S. Goodman and James T. Fleming (eds), 'Psycholinguistics and the Teaching of Reading,' International Reading Association, 1969. Reprinted by permission.

Chapter 16, On Valuing Diversity in Language: Overview, first appeared in 'Childhood Education,' December 1969. Reprinted by permission of the Association for Childhood Education International, 3615 Wisconsin Avenue, N.W., Washington, D.C. Copyright © 1969 by the Association.

Chapter 17, Up-Tight Ain't Right, first appeared in 'School Library Journal,' October 1972. Reprinted by permission of R.R. Bowker/A Xerox Corporation.

Chapter 18, Dialect Barriers to Reading Comprehension, first appeared in 'Elementary English,' December 1965. Copyright © 1965 by the National Council of Teachers of English. Reprinted by permission.

Chapter 19, Kenneth S. Goodman and Catherine Buck, Dialect Barriers to Reading Comprehension: Revisited, first appeared in 'The Reading Teacher,' October 1973. Reprinted by permission of the International Reading Association.

Chapter 20, Urban Dialects and Reading Instruction, first appeared in J.P. Kender (ed.), 'Teaching Reading - Not by Decoding Alone,' Interstate Printers and Publishers, 1971. Reprinted by permission.

Chapter 21, Kenneth S. and Yetta M. Goodman, Spelling Ability of a Self-taught Reader, first appeared in 'Elementary School Journal,' vol. 64, no. 4, December 1963.

Chapter 22, Manifesto for a Reading Revolution, first appeared in Malcolm Douglas (ed.), '40th Yearbook, Claremont Reading Conference,' 1976, pp. 16-28. Reprinted by permission.

Chapter 23, Acquiring Literacy Is Natural: Who Skilled Cock Robin?, first appeared in 'Theory into Practice,' vol. 16, no. 5, December 1977, published by the College of Education, The Ohio State University. Reprinted by permission.

Chapter 24, Kenneth S. and Yetta M. Goodman, Learning to Read Is Natural, first appeared in L.B. Resnick and P.A. Weaver (eds), 'Theory and Practice of Early Reading,' Lawrence Erlbaum Associates, 1979, pp. 137-55. Reprinted by permission.

Chapter 25, Do You Have to be Smart to Read? Do You Have to Read to be Smart?, first appeared in 'The Reading Teacher,' April 1975, pp. 625-32. Reprinted by permission of the International Reading Association.

Chapter 26, Testing in Reading: A General Critique, first appeared in Robert Ruddell (ed.), 'Accountability and Reading Instruction: Critical Issues,' National Council of Teachers of English, 1973. Copyright © 1973 by the National Council of Teachers of English. Reprinted by permission.

Chapter 27, Minimum Competencies: A Moral View, first appeared in 'Minimum Competency Standards, Three Points of View,' International Reading Association, 1978. Reprinted by permission.

Chapter 28, Promises, Promises, first appeared in 'The Reading Teacher,' vol. 24, no. 4, January 1971, pp. 356-67. Reprinted by permission of the International Reading Association.

Chapter 29, Military-Industrial Thinking Finally Captures the Schools!, first appeared in 'Educational Leadership,' February 1974. Reprinted with permission of the Association for Supervision and Curriculum Development. Copyright © 1974 by the Association for Supervision and Curriculum Development. All rights reserved.

Chapter 30, The President's Education Program: A Response, first appeared in 'Slate,' vol. 3, no. 2, March 1978. Copyright

Chapter 31, What Is Basic About Reading?, first appeared in 'The Arts and the Creation of Meaning,' National Art Education Association, 1976. Reprinted by permission.

The Afterword, The Know-More and the Know-Nothing Movements in Reading: A Personal Response, first appeared in 'Language Arts,' vol. 55, no. 8, September 1979, pp. 657-63.

We offer as an introduction this recorded conversation with
Kenneth Goodman. It should serve the purpose of providing
the reader with a quick overview of his work and focus. (A
detailed review of the Goodman work is to be found in the
introductory chapter to Volume I, the companion of this volume.)

INTRODUCTION
Reading: A Conversation with Kenneth Goodman

Dr. Goodman, you've been described as a 'psycholinguist.'
Could you explain what that term means?
It's not nearly so stuffy or difficult as it sounds. In a broad
sense, psycholinguistics is the intersection of interest between
psychology and linguistics. My point of view is specialized:
I'm interested in how the language process works in reading to
communicate meaning – how we get meaning from written language.

I know you've been involved in reading research for about a
dozen years. What I don't know is what got you interested.
A very simple kind of thing. I was finishing my doctoral work,
getting involved in psycholinguistics, and trying to familiarize
myself with the research literature on reading. But the more I
thought about language and the more I read about reading
research, the more convinced I became that a key mistake had
been made in not treating reading as language, in not being
concerned with how the reader gets meaning from print.

So when I got to Wayne, I made the simplest, most basic test
I could. I had children read something they hadn't read before,
orally, so that I could observe. And I discovered that people
don't always read what you expect them to read. That excited
me; here were all the things happening linguistically that I had
sensed would happen.

That is, kids were acting like language processors. They were
using their understanding of language, bringing it to their
reading. Even little ones were doing things like substituting
'the' for 'a.' Kids were making miscues – variations from the
text – that couldn't be a matter of simple word confusion, miscues that definitely had to do with the structure of the language. They were attempts to get at meaning.

For a while, I put everything in a single kind of cause-effect:
this child did that because of dialect; that child did that because of shape; another child did that because of sound. And
then I began to realize that reading is a complex process, that
all these things are interrelated.

So with my research staff, I developed a system for classify-
ing the miscues kids make. And what we're doing is comparing
what they do with what we expect them to do. From that we
get very powerful insights into how the reading process
operates.

What's your definition of the reading process?
It *is* a process, a process of getting meaning from print. And
this process has two characteristics. One is that the reader is
attempting to get at meaning. The second is that he or she is
using whole language to do so.

What do you mean by 'whole language'?
We read for information, insights, ideas, entertainment. We
read for meaning. This meaning is embedded not in individual
words but in the whole context – the sentence, the paragraph,
sometimes the entire selection.

*Many times, you've been quoted as saying that reading should
be taught as an extension of natural language development. But
is learning to read as natural as learning to speak?*
It *is* as natural if you consider the differences between written
language and oral language. Oral language is a face-to-face,
here-and-now kind of thing. Written language comes into existence when a society needs to communicate over time and space.
You need written language to survive in a literate society, but
children take a while to realize that.
    Kids learn to speak because they can and because they have
a need to communicate. We can put learning to read in the context of that need. I don't mean that you should say to a six-
year-old, 'Learn to read, because when you grow up....' Kids
don't learn under those kinds of circumstances. For children
to learn to read there has to be some kind of reason why they
need to read *now*.
    Children have an awareness of the need to understand print.
One of the things we're discovering is that we've underestimated the amount of natural learning to read that takes
place in society. We've been looking in the wrong places. We
put a book in a six-year-old's hand and say, 'Here, read it.'
When he or she can't, we say, 'See, that child can't read.'
Meanwhile, we're ignoring the fact that children can read
McDonald's and Burger King and Alpha-Bits and Count Chocula[1]
and all kinds of things that have meaning for them.

What can teachers do to build upon this natural reading ability?
The key thing in the early stages is to create what I would call
a literate environment, where kids are constantly exposed to
print, made aware of its functions, how it works, its subtle
differences and similarities. It's very difficult to grow up in
such an environment and *not* realize that what tells you whether
it's the women's room or the men's room is the stuff on the
door.
    We can help kids to be more aware of how print works and
what's in it for them. We can take a group of kids for a walk
around the school the first day – kindergarten kids. (And I'm
not for a strong push to get all kids reading before they get
to first grade. That's wrong, too, because some of them are

going to take longer to decide it's important for them.) We can
say to those kids, 'What can you read?' 'What do you think it
says on that door?' We can talk about safety on the way to
school. 'What's a stop sign?' 'What are those signs on street
corners?' 'Why do they have to be there?' We can get kids into
print awareness.

We can find simple, natural ways of letting print talk to kids,
get them to realize the meanings that are associated with print.
Lots of things teachers have done traditionally fulfil this
function: Calendars in the room. Attendance charts that the
kids are involved in. Little message boards. Those kinds of
things.

And of course, there's reading aloud to children. We can take
something the kids have particularly enjoyed, reread it while
they follow, then stop at an important word and let the kids
continue. Some people say, 'That's not reading, that's memoriz-
ing.' But these things that go on in the initial stages are the
things that make kids ready to read.

If children look at a McDonald's logo and say, 'That says
McDonald's,' they're connecting print with meaning. They're
responding to print and building the relationship between what
something says and what it means. Those are the initial stages.
That's how reading readiness is developed. When they're learning to talk, it works the same way.

*Can you explain the relationship between learning to read and
learning to talk?*
Children learn language from whole to part. We have the illusion
that very young kids learn words and then put them together.
But in fact, when kids say 'Eat!' that's not just a word, that's
a whole communication. Every parent knows that.

Wise parents come more than halfway. They answer 'Eat!' with
'You're hungry; you want to eat.' That way kids hear language
as it should be spoken, develop a sense of how to handle it.

Sometimes parents will say, 'It's not "Eat," it's "I want to
eat."' But in cases like these, kids continue to say 'Eat' until
they're ready to say more. Very young children feature the
most highly stressed parts of the language because they can't
control longer utterances. Then, for a while they may get by
with structures like 'No go there.' But in the course of their
development, as they have more complicated things to say, they
figure out ways of saying them. And as they gain control of
the language, things like prepositions, verbs, and articles
begin to appear in their *proper* positions. And that's because
children learn the structure of their language while they learn
the language itself.

Kids don't learn to talk by imitation. They don't learn to talk
by being given lessons in it. They learn by interacting with
language users. When parents respond to what kids are saying,
language learning is facilitated. Kids see speaking as worthwhile; it gets them what they want, what they need. And the

same thing is true in written language. For children to learn
to read, they have to have the opportunity to interact with
books. And they have to grow to see reading as a productive,
worthwhile experience.

Suppose we taught kids to talk the way we attempt to teach
them to read. Can you picture a parent standing over a crib
and saying sounds at the kid and then blending those sounds
into words? It would be terribly frustrating. The kid couldn't
handle it because it doesn't make sense. It doesn't make sense
in reading instruction, either.

*So the teacher creates an environment where children can
interact with books. How do children learn to read in it?*
Very much the way they learn to talk and listen. That is, they
become aware first of wholes and their relationship to specific
messages. And then with teachers' help they begin to develop
a sense of the structure and of the relationship of part to whole.
They develop a sense of what a word is, come to see that each
word has a unique configuration, grow to understand the parts
that make up the whole.

One of the big mistakes we've made in reading instruction was
to impose adult logic and afterthought. Sure it's sensible to
think that in learning you should start with the pieces and move
toward the whole. What we didn't understand is the fact that in
taking language apart, divorcing it from meaning, we're starting
with the most abstract and moving toward the concrete. That's
the opposite of how kids learn, particularly the opposite of how
they learn language.

*Do you have to be smart to learn to read through this kind of
whole-language approach?*
No, because language is learned from whole to part, not from
part to whole. To children the whole isn't a collection of parts,
it's a complete unit. So, paradoxical as it may sound, to go
from the whole to the part is to proceed from the simple to the
complex. The very kids we most worry about are the ones who
are least able to handle the abstractions we create when we
take language apart. The kids who have everything going for
them can deal with abstraction. Besides, they're so success-
oriented, they'll put up with stuff that doesn't make sense.
Those kids will survive. It's the other kids who need the most
meaningful, relevant things.

Teachers have got to get over the notion that learning to
read is by its very nature a difficult task. Some teachers'
reactions to a story called The Lion's Tail[2] is an example of this
kind of thinking. The Lion's Tail doesn't have a controlled
vocabulary. It's written in natural language so predictable
that it almost reads itself. Because children can read The Lion's
Tail so easily, some teachers say, 'But of course that isn't reading.' It isn't reading in the sense that if you put the words on
flash cards the kids could tell you what all of them are. But if

you accept that reading is learned from whole to part, from familiar to unfamiliar, then it is reading.

It'll be a while before children know every word in isolation that they can read in context – and it'll take longer for the slower learners. But as children find things that fit their predictions, they build confidence and ability to read. With the teacher's help, they learn to use some of the strategies for reading they've been using in listening. They discover that the grammatical patterns are the same, that they can predict meaning in print as they can in oral language.

How does language experience figure into your concept of beginning reading instruction?
Language experience as an approach has a very sound basis because it says, 'OK, here is an experience kids have had. We'll get them to talk about it and we'll write it down. That will be a good thing for them to read.'

The experience story has almost all the characteristics that reading material for children needs. It's meaningful. We know it's meaningful because they said it. It's language as they know and use it because they've just produced it. It's relevant in the sense that it's something out of their own experience.

The one needed characteristic it *doesn't* have is that it's not new. The kids already know what it means, and the basic task of reading is to get at meaning. So you have to be careful that you don't restrict the experiences kids have to their own language material. You've got to present them with something new, so they can figure out what it means. And this new material should be written in natural language patterns, language that reflects the way people speak.

One of the things that's most important in early reading material, maybe the only really important thing, is its predictability. Children have to find what they're looking for, what they expect to find. So the text has to be predictable in terms of ideas, concepts, language, whatever. 'Natural' isn't a mystic term, then. It simply means that language has to be what the kid expects.

And what determines what children expect language to be?
That's determined by the grammar of the language. I'm not talking about prescriptive grammar – the rules of how people 'ought to speak.' From a linguist's point of view, grammar is the structure of the language. Everybody, regardless of the status of their language, speaks in a manner that is structurally correct. Everybody learns this grammar, particularly the rules of grammar that make it possible to produce new sentences – things you haven't heard before.

These rules of language – can we state them?
No one can state them all. Children can state very few, if any. But some things that we know we can't state. They've reached

the level of intuition. Language is one of them. We learn it so
early and so well.... When four-year-olds say 'Jimmy hit
Tommy,' they're showing the basic control of the rule for subject, verb, object. Because they would never say 'Jimmy hit
Tommy' and mean 'Tommy hit Jimmy.'

Kids can play all kinds of games with language. They can
laugh at puns, at mistakes, at their own misarticulations. You
can say to kids, 'I was walking down the —' and they'll give
you a noun. They won't be able to identify it as such, but they
know what sounds right, what makes sense in that sentence.

*In a natural-language setting what does the teacher do to
facilitate the child's learning?*
Gets kids to feel the need to know by reading to them, questioning them about the print that plays a part in their everyday
lives. Keeps plugging away at the idea that printed language,
like spoken language, is supposed to make sense. Teaches kids
to recognize the various cues that will help them get sense out
of print – the context of the passage, the structure of the sentences, the graphic aids, their knowledge of sounds. And
within that, keeps asking, 'What would fit there?' 'What do you
think it's going to mean?' Gets the kids to use their own
language resources. Gets them to predict. Keeps asking them
questions that are designed to get them to look for the information they need.

Teachers also need to encourage kids to take risks: Say, 'You
may not know exactly what this word is, but what do you think
it might be? What would make sense here?' This is the way to
help kids get into the right area of meaning.

When children know the area of meaning, the teacher can say,
'Can you think of anything that looks like that and can fit
there?' This kind of question helps kids use their knowledge of
both graphic and structural cues to get to meaning. The ability
to integrate the various cues is what teachers should be building.

I don't think we should *just* teach kids the skill of attacking
words. We should teach them what to do when they're in a
situation of having some sense of what a word means but aren't
sure what the word is. Which is what an adult reader does.
When you're reading and you come to some term that is either
unfamiliar or vague, you try to get a sense of what it means.
Only when you think you know what it means but aren't certain,
do you go to a dictionary to check yourself out.

What about skills teaching, then?
You have to put skills in the context of meaning. That's where
they have the most value. That's where they maintain their
proper proportion. And there they won't lead to the development of problems that eventually interfere with learning to
read. In fact, children learn best this way because skills taught
in context don't result in incorrect generalizations which then

have to be overcome.

Take the common emphasis on phonic skills. When you isolate a letter or a sound, you make it more abstract, and you also change its relative value. If I give kids the sentence, 'The girl is in the garden,' I can talk about the initial letter of 'girl' and the sound that it relates to. But if I give the lesson backwards, if I start with the sound of 'g,' then I'm saying that each letter has a value - a meaning. That's not true. The value is dependent on the sequence that it's in. And the importance of noticing and using a particular graphic cue is exaggerated because in context it works together with everything else.

Readers use the same cues to get meaning as they would to identify letters and words. We depend upon features that are distinctive, that are significant in the system. But it's the mileage we get out of what we use that counts. If we focus children on identifying letters or words, they may have to use much more information with much less efficiency. The key to efficiency in reading is minimizing the amount of graphic information we need to get to meaning. Learning what *not* to pay attention to. And that contradicts what we've tended to teach kids to do, which is to concentrate on using all available cues.

Teachers can help kids learn skills, not by directing every step but by saying, 'OK, let's read,' and then letting the kids figure out how to do it. Giving help where it's needed, but letting kids make mistakes. That's how they learn. Sure, give skills instruction; alert kids to what they need to know to be good readers. But give your instruction in the context of meaning. Teach your kids to be intolerant of nonsense, to look for the sense in everything they read.

Can a child be taught to read for sense, for meaning?
The most natural thing for a child to do is to read for meaning. Right now, people are talking about a back-to-basics movement. Well, there isn't anything more basic to language than meaning. And in fact, back-to-basics ought to mean getting back to the clear focus on the relationship between print and meaning. Phonics isn't back to basics. Skills isn't back to basics. The basic thing in language is to get at meaning. So in this sense you don't have to teach kids to read for meaning. You have to encourage their natural tendency and not distract them.

Could you define what you mean by 'meaning'?
It's a hard word to define, because meaning varies from one person to another. In reading, you're trying to get as close as you can to the author's meaning. But your interpretation can't help but be colored by your knowledge, experience, background, needs.

So in the context in which we're talking, I use 'meaning' to mean comprehending. Comprehending is the process of constructing meaning. Now, one of the misconceptions about comprehension is that the teacher's goal is to get the kids to agree with his or her interpretation. That's not the goal at all. The goal is to make children meaning-oriented, to help them realize that if they keep saying, 'Does it make sense?' they have the resources to get sense out of it.

If we, as adults, read something that doesn't make sense, we're likely to blame the writer or at least conclude that the piece is something we're not prepared for. We don't often assume that we failed to get any sense out of it because we're poor readers. But children don't know that; their tendency is to think they've failed as readers. And they've got to be constantly reassured.

Reading is a psycholinguistic guessing game - and by 'guess' I mean the *informed* response that you make when you're not quite sure. That guess is based on many factors: your personal experience, your knowledge of the language, the context in which a word or sentence appears, the graphic cues provided by the text. You can dress 'guess' up in fancy terms and call it tentative information processing. But it really is guessing in the sense that you have an idea of what's coming before it actually comes.

Are you talking about an 'educated guess'?
Educated in the sense that you're using the sum total of the information that you have. It's a guessing game in the sense that you almost immediately form an hypothesis about the structure you're dealing with. You know it's a question before you've gotten to the question mark. You know it's a dependent clause because of certain grammatical cues - it started with 'when,' for example - before you get to the point where you have to know this in order to handle subsequent information.

It's guessing in the sense that you make predictions. And you're not simply predicting the next word, you're predicting the meaning. You gather information that either confirms or disputes your prediction. If it confirms, you're satisfied; you go ahead, you keep looking for meaning. Your focus is not on 'What's that word?' but on 'What does it all mean?'

Sure, there are going to be kids who substitute 'house' for 'home.' Both these words fit a lot of contexts; the kids are striving for meaning. If 'home' fits as well as 'house' and if they've predicted 'home' instead of 'house,' they're not even going to notice that they've miscued. And there's no need, at this point, for the teacher to correct them, because they've gotten the meaning.

I don't mean that teachers should settle for the miscue, never call the kid's attention to it. Both 'house' and 'home' have special nuances of meaning. We want kids to sense these. So later, the teacher can go back to the words 'house' and 'home.' She or he can put them on the board or on flashcards and ask the child, 'What differences do you see between these two words? How do they differ in meaning?' 'Later' is the key here. Keep that teaching procedure for later; don't let it interfere with the child's attempts to get to the right area of meaning.

How do you answer the people who talk about the rights of the writer?
It would be the ultimate arrogance on the part of the writer to think that he or she could totally control what someone else understands. Of course, it's the intention of the reader to get as close as possible to the writer's intended meaning – that's what communication is all about. But two people's interpretation of something is never identical.

How is a teacher to know if children have comprehended something?
You ask them. We've a long way to go in figuring out how to measure comprehension. We're tangled up in the issue of what the kids knew before and what they've learned. We get tangled up in being sure we understand their answers, being sure they understand the question. We get tangled up with the fact that we're judging children's comprehension after the reading in terms of their ability to give back information.

But the fact is that, if you read something, you're going to have a fairly good notion of whether you understand it or not. Kids can do that, too.

So if children can restate the ideas in terms that make sense to them...
...That make sense to them and hang together and are defensible in terms of the text. Of course, sometimes you'll want kids to do more with their own resources, to get closer to the meaning than they've come. So you give them the information they need to build background, understand concepts. But the real beauty of asking children, 'What did this mean to you? What did you get out of it?' is that their answers will provide you with insights into their thinking, will show you the kind of background and help they need to more fully comprehend something. Then, you start your teaching from that point.

There's a general proposition that I subscribe to, and a lot of other people have for a long time: The object of education is to take kids from where they are to as far as they can go. I believe in that for two reasons: One is because I think it's the legitimate function of education in our society, but the other is strictly in terms of pedagogy. You get the best success when you carefully try to understand what kids are doing and why they're doing it. You find out what they've learned and then you build on it. You draw on what they can do to expand their knowledge. You build on their vocabulary, concepts, the ability to handle print.

What about teaching the individual word – how does this figure into your ideas?
What does it mean to identify a word? Does it mean you recognize

the written form of a word you use? Does it mean you learn the meaning of a word you didn't know the meaning of? I don't know.

One thing I do know is that a person can correctly say a word and not know its meaning. On the other hand, somebody can stumble and mispronounce and yet give you a definition.

There's this pervasive tendency to think of language as a bag of words. But you can't get meaning out of language simply by processing individual words. As a matter of fact, though it contradicts common sense, it's easy to demonstrate that you can't really know what the words mean until you know what the sentence, the paragraph, means. If you take a word like 'read,' which can be pronounced rēd and spelled r-e-a-d, or pronounced 'red' and still spelled r-e-a-d, the only way you can identify it is to know the meaning of the sentence in which it appears. Over and over again this happens.

As I've said, you get to meaning and the words just kind of fall into place. And they fall into place in such a way that you suddenly know a word that you couldn't have known in isolation. Little kids have literally said to me when I've asked, 'How did you know that?', 'The words just came into my mouth.' The meaning creates the context that makes it all fit together. And within the meaning, the graphic cues make it more likely for the kid to come up with the right word.

Teachers ask, 'How will the kids read the sentence if they don't know all the words?' In thinking this way, teachers are discounting what children know about the structure of language. It's this knowledge of structure that makes it possible for kids to realize, 'I don't know what this word is, but I know what it has to mean. So I bet I know what it is, because what else would look like this.' This grammatical competence is a resource that is constantly dipped into. Look at all the words kids read without difficulty in context, words that can't be sounded out.

You've got to encourage kids to take risks on words. When they do take risks, they tend to be right or in the right area. If they don't take risks, they don't develop the confidence and strategies they need to handle the reading process. What we've tended to do with our focus on getting each word right is to penalize kids for taking risks. If children take a chance and it turns out they're wrong and they get called on it, they feel embarrassed or punished. So they shrink away from taking risks.

In writing, you get beautiful examples. A kid sits down enthusiastically to write, and when the paper comes back from the teacher, it's all bloodied up with loveless, unenthusiastic comments - comments that show no respect for what the child *has* accomplished. So when the kid turns in a revision, it's much shorter. Because that young writer has learned a simple lesson: The less you say, the fewer mistakes you make. Which is not a very good way to encourage people to write. Nor to read.

Teachers need to be encouraged to let kids move ahead. The teacher who complains that natural-language materials move too fast for the kids is probably holding them back, trying to get them to master every word, every skill that's introduced. When a teacher tells me that natural-language materials are difficult, I ask, 'What level are the kids at?' Then I take a story from farther along and ask the kids to read it. Most often, to the teacher's surprise, they can. Not without miscues, but with understanding. And that's the important thing.

What about skill mastery, then?
Some teachers feel that once part of a skill has been introduced, they can't let kids go on until they've absolutely mastered the whole thing. So these teachers spend days and days teaching vowel sounds to kids. And meanwhile, here's all this marvelous stuff to read that the kids don't get to read because the teacher's trying so hard to teach them all these vowel sounds.

The concept I propose is that skills be introduced, examined, learned in steps as part of an ongoing process. This method economizes effort by utilizing kids' interests and by developing skills as, one by one, they arise naturally in the reading.

Mastery should be an ongoing kind of thing. We adults learn so many things by doing - our jobs, our sports, our roles as parents. We all learned to talk by talking. Why can't we let kids learn to read by reading? Naturalness is inherent in the process of getting kids to continue reading. And continued reading is what we're striving for.

What about children who speak a low-status dialect - do teachers have the obligation to teach them to read in standard English?
One of the things there's very little controversy about among linguists and social linguists is that there's no profit in confusing the teaching of reading with the teaching of standard English or high-status forms of language. And when you do - when a kid is reading and says 'I lef' my books,' and the teacher says, 'You skipped the final consonant. See the 't.' It's not lef', it's left,' - the child gets confused.

If children say what to them sounds right, and the teacher says, 'No, that's not right,' they don't understand what they're being told. And they have to assume that there's something about reading that's beyond their understanding.

What about the teachers who like your ideas but don't want to - or can't because of pressure from various sources - abandon the more traditional methods of teaching?
There've been times where we've worked with teachers and they only bought a portion of what we were saying. What we've said to them is, 'Go ahead and do whatever makes you comfortable, what you need to do or what your school system is insisting you do. But don't ever let it interfere with keeping the

focus on meaning. Start with materials that are written in natural language patterns; supplement them, if you want, with things like flash cards, extra work on phonics. But keep that focus on meaning.'

There are lots of ways to do this. You can distribute a bunch of flash cards and ask kids to see how many meaningful sentences they can build out of them. Or you can give one child one flash card and ask that child to create a context for it. You might have kids name things in the room that begin or end with a particular sound. You can give them rhyming riddles, like 'He has a hat; his name is —.'

Also, we say to teachers, 'Accept the notion of the importance of risk-taking; don't make the kids uptight by complaining about the mistakes they make.' Reading is never miscue free; even the most expert readers make them. From kids' miscues you can learn a great deal about their strengths and about the kinds of help they need to become more effective, more efficient readers. And then we ask teachers to make sure that in teaching reading they don't spend so much time on the skill instruction that the kids don't get to read. These are things teachers can basically agree to. And when they try these ideas, they work. Kids learn to read.

I have a personal question to ask. I've got a son - a third-grader - who was a whiz at reading in his first two years at school. He could sound out anything. Suddenly, I've discovered that he understands very little of what he reads. Can you account for that?

There's a universally recognized occurrence in this country - recognized even by people who are staunch phonic advocates - that there's a falling-off-the-cliff phenomenon when kids reach middle grades. Kids who've had strong phonic programs look reasonably good - sometimes even great - the first year. But by the time they're in third grade they are regressing. Many begin dropping below the norm, falling farther and farther behind.

Some people say we've solved one problem - the decoding problem - and now we've got to solve the middle-grades comprehension problem. I think those problems are related. We have kids coming into middle grades not understanding what they read because we haven't helped them think about meaning.

The goal has to be, then, to focus on meaning. Sure, you're going to find in the middle grades kids who are very much handicapped. They're trying to do the things they were taught, and with them it's a question of patiently building up their confidence so that they understand what they're reading. We need to shift them away from the non-productive strategy of dealing with one word at a time. We need to move them toward the idea of dealing with the whole structure, predicting the meaning, checking their predictions.

What, then, ultimately, should be the goal of reading instruction?

What we should really be trying to do is to get kids to be critical readers – to get kids to understand more deeply, to think beyond superficial events, to use and interact with meaning.

The goal isn't to get kids to recognize words or simply to see what the author had in mind. Those are starting points. The goal is to enhance kids' ability to find the depth of meaning. When we do this – then we are truly teaching.

NOTES

1 These are registered trademarks.
2 The Lion's Tail appears in Level 2 (early grade 1) of Reading Unlimited, Scott, Foresman, Glenview, Ill.

The reader of this volume will notice that there is some overlap of content between articles. Because of Goodman's perspective, it is difficult to classify his writings into neat, self-contained categories or sections. His writings are a reflection of his approach, one that is always concerned with the total picture. There is a continual integration of theory, practice, and content that we would hope the reader will see as a strength.

Our basic intent in this volume has been to begin each section with one or more clear, simple articles that might serve as a good introduction for those with little familiarity with the Goodman writings. It is hoped that the introductory comments prior to each article will not only prepare the reader with valuable prior information, but will facilitate the selection of the most relevant material.

Part One
READING AND LANGUAGE

INTRODUCTORY

We begin with a simple, straightforward statement of Goodman's view of the reading process. He characterizes it as a search for meaning.

'It must be remembered,' says Goodman, 'that accurate recognition is not the major objective in reading. *The goal is always meaning.* A highly proficient reader is one who uses the least amount of information to make the best possible predictions. Such a reader has strategies for sampling, selecting, and predicting.

Instruction, he concludes, must be comprehension-centered in order 'to help children develop the strategies needed to engage in the search for meaning called reading.'

1   THE SEARCH CALLED READING

You may diligently examine the physical substance of this page and the black marks on it; you will find nothing that is intrinsically meaning. Yet, somehow you are able to react to the black marks on the page and get some version of the message this writer has intended you to get.

Preschoolers who observe adults reading seem to assume that reading is a game in which the reader looks at the page and makes up a story. Or they may regard the whole process as a mystery. To them, the meaning is somehow locked in the ink blotches, and readers possess a magic power to unlock it.

No adult, and certainly no teacher, would subscribe to the naive idea that readers make up the story as they go along. Obviously the reader is getting some kind of cues from the ink blotches. But many adults, including some teachers, still regard the getting of meaning from print as a mystery. If getting meaning from print is considered a mystery, then such superficial, easily observable phenomena as naming words or matching letters and sounds become targets for instruction. To understand the search for meaning, it is necessary to look below the surface behaviors and see what readers must actually do in order to read successfully.

Certainly what is on the page could be regarded as a collection of letters. But this theory would not account for your ability to read this sentence but not read the following jumble of letters.

Example A.   Wdefrrseefsrgiveeutaaaaaalmnorrrsr.

It would be expedient to say that the letters must be arranged in pronounceable spelling patterns (ones that can be matched to language sounds by readers). A sentence could be constructed as follows - and still be unreadable:

Example B.   Ag orrest ative deweni elawrg sufa resi.

If an additional qualification is made - that the spelling patterns must be real words - then the following sentence could be formulated.

Example C.   A a is language reader user written of.

The search called reading begins to become understandable only when it is clear that the black marks on this page are a written form of language and that the reader is a user of that language.

CHARACTERISTICS OF WRITTEN LANGUAGE

Written language is more than letters; it is more than spelling patterns; it is more than a collection of words. It is, in fact, a means by which a writer conveys a message to a reader. Though the ink blotches on this page have no intrinsic meaning, they are patterned in such a way by this writer that you, the reader, can reconstruct the message in your mind. As you reconstruct this message, you are responding to three essential characteristics of the printed display in front of you:

1 It uses the symbols of written English arranged in permissible spelling sequences with which you are familiar.
2 It is patterned according to the system of the English language. The system of a language is its grammar, with which each user of the language is familiar.
3.It represents an encoding of a meaningful message that will be understandable to you when you reconstruct it.

Notice that all three of the foregoing characteristics are essential to making reading possible. Furthermore, each supports and supplements the others in such a way that the reader may sample from the cues available to him rather than use each possible bit of information.

Example D. A _____ is a _____ of _____.

In the sentence above, the grammatical pattern can be determined from certain words that carry little or no meaning in themselves. These function, or structure, words create a syntactic, or grammatical, context that makes it possible to express a wide variety of meanings dealing with relationships between objects, concepts, and ideas.

Example E. A *clanbon* is a *borple* of *cordunt peft*.

The words that fill these slots are grammatically related to each other by the syntactic context in which they appear. If the reader has had experiences from which he has developed concepts that he relates to these words, then the words are meaningful to him. The only difference between the pseudo-words of Example E and real words is that the latter are meaningful to many, though, of course, not to all readers of English. In fact, the difference between sense and nonsense is a matter of the referents the reader has for particular words.

To sum up, it has been shown that the reader brings meaning to the search in order to get meaning from it. If he lacks relevant experience or concepts, he cannot read a particular story or book or article.

The reader creates, as he reads, a semantic or meaningful context for himself. What he has understood up to a point enables him to expect or predict what will be coming. Having created a context by prediction, he need only sample to confirm, reject, or modify his prediction.

Example F. A *clanbon* is a *user* of *written language.*

Though 'clanbon' is not a known word, in this sentence most readers could approximate an accurate meaning for the nonsense word in Example F. The two contexts, syntactic and semantic, work together to make the approximation possible. It has been well known for years that words are easier to read and learn in context than in isolation. If Example F was in a paragraph, 'clanbon' would be even easier to read. The semantic (meaning) context operates, not only over the paragraph, but over the entire passage being read. Syntax, except for such aspects as tense and antecedent agreement, tends to be confined to the sentence.

A reader always uses his knowledge of the graphic symbols within these twin contexts: syntactic context and semantic context. He may relate the graphic sequences to sound sequences, since he is reading alphabetic language, but he cannot really perform as a competent reader unless he has available all three kinds of information: graphophonic, semantic, and syntactic. If he is reading natural language that deals with ideas and experiences that are familiar to him, then all the information is present.

Example G. A r _____ is a *user* of *written language.*
Example H. A r_____ r is a *user* of *written language.*

Within contexts all that may be necessary to identify a given word is an initial consonant, as in Example G. Certainly initial and final consonants (Example H) will be sufficient. Reading teachers have always been aware that all letters in words are not equally important. Combining the foregoing concept with the view of the reader as a language user, one can understand that though reading starts with graphic input (print), the reader needs only to sample it. He has enough meaning and grammar cues available to him to predict what he will see. Then, by using a few key graphic cues, he can confirm or reject his prediction.

THE SEARCH FOR MEANING

Stated another way, reading is not the exact identification and response to letters or words. It is, in fact, a search - a search for meaning. What a reader thinks he sees at any time is always partly what he actually sees and partly what he expects to see.

The reader samples the text and selects the most useful cues so that he can make the best predictions. A highly proficient reader is one who uses the least amount of information to make the best possible predictions. Such a reader has strategies for sampling, selecting, and predicting.

Of course, the reader needs to know what to do when his prediction is wrong - he must gather more information and make another prediction. Sometimes the reader knows immediately that he is wrong because his prediction does not fit what he has previously read or predicted. Sometimes he discovers later that his prediction has not been correct. A proficient reader has correction strategies to deal with both situations.

What makes it possible for a reader to recognize his miscues and to make corrections is his concern for meaning. He continuously asks himself whether his predictions make sense. Because meaning is dependent on grammar, he also asks himself whether his predictions are producing language as he knows it. If a reader is not concerned with meaning, he is not truly reading. His concern for meaning is expressed through the development of comprehension strategies. These strategies control and make the other strategies work as he reads, and they also carry him beyond reading into reflective thinking, concept formation, and acquisition of knowledge.

Even among proficient readers there are times when the predictions are wrong, but predictions go uncorrected as long as they do not seriously impair comprehension. It must be remembered that accurate recognition is not the major objective in reading. *The goal is always meaning.* Because even proficient readers make errors on unfamiliar material, teachers must resist the temptation to correct meticulously all inconsequential mistakes. They must always ask whether a particular miscue really makes a difference.

If teachers make their instruction comprehension-centered, they will arrange their instruction in proper perspective. Then they will be able to help children develop the strategies needed to engage in the search for meaning called reading.

The need for reading instruction to be based in whole language is extended in this article. Teachers are urged to 'get it all together' rather than fragmenting instruction into bits and pieces.

'When we force beginning readers to move from letters to words to phrases we are forcing them to process all the information. And there is such an excess of graphic and phonemic information available on any page that complete processing makes it nearly impossible to deal with text as language.'

2 READING: You Can Get Back to Kansas Anytime You're Ready, Dorothy

No quest among educational endeavors in America within the past century has been more diligently pursued with more energy, more resources and more urgency than the search for universally effective reading instruction. Reading researchers, teachers, text authors, have followed every promising path, explored every blind alley, turned every stone, rubbed every magic lamp, indulged every faith healer, bought every patent medicine. We've borrowed treatments from general medicine, psychiatry, physical therapy, industrial management.

And when the dust settled, when the parade was over, when the band wagon lost a wheel, when the revival pulled down its tent and moved on, there we were with the same sobering truth; some kids learned to read easily and well and some didn't. And, if we were honest, we had to admit it was possible that some kids learned to read in spite of what we did to and for them rather than because of it.

Well, I'd like to say, Dorothy, that you don't need a carnival balloon to get back to Kansas. There isn't any yellow brick road to follow, no wizard is standing in the wings ready to show you how to pop a magic pill or wave a magic wand. Rather the truth has been around us all the time. All that's necessary, Dorothy, to get back to Kansas is to see beyond the superficial. A new way of looking, a new vantage point to look from, a new orientation in harmony with reality and suddenly we can see that the greatest significance is in things we never noticed that have been right there all the time.

To establish this new vantage point I'm going to ask you to set up certain audio visual devices within your own head. Then I'll flash some graphics on these screens in your mind and play an occasional mental tape recorder for you to listen to. Ready?

The first picture I'm going to flash on your In-the-Head Projector is a water glass with a water line mid-way up between the bottom and the top. Got the picture? That's right, it's the one the Peace Corps used in their recruitment campaign. OK, the first step that you must take toward Kansas is to see that glass as half full. If anyone sees a half empty glass adjust the focus so that it appears half full. We're going to content ourselves with what is present and not be distracted by what is not. The first requirement in building the new view is to build on strength and avoid preoccupations with deficiency.

Now I'm replacing that slide with a new one. On your screen you should now have a child, age, roughly six, average height

25

and weight. Sex is unimportant but the child you're looking at is a boy. We're using a moving picture projector now. It's too hard to get a clear still picture of a kid this age. They move around so much.

If this child looks to you like a small imperfect adult, again please adjust your focus. If he bears any resemblance to a rat, a pigeon, or a chimpanzee use your zoom lens to move in closer so that you can see clearly that he is indeed human. Did you hear what he said just then? Oh, you noticed a kind of whistle on some s's! Well if you'll take a look at his mouth you'll notice that he has some missing front teeth, a quite normal condition for six-year-old humans.

I'm going to play back what he just said so that you can listen again. Did you notice when he was talking about the game he played with Bob that he was using some pretty complex grammar? Did you notice how easily he expressed the relationship between the winner and the loser, never confusing object with subject? We know a lot about a kid's ability to use language now, but it all adds up to one thing. If you're going to teach kids to read, you're going to have to show a healthy respect for the prodigious language achievements and language learning ability of the human young.

Now I want you to see another slide on your screen. On the slide is a big red circle labeled psychology and a big yellow one labeled linguistics. The two circles overlap forming an orange area labeled psycholinguistics.

Psycholinguistics is the scientific study of the relationships between language and thought. As such, it is basic to understanding how anyone reads or learns to read, because through reading we're able to process written language and create in our minds thoughts that match or relate to thoughts in the mind of a writer who may be far away in time and space.

But psycholinguistics is also a way of seeing and organizing what we see when we look at reading and learning to read. We see through psycholinguistics, reading as a process of getting to meaning from print, looking beyond the superficial behaviors of oral or silent reading.

Through psycholinguistics we see a writer as a producer or generator of language. The writer is an encoder who has a message in his mind and who creates, in print, something tangible and observable to represent his message. We see the reader as a user of language, able to use the writer's product, to draw on his own experience, concept, and language ability to comprehend.

Reading is then not a mystery but an understandable describable process.

Through psycholinguistics we see the child just beginning to learn to read as a marvel of nature, a unique individual but sharing with the human species the competency, unique among all living creatures, to create, use, and learn language.

Through psycholinguistics we see literacy, reading and

writing as an extension of natural language learning and development both for the individual and human society. All human
societies have language regardless of the stage of cultural
development they have achieved. When human societies reach
the point where communication must be carried on over time
and space, then written language develops though oral language continues to be the medium of face-to-face communication.
The individual learns the oral language as a first form of language and extends his language competence to include reading
and writing when he must communicate personally over time and
space.

Whenever we study language processes – reading, writing,
speaking or listening – we are dealing with psycholinguistics
questions.

Now look at another slide. On one side is a desk. Seated at it
is a stick figure we've tagged the writer, on the other side of
the slide is a stick figure laying on the floor with a book open
in front of him. He's labeled the reader. Written language, a
page of print, occupies the center of the picture. The writer
and the reader communicate through the page of print. It's
output for the writer and input for the reader. The author's
message grows out of his life and his view of the world. The
reader's message is just as much a result of his life and his
view.

In this written language communication, meaning is never
in the print but always in the head of the writer and the
reader. Now we'll switch to the next slide which is a blowup
of a paragraph from the page of print we just saw. See the
line with these words: 'I switched off the head lamps of the
car.' Now listen to the reader. Did you notice that he said
'head lights'? As he did so, you noticed that the neon sign in
the corner of the screen lit up and began flashing 'miscue.'
The reader produced a miscue. His observed oral response
'lights' didn't match the expected response 'lamps' so the 'miscue' light lit up.

Now here's where we begin to find great significance in the
familiar and hidden truth in the obvious. When people read out
loud, they often produce miscues. Testers for years contented
themselves with the obvious – simply counting these miscues
(they called them errors). They assumed that accurate reading
was the only acceptable reading.

But now let's consider again that reading is an active process,
one in which the reader interacts with the writer through the
print. Our psycholinguistic viewpoint requires us to consider
how, in response to *this* print, *this* reader could have been led
to produce *that* response. Why did he say 'head lights' when the
writer said 'head lamps'? Is it possible he said that because he
expected it to say 'head lights' and since it made sense he didn't
notice that it didn't say that? Does it matter that the words have
the same letters and sounds? That they both are common nouns
that fit the syntax? Is it significant that the writer is British

and the reader is American? If reading is a process the reader
uses to get to meaning why should we be surprised if some of
the words don't match in his oral rendition with the writer's
version.

Miscues viewed in this way are windows on the reading process in general and as it is used by a particular reader dealing
with particular text.

The miscue is observable, but through it we see the underlying process that produced it.

The miscue view of linguistic behavior need not be confined
to reading. For instance, consider literature. On this next slide
you see a volume of Shakespeare, a teacher and a learner. The
teacher, as you can hear on the tape, is lecturing to the class
on what Shakespeare meant to communicate through his character Hamlet. As you can see on this next slide the student has
received a C- on the quiz on Hamlet. He didn't seem to understand what Shakespeare intended him to understand. But now
in this next slide you see another view. Shakespeare and our
student are attempting to communicate through a play, Hamlet.
You'll notice that the teacher is visible in the corner observing
the interaction. The voice you hear is the student's. His understanding of Hamlet is not the teacher's. It reflects in fact his
culture, experience, life view as well as some dialect differences
between the writer and reader. Can the teacher contribute to
better comprehension of Hamlet? Yes. He does so by seeing
'where the student's coming from,' how far he's gotten, where
he's going.

Miscues are not simply errors. They show more about the
learner's strengths than about his weaknesses. In reading,
they are the best possible indications of how efficiently and
effectively the reader is using the reading process.

Whatever a reader does is caused as he engages in this
psycholinguistic process. The reader uses the print and his
language competence to get to the meaning. The miscues he
makes reflect what he's doing.

When we teach people to read, we aren't teaching them letter
sound relationships or word names, or sets of skills. We're
helping them to develop strategies to get to meaning from
print which parallel and draw on the ones they use to get from
oral language to meaning.

We learn to listen to what miscues a reader makes, what effect
they have on meaning, whether the reader corrects when the
meaning is lost or disrupted. We find the strengths that the
miscues reveal and build on them. We teach for comprehension
strategies, confirmation strategies, correction strategies.

We encourage readers at all levels of proficiency to take
risks, to use their language competence to guess what would
make sense when they're unsure. We rejoice in choice miscues and drop our preoccupation with accuracy and isolatable
skills.

This last slide at first may seem so bright that it looks like

the rising sun. But if your eyes can become adjusted you'll
see that it's only the reflected glow of an enlightened teacher.
If you can see that, you're ready to go home now, Dorothy.

READING AND LANGUAGE IN THE CLASSROOM

'The goal of school instruction is not to teach children to talk. They've already learned that. Nor is it to teach them to talk properly. That imposes a strait-jacket on language at a time when the teacher should be encouraging children to stretch language and experiment with it. The school's purpose is to help children use language more effectively, in communication, in thinking and in learning.'

This section begins with a clear account of the language competency that children bring with them when they first come to school. Here Goodman explains what language is, how it is learned, and how important it is to value the individual's unique language and language background. Teachers are encouraged to build on children's natural language strengths.

3 THE LANGUAGE CHILDREN BRING TO SCHOOL: How to Build on It

When it comes to language, teachers have tended to underestimate the competence that the child brings to school with him. Now linguistic and psycholinguistic research on children's language development is providing a clear picture of just how great this competence is, and many teachers are learning that children have much more strength to build on than they have weakness to overcome.

Even so-called disadvantaged children have mastered, to a high degree, the language of their communities. They, like all other children, can communicate their needs and thoughts to the people most important to them – their family and peers – in language that their listeners easily understand.

We've known in education for a long time that children have extensive vocabularies at the age of five and six. We've tended to underestimate the vocabularies of children from lower socioeconomic groups because we have given them tasks and situations that are unfamiliar to them and not conducive to getting them to use their vocabularies more extensively.

We've been largely unaware of the control children have over the symbols (phonemes) and the system (grammar) of their language. We tend to be distracted by the few immaturities and miss the significance of the immense learning achievement that children have already made in language.

But even the immaturities are signs of learning. When a child says 'I bringed it,' he is demonstrating that he has acquired a basic rule for past tense formation. He is also demonstrating that he does not simply produce sentences by imitating adults, but that he generates his sentences through use of grammatical rules induced from the language as he has learned it.

WHY CHILDREN LEARN LANGUAGE

Of all the living creatures, man is unique in his ability to symbolically manipulate his experiences and to organize them into concepts which he can express, through language, to his fellow men. Human infants are born both with this capability and the need to communicate. In the course of their early years, language becomes not only their means of communication, but also their medium of thought and learning.

Whatever language the child has learned serves him well in all these respects because it is the language of his community and his family. His need to communicate and express his needs and understandings is so strong that he constantly moves toward the language norms of his community. He keeps what works and drops what doesn't. His language develops in the mold of his community's language but isn't really an imitation of it.

The extent to which he uses the sounds, patterns and vocabulary of his community is the extent to which he communicates effectively. So he zeros in on sounds, patterns and vocabulary. And while doing so he acquires a symbolic means for communicating with himself; for representing his experiences, reflecting on them, reorganizing them and trying them out on his family and acquaintances. Without language, not only communication but thought and learning would be severely inhibited.

It should be obvious that teachers not only should capitalize on this medium of thought and learning but should watch very carefully the ways in which they react to a child's language. If the child is confused or made to feel ashamed of his language, however well meaning his teacher, the learning process itself may be disrupted. If, on the other hand, the teacher carefully cultivates the language base of the child and nurtures his pride and confidence, then he continues to use language to learn in school just as he has been doing outside of school.

SYMBOLS AND SYSTEM

Language is not simply a collection of symbols. It is a 'system' of symbols. In Morse code, a very small set of symbols – dots, dashes and long and short pauses – are used. But when these symbols are arranged in patterns representing 'letters,' and these patterns are arranged in patterns representing 'words,' and these in turn are arranged in patterns representing 'phrases' and 'sentences,' then it is possible to communicate any thought which a user is capable of thinking.

We call the system in language 'grammar.' It is a pattern of symbols that fit together in systematic ways. In learning language, the child learns both the symbols and the system at the same time. He hears language around him in recurrent situations. He notices, for example, that certain language accompanies the sensations of taste, smell, touch and sight which are in feeding situations. Eventually he learns that he can use this language to indicate his need to be fed. His sounds in the beginning are only approximations of what he hears, just as his patterns are abbreviated approximations limited by his ability to coordinate all of the organs – lips, tongue, teeth, etc. – that produce speech. Similarly, his meanings begin as vague and general and move toward the precise and specific.

Humans have a great many ways of varying the sounds they produce. Languages arbitrarily over the centuries develop a small number of bundles of these sounds to use as symbols or phonemes. The differences between these bundles are significant ones in the language. The child, to be an effective listener, must be able to discriminate these differences. But there are many sound differences that are not significant in the language the child is learning (though they may well be in another language). He must learn not to pay attention to those differences which are not significant.

Perception in language is a selective process. The young child learns what to expect and learns to ignore what is insignificant. Even a three-year-old can repeat with relative accuracy a long sequence in his native language, but is quite unable to repeat with any accuracy a short one in a foreign language. (Adults are often even less able to repeat foreign sequences.)

While he learns this selective perceptual process, the child acquires control over the syntax (sentence patterns) and other grammatical features of his language. He learns to recognize the markers, function words like 'the,' 'a,' 'was,' 'and,' 'of,' 'not' and word endings which indicate the patterns. When a child hears 'I want a —,' he is able to predict that a noun is coming (even though he has no terminology, he can provide acceptable examples of what must come next).

Children learn to recognize the basic syntax of English and eventually they derive the rules that make it possible to generate their own sentences. They may make mistakes in the process, but that's part of learning – the ineffectiveness leads them to try alternate ways and thereby perfect their rules and gain control over the process. As the child learns the system of language his perceptual process becomes one in which he predicts and selects.

The child continually narrows the situations in which he uses language so that meaning becomes more exact. What starts as a general call for food becomes a specific, 'I want some milk.' He begins to be aware that within recurrent globs of language there are pieces which have meanings. And he starts saying, 'What does — mean?' He is becoming aware of words and word meanings. But the whole comes before the part. We do string words together to get meaning. We differentiate the parts from meaningful wholes.

Of course, no language has meaning apart from the experience of the user. The child uses his developing language in relation to his experiences. All children have experiences, but they vary and so will their vocabularies vary.

Research indicates that, except for a few complex refinements, children have mastered the grammatical system and rules of their community language by the time they are in school. When a child says a simple sentence like 'Jimmy hit George,' he shows his ability to control the syntax of the language because the only way in English to differentiate subject from object in this statement is to place one before and one after the verb.

LOW STATUS LANGUAGE

Everyone learns and speaks a dialect of his native language. In fact, language itself is nothing more than a collection of dialects. No one speaks just plain English.

Unfortunately, there has been a lot of confusion about dialect differences. People tend to put all language on a single ladder with good language at the top and bad at the bottom. But each infant learns his dialect in much the same way and it serves him in all his language needs. He learns its phonemes, its syntactic patterns and its rules. Its vocabulary and distinctive idioms help to express those of his experiences that are common to his culture. In no sense is his language less systematic or less useful to him than any other speaker's, except in unfamiliar situations or in communicating with speakers of other dialects who are unfamiliar with his dialect. (This problem is not unique to any one group. Communication is a two-way street, and teachers would do well to remember that if children sound funny to them, they must also sound funny to the same children.)

OUTWARD EXPANSION IN SCHOOL

Teachers who wish to make use in class of the language resources of children will start by building the pride and confidence children have in their own language and their ease in using it in school. The goal of school instruction is not to teach children to talk. They've already learned that. Nor is it to teach them to talk properly. That imposes a strait-jacket on language at a time when the teacher should be encouraging children to stretch language and experiment with it. The school's purpose is to help children use language more effectively, in communication, in thinking and in learning.

More effective language may require more variety, more flexibility, more appropriateness - in fact, more language as children meet new situations and concepts. But in all cases this must be an expansion of the existing language not a substitution or extinction of it.

USING THE CHILD'S LANGUAGE

Reading is very much like listening. The reader uses his language system knowledge, his syntactic knowledge, his semantic knowledge and his sum total of experiences and concepts. If the child is reading material that deals with familiar situations and ideas, and this material is written in a language which is like his own oral language, then he can bring all of his language strength to bear on the task. Ours is an alphabetic system. The child needs to learn to use print rather than the sounds of oral language as input. This will help him form his own associations between the written language and the oral language. The alternative - teaching him to produce sounds that are not his own - is less than useless.

There is a good deal of merit in using a language experience approach if the teacher avoids tampering with the language that children use in creating their stories. Experience stories are bound to meet the criteria of being about familiar experiences and in familiar language. But if the teacher 'corrects' the child's language or makes it look like the pre-primers, then the language becomes changed and the child will find it harder to read.

It requires neither great skill nor sequences of courses in linguistics for teachers to begin to utilize the language competence of their pupils. All that is required is a willingness to listen carefully to them, to take the time to understand them, and to treat their language, however low it is on the social totem pole, as legitimate. And what a great pleasure it is to work *with* children rather than against them!

Here Goodman points to the need for a sound theoretical understanding of the reading process and of language learning so
that we might stop interfering with the learners in attempting
to help them. He argues that in the past we have not always
helped the learner as we might have, largely because our theory
was inadequate or inappropriate. Goodman believes that the
key to our understanding is in the children themselves. The
article concludes with appropriate principles and guidelines for
teachers.

4 READING: The Key Is in Children's Language

It is entirely possible that within the next decade virtually all children will be learning to read, easily and effectively. That goal will not be achieved through a marvelous new breakthrough in the form of a simple new method, nor a rededication to an old method, an ingeniously devised new alphabet, a well-stocked bank of behavioral objectives, a highly structured and sequenced set of programed materials, a super basal reader, or a scheme for paying teachers and publishers according to their evident success or failure.

Universal literacy will be achieved only when we have understood enough about the reading process and its acquisition to stop interfering with learners in the name of helping them. Man has a marvelous natural facility for creating and learning language. Reading is a language process, the direct counterpart of listening. It is no small source of embarrassment to organized education that children are far more uniformly successful in learning to talk and listen than they are in learning to read and write. They accomplish the former with no systematic instruction, no teachers as such, no programed materials. A human infant need only be exposed to language, any language, and he quickly becomes competent in it. And all this occurs at an earlier age than that at which literacy instruction normally begins.

NO MYSTERY

There is no deep mystery here. Linguistic science during the past quarter century has made giant strides in explaining how language works. Research on child language development is helping us to see how language acquisition takes place. Sociolinguistics is clearing away the cobwebs of misconception surrounding language differences, particularly as they relate to social attitudes toward language. Psycholinguistics is making it possible for us to understand how language is used to communicate thoughts, and how experiences are manipulated through language.

To put this basic knowledge to work, it is essential for educators to view reading as a receptive language process and readers as users of language. Viewed from these vantage points, it appears clearly that our failures in reading instruction result as much from what we have been doing as from what we haven't.

We have been teaching reading as a set of skills to be learned
rather than as a language process to be mastered. We have
been teaching children who are competent users of oral language as if they were beginners in language learning. We have
ignored the language structure and in the name of teaching,
fed children strings of letters or strings of words. We have
taught children to match letters to sounds without giving them
basic knowledge of the complex relationships between oral and
written English, and without evidence that such a step is either
necessary or desirable in getting meaning from written language.
   What has saved us from even greater failure, considering how
unsound our instructional programs have been, has been the
remarkable language learning ability of the children we teach.
They have been able to surmount obstacles we have placed in
their way. They have been able to unlearn unsound strategies
and to ignore or delimit questionable generalizations. No method
of instruction, no matter how absurd, has ever succeeded in
preventing even half the learners from learning. As long as
they get some exposure to written language, most learners will
acquire at least a modicum of literacy.

MISDIRECTED MATERIALS

Materials for reading instruction have been built largely around
inappropriate learning theories. Behavioral, stimulus-response
learning theories view learning as an accumulation of bits and
pieces and encourage programs designed to break learning down
into sequences of small easily managed tasks, each related to a
measurable, isolatable behavior. For decades authors and editors of reading materials and curriculum builders pursued this
will o' the wisp in reading. Phonics, sight words, word attack
skills were strung along, one after the other, like beads on a
thread. Though sequences were developed and implemented,
no one was ever able to justify scientifically such a sequence
in terms of what a learner must know as he proceeds. Tests
were constructed on the same premise, with most of the subtests dealing with subsidiary skills rather than the purposes
of reading. New tests are validated by correlating them with
old tests, insuring that new understanding of reading is kept
out of them.
   Programed learning carries this view of learning to a kind
of ultimate application. The problem programed materials face,
however, is exacerbated because they are built entirely around
the principle of learning a totally sequenced set of items, each
one a prerequisite to the next. To be successful, such materials
would have to be based on a very thorough knowledge of reading as a process. Furthermore, the reading process would have
to be composed of isolatable steps, and the way to learn reading would necessarily have to be through such a sequence.
   Careful examination of programed materials reveals no such

detailed understanding of the reading process. Usually the skills are borrowed directly from pre-existing materials and the sequence is quite arbitrary, based on assumptions or narrow concepts borrowed from psychology, such as frequency of exposure, or from linguistics, such as phoneme-grapheme correspondence.

READING AND THE REAL WORLD

But, reading does not work that way, and neither do readers learn that way. Just as in learning to talk, the child learning to read needs all the strategies right from the beginning. His progress is not a matter of mastery of parts leading to mastery of the whole, but rather a matter of successive approximation of proficient reading. Children's speech moves rapidly from unintelligible babbling to effective speech. They increase their control over the whole process, mastering details only after the whole has moved forward. In reading, much the same is possible provided the learners are exposed to whole, natural, meaningful language.

Language cannot be broken into pieces without changing it to a set of abstractions: sounds, letters, words. When it is all together, the learner can use his knowledge of the language structure and his conceptual background as a framework in which to utilize graphic input. Broken into bite-sized pieces, on the other hand, language has to be learned abstract piece by abstract piece; the learner then needs to relearn how to use the pieces in the reading task.

Children who have trouble learning to read are those who are unable to take the abstract bits and pieces of their instruction and put them together. Ironically such children are given extra doses of 'skill instruction' as remediation. While their more fortunate classmates are getting a chance at increasingly more natural and more interesting language, they get more phonics (the chicken soup of reading instruction), more word attack skills, more splintered instruction.

Since reading tests mostly test 'skills,' programs designed to teach such skills usually present an illusion of great success, particularly over periods no longer than a year. Any progress the learner makes in comprehension, however, is largely his own doing. Frequently sequential skill instruction will interfere with comprehension since the learner's attention is diverted from meaning.

SOLUTIONS WITHIN REACH

Sometimes one can search for solutions to complex problems only to find the solutions were within easy reach all the time.

In reading, the solutions to the teaching-learning problems

are in the children themselves. If we view them as users of
language, our goal becomes one of making literacy an extension
of the learners' natural language development. Instruction will
be successful to the extent that it capitalizes on children's
language learning ability and their existing language competence.

We have been so busy searching for weaknesses in learners
that we overlooked their language learning strengths. Motivation for reading as for all other language learning is intrinsic.
Language is learned because people need to communicate.
Children growing up in a literate society need to understand
certain written language: signs, warnings, directions, messages.

Comprehension of such written language will motivate learning far more effectively than candy or Green Stamps. But the
message must be one the learner cares about. Relevancy is vital
in reading instruction.

COMPREHENSION FIRST

Teaching and learning in reading must always be centered in
comprehension. The importance of any particular letters and
words in a sequence can be determined only in relationship to
the message the whole sequence is conveying.

That means that right from the beginning of instruction
learners must be dealing with meaningful, natural language.
Perhaps the best place to begin is their own language as they
use it to cope with their own experiences.

As children strive to get meaning by processing written
language, they begin to develop comprehension strategies.
These are strategies for selecting and using the graphic
information, predicting an underlying grammatical structure,
and relating their experiences and concepts to written language. They develop strategies for recognizing when they have
gone wrong and strategies for correcting. Though these strategies seem more complicated than the skills we are used to
teaching, they are much the same as those the learners have
already learned to use in listening, and are learned with no less
ease.

THE TEACHER'S ROLE

Perhaps the most crucial aspect of making literacy an extension
of the natural language learning of children is the role the
teacher must play.

Teachers must understand the reading process well enough
that they can be true facilitators of learning. Undergraduate
training must include work in linguistics and applied linguistics
so that teachers will be able to understand the reading process,

language learning, and language difference. Inservice education must accomplish the same purposes for teachers already in the field.

If teachers can understand the significance of what children do as they read, they can provide useful, relevant materials, detect hangups children acquire, help a child to acquire useful strategies, and let go of nonproductive strategies. The teacher will be able to monitor the reading process as it develops.

The alternative to such effective teaching is not 'teacher proof' material. Interesting, varied material which is keyed to the backgrounds of learners will be helpful. But no instructional package can replace enlightened teachers. That is because solving the literacy problem depends on working *with* learners rather than at cross purposes to them.

This is a hard hitting direct account of what we should and should not be doing as teachers of reading in the classroom. This article warns of the dangers of some traditional practices and trends in education and gives valuable guidance both theoretical and practical in the form of key principles about reading and learning to read that teachers everywhere should find relevant.

5 EFFECTIVE TEACHERS OF READING KNOW LANGUAGE AND CHILDREN

It is popular in modern educational groups, particularly those dealing with research, to cultivate objectivity by sticking very close to observable behavior without dealing with values, questioning assumptions, or probing beneath behavior to the underlying processes and competencies that produce it. Furthermore, educational speakers and writers seldom are direct in attacking specific programs and methods. While supporting my position on a base of sound research and theory, I do not claim that it is value free. Furthermore, I do not want you to draw the conclusion that in this position I am rejecting others. I wish to be explicit about what I reject and why.

My basic tenet is this: All children have immense language resources when they enter school. By understanding and respecting and building on the language competence of kids we can make literacy an extension of the natural language learning of children. Teachers must know and understand kids, their language and the reading process in order to bring this about.

If this position is valid then I must reject the position of those who treat children as defective adults, as deficient in language, as so many lumps of clay to be forced into a mold and reshaped as look-alike, think-alike, talk-alike robots. I must reject directly and unequivocally programs and practices which I believe threaten to create a new dark age in reading and language instruction.

If children are our concern then we are accountable ultimately only to them. Those who believe in kids must speak up in their defense. How can we face these kids, now, and later when they are grown, if we abandon them to the behavior modifiers, to the interveners in their lives who want to buy their souls for a handful of candies and win their parents' consent for a book of green stamps?

We've got to tell the operant conditioners and the contingency reinforcers that kids can learn like pigeons but pigeons can't learn like kids and that learning theories that try to reduce learning to read to bite-size pellets that pigeons can swallow are inappropriate and theoretically wrong and ultimately harmful to at least some kids. We've got to assert that if kids learn to read with these pigeon pecking programs, that's a tribute to the language learning competence of kids which makes it possible to overcome the absurdities of programs like Distar and BRL and learn to read anyway. Most children can learn in spite of such programs which fragment reading into sequences of

measurable irrelevant trivia. But enough children suffer that I
would like to see signs displayed all over the walls of the
exhibit areas of professional conferences of groups like IRA
and NCTE which say: 'Caution: instructional materials displayed here may be injurious to the mental health of your
pupils.'

Following the initial commitment of this paper I'm going to
state a series of key principles about reading and learning to
read and will discuss these in relationship to some current
practices and trends.

Reading is language. Reading is one of four language processes. Since literate societies have two alternative forms of language, that is, speech and writing, reading must be viewed
as the receptive written language process, parallel to listening,
the aural receptive process. Speech and writing are the productive processes.

Readers are users of language. Readers are people who use
this receptive process to construct meaning from written language. Reading is successful to the extent that readers can
construct meaning. The writer encodes thoughts in language.
The reader goes from language to thought. The reader decodes.

Reading beginners are competent language users. When children learn to read their native language they bring to the task
a competence in language which they use in listening and speaking. They can process an aural language sequence, get to its
underlying structures, and construct meaning. They are limited
in doing so successfully only to the extent that cognitive development and relative lack of experience limit them. They have
mastered the system of language, its symbols, rules and patterns. If they lack vocabulary it is more a result of limited
experience and cognitive development than a cause of lack of
comprehension.

Every child, in every stratum of every society, leans well at
least one language form, the one most useful for purposes of
communication in the community. Only the most severely handicapped children are hindered in this achievement. Unfortunately, through ignorance and prejudice, a stereotype has developed of 'linguistically deprived,' 'non-verbal,' 'culturally
disadvantaged' children. Researchers and authoritative writers
are not immune to elitism and racism. Ethnocentrism, a tendency
to judge others by the extent to which they deviate from one's
self, contaminates a good deal of the professional literature
dealing with the language competence of low-status children.
The stereotype is a vicious one but not new to America nor
restricted to poor blacks or Appalachian whites. The 'Dumb
Swede,' 'Dumb Dutchman,' 'Stupid Polack' stereotypes attest
our willingness to equate difference with deficiency and assume
that people who don't speak our own version of good English

thereby demonstrate an ability to do so resulting from inferior ancestors or inadequate home environment, or some combination of both. Compensatory education, through which we will help these unfortunate wretches to overcome their deficiencies and inadequacies and become as much like ourselves as is possible, considering the long way they have to come, is the solution offered for problems that don't exist.

Instead of this stereotype we must recognize the competence of children in their own language, whatever its social status. Literacy can become an extension of the existing language competence of the learner if we understand it and encourage children to rely on their language strength in learning to read.

Language exists only to communicate meaning. Language is an arbitrary code, a social invention, to meet the needs of its users for communication. Apart from this purpose it becomes a set of abstractions. In its relationship to meaning it becomes, for its users, almost a part of the concrete world which it is used to represent and manipulate. Language learning when it is in this communicative context is like concrete learning. Learning to read requires relevant meaningful language in order for language users to make use of their existing language competence and of the meaning context in which language processes function.

Any attempt to reduce the complexity of language in reading by sorting out letters or word parts or words increases the complexity of the learning since it substitutes abstract language elements for meaningful language.

There is no need for extrinsic motivation in teaching reading such as raisins, Green Stamps, candies or grades. The motivation in all language learning is successful communication. Communicative need, the need to understand and be understood, is the driving force behind language learning. It is only when language is divorced from meaning or the meaning is irrelevant to the learner that extrinsic rewards are needed to spur learning. Furthermore such rewards work regardless of the value or validity of what is being learned. Behavior that ultimately interferes with successful reading may be fostered with extrinsic rewards since they do not relate to the process itself. One might safely conclude that the less soundly based on knowledge of language use and language learning a program is the more likely it is to require external rewards to keep the pupils involved.

There is no defensible sequence of skills in reading instruction. Since reading must, like all language processes, be always related to the communication of meaning, there is no time, in reading acquisition when the reader may dispense with any aspects of the process that would result in the learner dealing with anything less than whole natural meaningful language. Only in its communicative use are all elements of the reading process in proper perspective. The actual importance of any letter, letter part, word or word part at any point in reading is totally dependent on all other elements and on the grammar and meaning of the language sequence.

Isolating and sequencing skills appeals to the logic of the adult literate as a means of being sure that the novice encounters and learns to control each thing that a proficient reader controls. But such sequencing was not a necessary prerequisite to the original language acquisition of the same learners. They learned to understand and be understood through oral language at an earlier age, with no prior language competence, and without the professional help of teachers. Imagine putting infants through a program where they were first taught sounds, then the blending of sounds into sound sequences, then production of words, then phrases, and then sentences, after which they were permitted to engage in meaningful purposeful discourse. Such a program would not foster language learning; it would yield large numbers of children who were candidates for remedial talking classes.

But children learn language because they encounter it whole and within the context of meaningful use in meaningful situations. Out of all the sensory input which bombards them and out of all the noise, both linguistic and non-linguistic they encounter, they are able to sort out language, relate it to the accompanying experience and reach the point at a tender age when they can easily express any thought they can think through utterances that they generate but have never heard before. It is absurd to think that these competent language users need to have the process of reading turned into an academic exercise in pseudo-scientific linguistic analysis. All they need to become as effective in reading as they are in listening is meaningful written language which they need and want to understand.

No researcher has ever been able to support any particular sequence of skill instruction as having any intrinsic merit which derives from linguistic or psycholinguistic analysis. All sequences are arbitrary, often frankly stated to be so by those who originally formulated them, though not always by later borrowers.

Accuracy in reading is inconsequential. Successful readers are those who are most effective: they can construct a message which substantially agrees with the one the writer began with, and most efficient: they use the least amount of effort to achieve that end. Accuracy, correctly naming or identifying each word or word part in a graphic sequence, is not necessary for effective reading since the reader can get the meaning without accurate word identification. Furthermore, readers who strive for accuracy are likely to be inefficient. They use too much available graphic information since the amount of information needed to identify graphic elements far exceeds the amount needed to predict the underlying structure and construct a related meaning. Efficient readers sample from the distinctive features of the graphic display using only enough to make a useful prediction about the structure and the meaning. Then they sample again to confirm or contradict their predictions. Too careful reading becomes bogged down in detail so that meaning is lost. The too careful reader is like a driver who has not yet learned to sort out the realities which assault his or her senses which are needed to make effective decisions: when to stop, to speed up, to turn. Using all the available information is little better than using none. There is too much to sort and evaluate. An efficient driver predicts, anticipates and therefore is able to ignore the insignificant and capitalize on really significant information bearing cues.

Readers who are efficient and effective operate in much the same manner as such drivers. If they do make miscues they become aware of them only if they result in loss of meaning, since they are constantly monitoring the process for meaning. They are trying to comprehend, not say words. Furthermore, such readers know how to recover from significant miscues which do disrupt meaning and correct. Better readers don't just make fewer miscues they make better miscues. Their miscues are more likely to retain meaning and acceptable syntax. The process of reading is such that even very efficient readers make miscues. But efficient readers know how to recover meaning when miscues have caused a loss of meaning.

Reading is a single process. In recent years some writers building on a few narrowly interpreted linguistic principles have argued that the teaching of reading could be divided into two parts; a code-emphasis stage during which the learner is taught to 'crack the code' by matching graphic patterns at phonological ones and meaning-emphasis stage that would follow where the reader learns to comprehend. Such arguments are based on two key misconceptions.

The first is that oral language is not a code but written language is. Such a view is not consistent with linguistic reality. Both the phonological and graphic surface representations of language utilize arbitrary symbols systematically patterned by English grammar to represent meaning. Spoken language is no less a code than written. Learning to *recode* from a graphic code to a sound code is not *decoding* which must result in going from code to meaning. Even in alphabetic writing systems, such as English uses, though the graphic system in origin relates to the phonemes and patterns of phonemes in oral language it becomes, in practical use, an alternate way of representing meaning.

The second misconception is that one can usefully separate concern for the aspects of the written code from the use made by the reader in reconstructing meaning. As indicated above, such a separation at best results in inefficient reading and at worst creates barriers to effective comprehension.

Behavior and competence are not the same. There is rampant in education today a mindless empiricism largely based on behavioral learning theory that equates behavior with competence, that makes change in behavior the only defensible goal of instruction, and which asserts that all curriculum and instruction must be judged in terms of observable, measurable changes in behavior. I call this mindless empiricism because it accepts only what can be seen. Where would astrophysics be if Galileo had believed that? Science always starts with the observable but then it creates theories to explain the processes by which these phenomena are produced. Then the theories are tested against observable reality and either rejected or modified if they do not adequately explain and predict.

In reading instruction the goal is not to produce behavior in the form of performance on tests; the goal is comprehension. We seek readers to achieve a competence in reading which is both efficient and effective. We may use tests, or oral reading, or other performances as evidence of this competence, but we are never justified in saying that the performance we can observe and measure is the competence itself. In fact a pupil may be taught to perform well on tests of reading without acquiring reading competence. This is particularly true if the tests deal with sequenced skills and not reading comprehension. Children may learn to say letters or name words but not to construct meaning from written language. Only with a thorough understanding of the reading process and how it is used can one interpret behavior in reading to get insight into the strength of the reading process as it is being used.

Nuclear physics is based on a theory that Einstein developed on the basis of interpreting the behavior of the stars and planets. But it extended knowledge in directions which could not be confirmed until decades later through any observable and measurable phenomena. The theory of gravity that Newton developed was a basic tool in planning moon explorations. It required modifications when it was applied to the new conditions of the moon. But what would have been the fate of our first manned flight if we had relied only on observable phenomena in planning their trip? How many crews would have perished while we shot off rockets and watched where they went?

Theory in reading, built on a base of psycholinguistics, the study of the interrelationships of thought and language, has progressed to the point where it is possible to interpret reading behavior and even predict it. There is no justification to superficial focus on behavior without relating it to underlying competence.

Nor can we justify narrow behavioral objectives which reduce reading to a collection of measurable trivia and erroneously force on to the reading process an inappropriate sequence of isolated skills. Objectives in reading relate to the efficient, effective control over the process and a flexible competence in the use of reading to comprehend a wide range of written language. If these objectives are not as finite and precise as the ones conjured up in the name of specificity then that is one more demonstration of the inappropriateness of behavioral learning theory to language learning.

Tests in reading are anchors against progress. Reading tests in current use lag far behind current theoretical insights into reading and learning to read. They lag farther behind than practice and, particularly with the current emphasis on accountability which is equated with test performance, serve to pull practice away from innovation and the application of new knowledge. Teachers teach to the test particularly if they and their schools are going to be judged by pupil performance on tests. Sound tests of reading performance would need to be built even more carefully on a modern theoretical base than methods and materials. They would need to be used by practitioners capable of interpreting performance to get at underlying competence.

Test markers are not going to provide adequate tests however until those on the market cease to be profitable. Even new tests are measured today by the degree to which they correlate with the older ones. Educators need to declare a moratorium on the use of reading tests until publishers get the cobwebs out of them. In the meantime the immense expense in time and money that goes into tests could be used for in-service education to provide teachers with the knowledge they need to assess pupil progress toward reading competence.

People not technology. No new teacher-proof materials or child-proof machine is going to solve the problem of assuring all children become functionally literate. But teachers who believe in kids, who understand how language works and who can help kids capitalize on the language resources which they bring to school can solve the problem. We know now how reading works; we know how it is learned; we understand its uses and limitations better. And it turns out that the help kids need from school in acquiring literacy is assistance in using strengths they already have and resources they already possess.

John Hersey's Child Buyer is alive and well and doing business in every school house in America. He promises to teach kids to read, to raise their IQs, to purify and cleanse them, and to modify their behavior so they'll be docile, obedient, and conformist. Are we on his side or that of the kids?

This is a practical article dealing with the place of language experience activities in helping children learn to read. Here Goodman suggests that the language-experience story is the most natural starting point for beginning readers, one that has many advantages:

> ...this procedure enables children to use in learning to read the competencies they already have developed. Literacy becomes a natural continuation of a child's growing competence in language if it is not presented as something new and unlike language as he has known and used it.

> Every child comes to school with a strong control of his mother tongue. Only if the school rejects or ignores his language is he truly disadvantaged. Teachers must be careful, when they evaluate language and experience, not to equate difference with deficiency.

6 CHILDREN'S LANGUAGE AND EXPERIENCE: A Place to Begin

Variants of the experience story - a narrative produced by children and written by the teacher on a chart or on the chalkboard - have been used for many years. It has always made sense to teachers to get children to draw on their own experiences and to let them see their own spoken language in written form. Furthermore, teachers found experience stories successful: children read them easily and with pleasure. There has, however, been confusion over the purposes of such activities and their relationship to the teaching of reading.

Frequently teachers have seen experience stories as a bridge to the reading of preprimers. It is not surprising that the stories looked very much like the preprimers by the time the teacher had finished recording them. In fact, the teacher had used many of the words presented there.

An old cliché in education is that any teacher must 'start where the child is' and take him 'as far as he can go.' The five- or six-year-old child coming to school for the first time is not a beginner because he has already learned his native language. He has learned to communicate his needs, wishes, feelings, and his wonder. He has learned to use language, not only to relate his experiences to others, but also to organize, manipulate, and reflect on those experiences. He has begun to use language to build concepts out of the novel and recurrent experiences that he, like all other children, encounters in every waking hour. In short, before he undertakes the task of becoming literate in his native language, his language has already become his medium of expression, thought, and learning.

Thought and language develop together in a dependent interrelationship, both nurtured by experience. The understandings and concepts a particular child develops are limited by the experiences he has, just as his language is; thought and language must develop simultaneously in order for either to prosper. Fortunately, all children, regardless of the setting in which they grow up, encounter many experiences common to all human beings simply by living. Such experiences are so recurrent that children learn well what they need to know in order to survive. The forms of these experiences vary, but they have a common core. All children eat, for example. What they eat varies according to their culture and circumstances. How they eat varies, too, though all must have some means of conveying food to the mouth. All may start with the hand as the sole means. Some will move to the use of spoon, fork, and eventually knife; others will move to chopsticks.

The language a person needs in order to survive in human society develops in relationship to the common core of experiences all humans share and the variable forms these experiences take.

There is no social, ethnic, racial, economic, or religious groups that are deprived of experiences; hence, there are no groups deprived either of language or conceptual development. The types of experiences differ, and the language may differ somewhat. However, children of each group develop the ability to cope with the common experiences of all children and the special experiences of the children who share their culture. The form of language a particular child learns is the one his community uses. Regardless of the social acceptance of his language, that form is the most useful one for him to learn. It is the one best suited to the common experiences of his group and best understood by the people with whom he needs most to communicate.

Every child comes to school with a strong control of his mother tongue. Only if the school rejects or ignores his language is he truly disadvantaged. Teachers must be careful, when they evaluate language and experience, not to equate difference with deficiency.

WHY USE EXPERIENCE STORIES?

It is vital to build reading instruction on the language and experience of the children because this procedure enables children to use in learning to read the competencies they already have developed. Literacy becomes a natural continuation of a child's growing competence in language if it is not presented as something new and unlike language as he has known and used it.

Many teachers, underestimating children's language abilities, have not made maximal use of language-experience activities. Often, they have regarded language-experience activities as prereading experiences rather than using them as the first steps in teaching reading.

Because these teachers did not fully understand the function of language-experience activities, they restated and restructured what the children said. In the process, the teachers were sure to introduce the vocabulary that the child would be encountering in his reading texts. The net result was that a common experience related by the children in their own language was rewritten in an unfamiliar language that sounded quite foreign to the children. In fact, such a procedure defeats the intent of the activity; teachers might just as well begin with commercially prepared materials.

Also, many teachers systematically correct children's language while the youngsters construct an experience story. For example, 'Me and James was chunking a ball around' becomes 'Jim and I were throwing a ball around.' The child who made the statement is probably not able to recognize the restatement.

Language is by nature systematic, it cannot be used in an unsystematic way. What teachers may interpret as incorrect in fact turns out to be a somewhat different system. The learner, when corrected, becomes confused; he is told that what he has said is wrong, even though it fits his system and sounds right to him. This confusion leads to a feeling of linguistic isolation.

Children know both the sound system and the grammatical system of their language by the time they come to school. The few immaturities in pronunciations stand out precisely because the remainder is so well learned. Similarly, an occasional immaturity, usually a misapplied generalization like 'I taked it,' stands out. It is true that young children do not use certain complex aspects of the grammatical system; perhaps their thoughts are not so complex that they need such constructions.

Vocabulary is, in a sense, the most open-ended aspect of language. As stated earlier, all children have sufficient vocabulary to express their reactions to experiences common to all people. But even users of the same language do not necessarily choose the same terms for the same experiences and do not necessarily have common definitions for the same words. What one American calls a glass of 'pop' is 'tonic' or 'soda' to another American, while to a Londoner it's a 'mineral.'

Furthermore, children, like adults, have rich, varied, and precise vocabularies for discussing topics in which they have strong backgrounds and interests; they have more limited, more generalized vocabularies for dealing with other topics. Contrast the farm child, six years old, with his suburban and city counterparts. Whose vocabulary would show to the greatest advantage in discussing cattle? Who would have the richest vocabulary for explaining freeway travel? And if each child had had some experiences with fishing, would they use the same terms for the equipment, the procedures, or even the fish?

The experience story, created by children in their own language, is a vehicle by which each child may use his own strengths, dip into his own vocabulary reservoir, and find himself at equal advantage with other children.

Formerly preoccupation with controlled reading vocabulary caused teachers to worry about using the right words in experience stories. Now the right words are considered to be the ones that the children want to use. If they are dealing with an experience in which they have been really involved, they will have something to say about it. They will use some key words related to the subject repetitiously. Common words, including those which have caused teachers the most concern, will occur naturally, since they are needed in everyday language.

In the experience story, beginning readers will see familiar language in written sentence form. They will learn to recognize

these familiar wholes – sentences – in familiar stories; then they
will become familiar with the smaller units – words – first in
familiar sentences, then in unfamiliar ones. And finally they
will generalize about the relationships between the patterns of
written English.

STEPS TO EXPERIENCE STORIES

Here are some points to consider in making plans to use the
experience story as a major element in teaching children to
read.

*Capitalize on children's interests and plan real experiences
around them.* The key to success is to provide relevant experiences and to be alert to ones children are having out of school.
If teachers will become keen observers of their pupils, there
will be no dearth of experiences to pursue. Remember, however, that what is relevant for one group may not be for
another. Here are a few examples of experiences that children
might find highly interesting, which teachers can take advantage of:

> The first rainfall in Los Angeles after the long dry
> summer
> The first snowfall in Chicago
> A windstorm in Tucson
> Bulldozers knocking down houses in a nearby urban
> renewal area
> A car accident observed by children on the way to
> school
> A popular television program (Television is a real part
> of the child's world.)
> A protest demonstration in the community
> A visit to a county fair or a street carnival

Any major event such as a moon walk, an election, a weather
happening, or some disruption in the lives of the children
can be a good base for an experience story. Mass media have
made every child a participant in the events of his time. By
drawing on such events, the teacher not only builds on high
interest but also helps children cope with their world.

Trips are desirable as a means of broadening experience,
but they are not essential if teachers take advantage of the
experiences in which pupils are already immersed.

Classroom experiences relating to social studies and science
and individual experiences are other sources. Individual
experiences can be the basis for either class or group stories
as a child shares a major or minor event in his life: the new
baby in the family, a fishing trip, a gift, a movie he saw.
Children can create their own personalized charts and stories

by dictating to the teacher or to an older child.

Talk about the experience before making a chart or writing a story. What is written down will be a small part – the distillation of what the children have to say about the experience. After the children have expressed their individual reactions and have reacted to each other, then the teacher can ask them what they would like to include in the written account.

Establish a purpose for the writing of the experience story. To say it's a reading lesson is not enough. The children must have a better reason for the activity. Writing a story for a class newspaper, enlarging a social studies unit on the election or a safety campaign – these are examples of intrinsic purposes.

Use the children's own language. No special spellings need be involved, since spelling is standard for all dialects (though American and British spellings are not always identical). 'Pumpkin' is spelled the same whether or not one says 'pump' for the first syllable, and 'help' has an 'l' whether it is pronounced or not. In general, final 's(es)' and 'd(ed)' may be included in the recorder's spelling even when they are not used by the speaker: 'Then I walked right by it' is a suitable way to record what might sound to the teacher like 'Den ah walk raht bah it.' The important thing the teacher must do in these cases is to accept the child's reading of what has been written as long as it is consistent with his own speech. The goal is to build bridges between his speech and written language. Correcting or attempting to change his sound patterns will only confuse the child.

The grammar of the children's language must be kept intact. If the child says 'Me and James seen a crash,' substituting 'James and I saw' may cause confusion. Vocabulary choices must also be maintained. Calling a 'crash' an accident may be more elegant, but it is not what the speaker meant. Similarly, if the child says 'His arm was busted,' to substitute 'broken' would defeat the purpose of using the child's language; 'broken' and 'busted' may well not be synonymous to him.

Teachers often worry about the reactions of parents and administrators to the use of the children's own language. If the purpose is clear in the teacher's mind, there should be no difficulty in explaining it to others who share an interest in the children's learning to read. Parents support teachers if the parents are informed and if they feel that the teacher has a purpose.

Consider the experience story a significant part of the reading content. Through the use of experience materials comprehension strategies are built. These strategies can be used later by the children as they perform other reading tasks and use published reading materials.

Though the focus in this chapter has been on the place of experience stories in beginning reading, the same basic techniques are applicable at later stages, and the same benefits may be derived. Alert teachers can find frequent opportunities to have children, individually and in groups, create their own materials to read and share with others. Such activities can direct the teaching of reading into personalized channels, the better to meet each child's needs.

Language is learned from whole to part, from general to specific, from familiar to unfamiliar. Learning to read follows the same pattern. There is one place to begin - with the language and experience of each learner.

This is an important article for teachers who want sound advice about strategies that help readers get to meaning, an ultimate aim of all reading. Here Goodman provides a wealth of information concerning scanning, selection, confirmation, and correction strategies based on his extensive research with young readers. The article concludes with valuable advice as to how teachers can analyze children's miscues and work with them in helping them become both efficient and effective readers.

7 STRATEGIES FOR INCREASING COMPREHENSION IN READING

Reading teachers in past decades have been so close to reading and so anxious to help children develop into good readers that they have sometimes lost sight of the essential nature and purpose of reading. Sometimes we have even let ourselves slip into thinking of reading as the score on a test or the ability to deal with skill exercises. We must remind ourselves that reading is a language process. It is a receptive process similar and parallel to listening. Its purpose is to construct, from language in written form, a message that will match to a high degree the one the author intended to convey. *We read to get the meaning.*

A reader, then, is a user of language who constantly seeks sense from what he reads. His success in any reading task can be judged primarily on the basis of what he has understood. Teaching someone to read is a matter of helping him become competent in getting meaning from written language. Reading is not matching sounds to letters or sound patterns to spelling patterns, or naming, recognizing, or perceiving words, though in the process of reading a reader may do any or all of these things. Yet he may do them all with relative success but not get the meaning. Only getting intended meaning is the test of the success of reading instruction.

The ability of a reader to get the meaning from written language is his effectiveness as a reader. This is not a matter of exact agreement with the author. In fact, exact agreement is unlikely many times because of the differences in attitudes, concepts, and backgrounds of the reader and the writer. Furthermore, much written language presents complex multi-layered meanings. One may understand the basic theme of a story while missing some of its fine details because of an unfamiliarity with the settings or some of the activities in which the characters engage. Or one may gain a superficial understanding without grasping the theme because it involves subtleties and concepts which the reader does not have in his background. If teachers expect and only accept exact agreement with the way they understand the author's message, they are expecting an impossibility. At the same time teachers may impose a convergent view of meaning in which creative and divergent views are discouraged. If meaning is viewed as absolute, then critical reading will be discouraged.

EFFECTIVE AND EFFICIENT READING

'Efficient reading' gets to the meaning with the least amount of effort necessary. This efficiency is gained by using the fewest number of graphic cues and making the best possible predictions on the basis of what the reader knows about language and the content of what he is reading, without sacrificing meaning. Slow, plodding, careful reading may be effective, but it is likely to be inefficient if only because of the time and fatigue involved. It may well be ineffective, too, because of the load it imposes on the memory of the reader who is attempting to store too much information and delay making decisions about meaning until he has all the information. By the time he is ready to make a decision, he may have lost some of the information he needs. As a result some rapid readers may have higher levels of comprehension. Speed in itself is of no particular significance in reading comprehension. But increasing speed often requires the reader to use more efficient strategies and to be more selective in the information he uses as he reads.

The word 'strategy,' which has been used here, grows out of research and theories of reading. As one reads, one must have means to get from print to meaning which are flexible enough and varied enough to deal with a wide range of demands. These general approaches for using available information are called strategies.

SCANNING STRATEGIES

Written English progresses from left to right. Consequently a reader must develop 'scanning strategies' which respond to this characteristic of the language. However, some graphic information encountered later has important effects on the value of that which precedes it. A final 'e,' for example, marks the preceding vowel letter's relationship to a vowel sound. The reader, then, must accommodate his use of scanning strategies and the information they provide, so that he anticipates or seeks out information which may not be in a simple left-to-right sequence. To get to the meaning of a passage, a reader must assign a grammatical structure. He knows then how the elements fit together and anticipates what to expect as he gathers more graphic information. He seeks cues early in the sentence to help him identify a first element in a pattern and predict what follows. He may identify a common statement pattern (subject, verb, object) by finding that the sentence starts with a noun phrase: 'Franklin had a marvelous sense of humour. His brother printed a newspaper.' Or he may predict a question if the sentence starts with a question marker like 'what': 'What good could a balloon be?' Or his cue that it is a question may be that it starts with a verb marker: 'Do you know what my favorite is?' Punctuation that comes at the ends of sentences can confirm a prediction about the grammatical pattern of the sentence, but it is of little help in formulating one.

SELECTION STRATEGIES

The efficient reader selects graphic cues, letters or letter parts, or configurations of letters, which will identify for him most directly a grammatical structure resulting in meaning. The brain can only handle a limited amount of information at a given time. One may think of one's eye as transmitting visual information to a tiny television screen which can hold a small picture for only a very short time before it is replaced by a new image. Therefore the reader must select carefully what is to be fed into that screen, or he will waste a great deal of effort and be inefficient. He has 'selection strategies' that draw on his familiarity with language structure, his expectations as he reads, and his ultimate concern for meaning. Meaning is very important because if the reader is concerned with correctly identifying letters one at a time, he will use more graphic cues than he needs and use them differently. For example, try to read this sequence of letters: tygizdziezagizdozony. Since it has no apparent pattern, one is forced to concentrate on letters. Even when word spaces are inserted, a great deal of graphic information is required to say, remember, and reproduce it: Ty gizdzie zagizdozony. On the other hand a native speaker of Polish will be able to not only remember and reproduce it with ease, but will know what this line from a fifth-grade Polish reading text means. The difference is basic competence in the language. A native speaker of English can go directly from minimal graphic cues to meaningful grammatical structures when he reads English, and he has no need to identify inefficiently every letter or word to do so. In fact, even what he thinks he sees is largely what he expects to see. 'Prediction' or 'expectation strategies' are used in close harmony with selection strategies. Simply speaking, the reader uses minimal cues, graphic as well as grammatical and semantic (meaning), and guesses at what is coming. How good his guesses are, is dependent on how efficient he has been in using his selection and prediction strategies. Again the most important factor in his success is his concern for meaning.

CONFIRMATION STRATEGIES

Having made predictions, the reader must use 'confirmation strategies' to check on the consistency of his expectations with the cues he is encountering as he reads on. He must ask himself whether it is making sense and whether the grammatical pattern he had predicted is the one he is finding. The same graphic cues that he uses to make subsequent predictions are used to confirm or reject prior predictions.

Two contexts are created as the reader checks his guesses. One is a semantic or meaning context as he looks for sense. The other is the syntactic, sentence-pattern context which relates elements to clauses and clauses to each other. Efficient and effective reading requires that the reader closely monitor his reading through these confirmation strategies. Knowing when and where he has lost the meaning is as vital to successful reading as making strong predictions in the first place. The reader uses correction strategies to reprocess information when he needs to do so, in order to recover from miscues that have resulted in meaning loss. Sometimes he can rethink the significance of the information he has and try an alternate prediction consistent with the cues he has. At other times he will need to regress with his eyes to the left and up the page, seeking more information and additional cues showing where he got off the track. Knowing what to do when one has lost meaning is a vital part of learning to read. All readers make miscues. Efficient, effective readers know what to do when they need to correct them.

It is also necessary for an efficient reader not to waste his energies and time correcting miscues which do not result in loss of meaning. Preoccupation with accuracy in word identification for its own sake requires the reader to use more information than he needs and to use inefficient selection strategies. This view of efficient reading contradicts the commonsense notion that there is value in being careful and accurate in all reading situations. But it is not difficult to see that if the reader makes confident predictions, keeps his concern for meaning constant, recognizes when he has lost the meaning, and corrects to recover the meaning, then that correction only for the sake of accuracy alone is more of a distraction than an aid.

There is also a time in reading when correction will not be of value. The reader is aware that he has not understood the author's meaning and checks to make sure that his lack of meaning is not because of miscues. He rereads to see if he can make more sense of what he has read, but can not make any sense of it. He can read ahead, hoping that subsequent reading will make the meaning clear. If that does not help, he may have to conclude, as even proficient adult readers often do, that he lacks the background necessary to read the particular selection. He must either get the experience or find a more relevant selection.

Research on the reading process has shown that in children's oral reading, the most important indicator of their basic reading competence is the extent to which they retain meaning even when they produce miscues. Teachers should be concerned with the effect of miscues and not with their quantity. If the miscues do not disrupt the meaning, then the reader is being effective. If he corrects when his miscues do disrupt meaning, he is indicating his pervading concern for meaning.

Here is an example of a miscue that does not affect meaning:

> in
> 'How come everybody is zonked out ~~on~~ the living room floor?' Brian asked.

Here is one that did disturb the meaning and grammar but was corrected:

> 'You can be a nutseller!'

Note 'a' is omitted but the reader realizes as he starts the next word and goes back to correct. He is using confirming strategies to check himself out.

Teachers can help developing readers to build the strategies they need for effective and efficient reading. In doing so the teacher helps the pupil build on his strength and fill in his areas of weakness. Thus the teacher is working with the learner rather than at cross-purposes with him. The teacher is not so much a source of wisdom in sound reading instruction as a guide and aid, monitoring the learner's progress, offering help when a hang-up is detected, stimulating interest in reading, helping him find relevant, worthwhile materials to read, and offering continuous encouragement.

Everything that the teacher does for and with the learner must be thought through in terms of how it contributes to his attainment of meaning. Perhaps the most important question a teacher can ask a pupil is 'Does that make sense to *you*?' The teacher must help the learner to keep in mind at all times that he is seeking meaning.

It is also very important that the teacher build up the learner's confidence in himself as a user of language. Every child who speaks a dialect of English has the language competence necessary to predict English sentence structures and get meaning from them. But the developing reader must come to trust his own judgment and linguistic intuition. He needs to be assured that what has worked for him in listening can work in reading, too, if he approaches reading with ease and confidence.

It is doubly important that the teacher does not confuse teaching pupils to speak a high status dialect of English with teaching them to read. If the teacher 'corrects' a reader's pronunciation from what sounds right in his dialect to what sounds right in the teacher's, the reader may become confused and think that he is not a successful reader. Furthermore the information the teacher is providing him by such a correction does not help him relate print to speech as *he* knows it, but rather to relate it to another sound system he does not control.

A rule of thumb for teachers in cases where they are doubtful is that if the pupil reads the way he speaks, he is not having a reading problem.

It is very important that the teacher help the developing reader to use his own resources, to build his own strategies. When a reader pauses, many teachers assume it is because the reader doesn't know the next word, so they tell him what it is. But he may have a very different problem. He may know what it is but not be able to figure out how it relates to the pattern or meaning of the sentence. Telling him the word is like saying 'Even if it doesn't make sense, say it anyway.' Rather, the teacher should probe to find out what the reader considers his problem to be. Even if he says 'What's that word?' a perceptive teacher might say 'What do you think it is?' The pupil's response may contain some surprises such as: 'I think I know, but that doesn't fit' or 'I know all the words, but I can't get any sense out of it.'

The teacher can be very helpful at times when the reader is groping for meaning to help him crystallize his strategies. 'What would make sense here?' is a good first question. It puts everything in the context of a search for meaning. 'What would sound right or fit here?' is a good next question if further help is needed. Such a question directs the reader to use his sense of English grammar. Having established these meaning and grammar limits, if help is still needed then one might add 'What looks like this word that could fit and make sense here?' The teacher must remember, however, that the goal is to help the reader get to meaning, and that is more important than getting each word exactly right.

CORRECTION STRATEGIES

When the reader knows he has lost the meaning, the teacher can help him develop correction strategies. Some suggestions a teacher might make are:

1 Go back and see if you can find a place where you might have gotten off the track.
2 Think about what you think the page should be saying. That may help you find where you got off.
3 Read ahead and see how things work out.

Sometimes readers indicate a kind of inefficiency by correcting themselves when they do not need to do so. Only when the meaning is disrupted is there any real need for correction. If the teacher is relaxed and at ease about deviations that do not upset meaning, the pupils are likely to be more relaxed as well.

When the problem the reader faces is an unfamiliar word, phrase, or word usage, the teacher can help the child understand that:

1 The way the word or phrase is used is a good clue to its meaning in the particular passage.

2 Authors frequently provide simple definitions right in the text: 'To measure wind speed, meteorologists use an anemometer.'

3 If the word is important it will occur several times. Each subsequent occurrence will provide a new context to help the reader zero in on its meaning.

4 If the word is unimportant to the reader's comprehension, he will need only a vague notion of its meaning to go on. Usually its context provides that. Most proficient readers have learned to be undisturbed by a few unimportant words, the meanings of which are uncertain.

5 Dictionaries are most useful for confirmation when the reader has formed a fairly strong notion of a word's meaning from the context.

6 If the word or phrase is a name difficult to pronounce or a foreign word, it may be sufficient to use a place holder to facilitate reading. Calling the character with the Slavic name Ivan may be good enough - and save a lot of time while avoiding distraction.

7 One need not be able to pronounce every word to get its meaning. Most proficient readers have many words in their reading vocabularies they do not use or have not heard used orally.

Our research has shown that less proficient readers dissipate a lot of energy working at every word while more proficient readers have the confidence that they can get the meaning without word-by-word accuracy.

TEACHER ANALYSIS OF MISCUES

Teachers can learn to infer from the miscues a learner makes, what his strengths and weaknesses are. This may be facilitated by having a pupil read orally to a tape recorder. The teacher can then analyze his miscues at a later time, using the steps listed below:

Consider whether the reader's response is simply an evidence of his own dialect. If so, then it is not a miscue to be concerned about since the reader has shifted to his own dialect while getting to meaning. Most dialect miscues are phonological. In oral reading the reader says the words as he does in his speech: 'help' may be 'he'p,' 'pumpkin' may be 'punkin.' There are four ways that 'almond' is pronounced in various parts of this country, two with 'l' and two without. Clearly, if the reader uses his preferred pronunciation, he shows he knows the meaning. If a teacher insists on a preferred or standard pronunciation, it is likely only to confuse the reader.

Other forms of dialect-related miscues may involve inflectional suffixes; the 's' or 'ed' endings in the speech of many black youngsters are dropped. Appalachian pupils may not use 's' forms after numbers: 'two miles' becomes 'two mile.' Sometimes readers may switch to a different grammatical form as they go to meaning. They may, for example, use a different form of 'be': 'There was lots of goats.' Again these are shifts to the reader's own dialect and show that he has understood. Readers will even, at times, substitute a preferred word in their own dialect, 'minute' for 'moment,' for example.

If teachers make themselves aware by listening objectively to how the dialects found in their classrooms are used, they will easily be able to separate miscues that matter from these dialect shifts.

Consider the effect of the miscues on meaning. The best indication of the strength the reader brings to any reading task is the extent to which his miscues still result in acceptable meaning. Such miscues show the basic preoccupation of the reader with meaning. If upwards of 40 percent of the reader's miscues produce acceptable meaning (before any correction takes place), the reader shows this vital ability to get to meaning. There is no need for teachers to be concerned about correcting miscues that produce acceptable meaning. Such miscues may produce changes in meaning even if they make sense, however. The teacher should consider how the meaning is modified in judging whether the pupil is showing strength or weakness. Often the change is more an indication of a conceptual problem than difficulty with reading.

Consider the ability of the reader to handle the grammar. Often, even when the reader loses meaning, he stays with the grammatical pattern of the author or produces another acceptable pattern. Even when pupils produce non-words they may preserve the affixes of the original word, showing their sense of its grammatical function. In word substitutions pupils who are operating with reading as language may substitute only nouns for nouns, verbs for verbs, and the like.

Among intermediate-grade readers a strong disparity between the percent of their miscues that produce acceptable grammar and those which produce acceptable meaning may indicate that the conceptual load is heavy for the readers. If they are not able to comprehend, they may treat what they read as grammatical nonsense, manipulating the English structures effectively even though they cannot understand. Even proficient adults behave this way with difficult texts, such as legal documents.

Consider the relationship between the miscue and the text in terms of sounds and shapes. The reader's miscues, when they are word substitutions, may be considered on the basis of how much they look or sound like what was expected. Ironically, teachers have often assumed that when pupils produce a number of substitutions that vary in minor aspects from what was expected, the pupil is showing evidence of a phonics problem. In fact such miscues show the opposite. They show the reader is able to use phonics to get close to the right pronunciation. If the miscues also produce sense, then the reader has no serious problem. If, on the other hand, his phonic 'near-misses' produce nonsense, his problem is not phonics but may even be the result of preoccupation with letter accuracy and too little concern for meaning. In that case the teacher will try to help the reader develop his ability to use meaning and grammar contexts and temper his use of phonics strategies.

Consider when the reader corrects. Effective readers know that when meaning is disrupted, when they cannot get sense from their reading, they must correct; that is, go back over what they have read to make sense out of it.

Correction in reading is a complex phenomenon, however, because the reader who is proficient produces a majority of miscues which have acceptable meaning and do not need correction. Less effective readers may correct by persevering on individual words until they get them right while they do not correct on other types of miscues which produce nonsense. The teacher, then, must observe whether pupils correct miscues where the meaning is affected.

Helping pupils to build sound, useful correction strategies requires that they learn to detect miscues that need correction. Teachers must resist the temptation to tell the pupil when and why he needs to correct; furthermore the teacher must help the reader use his own resources in correcting. Rarely is it ever desirable for the teacher to tell the pupil what he should have said. If the pupil develops his own correction strategies, it will not only build his confidence and success in getting to the meaning but will lead to his producing fewer miscues that need correction as he becomes more aware of the importance of keeping meaning his main concern.

DIFFERENT STRATEGIES FOR DIFFERENT TASKS

Though general reading strategies are essential for all kinds of reading, different materials may vary in ways that require the reader to employ special strategies.

The language of literature, for example, has the general characteristic of being less predictable than everyday conversation. Authors avoid using common, repetitious vocabulary. This rich language full of surprises adds to the pleasure of reading but it creates problems for a reader for which he must have flexible strategies to apply. Consider this passage:

A feeling of panic surged through Stan as he tried to wriggle free. Then he fought back the terror, realizing that panic was as big an enemy as the current which held him fast.[1]

Suppose the author had written it this way:

Stan was scared. He tried to get loose. Then he knew he shouldn't get scared because that was as bad as the current that kept him from getting loose. So he tried not to be scared.

Both passages mean the same thing, but the original will be less predictable and harder to read and understand. The more predictable language is dull and flat-sounding. The teacher must help the children develop strategies for dealing with the language of literature.

In contrast, the language of the content areas may be expository, designed to present new concepts and ideas. It employs a technical vocabulary and uses some common terms in specialized ways. Teachers must provide relevant experiences and must help pupils acquire the necessary concepts so that the technical vocabulary will become useful and easily handled. Language and concepts depend on each other. Moreover, most content-area texts are heavily laden with concepts. Thus they are written with an economy of words to express complex ideas. In these areas it is more difficult for pupils to comprehend unless the teacher builds concepts through advance preparation for reading, even if the author is careful to define his terms.

The language of literature provides central characters, plot, and mood around which rich and continuous context is developed. In contrast, continuity in social studies or science may be weak as the text moves from idea to idea and may be interrupted by reference to maps, charts, graphs, and tables. The child must build comprehension strategies to learn these aids.

The language of mathematics has a special logic and grammar. There is less redundancy so that the omission of a word may change the meaning entirely. These special comprehension strategies are most readily learned in the materials and situations that approximate their use. Thus the social studies strategies are learned most easily in social studies materials. The quantitative language of mathematics calls for more careful concern for detail within a search to determine the problem-solving steps and the relationships between the quantities.

CHECKING COMPREHENSION

All of the foregoing strategies help make pupils independent and effective readers. In most instances they will approach the meaning that the author intended, although special features of the author's style may complicate this. For example, some authors use exaggeration or analogous statements to emphasize a point. It is important for teachers to help pupils develop strategies to comprehend particular features of literary style. Moreover, there are times when pupils achieve a meaning which is quite far from the one the author started with. It is important for the teacher to be aware of how much the pupils have understood.

Comprehension of subtle and implied meanings, as pupils encounter complex materials, develops gradually. A good story almost always has more than any one reader can find in it. Teachers, with patience, can help pupils find this richness.

CONCLUSION

Pupils in the intermediate years can be helped to analyze their own strengths and difficulties in reading. After a pupil has read to a tape recorder, the teacher may find it useful to analyze his reading with him, encouraging him to consider what he is doing as he reads and perhaps helping him gain insights into how he can become more proficient. Together they may find that the pupil is either too cautious or too impetuous, too much concerned with accuracy when it is not essential, or too quick to leap to a conclusion. He may be helped to think through what information he could have used, or what strategy would have helped handle a particular problem. Such a joint analysis may provide the teacher with additional insights into the reader's strengths and weaknesses, so that the teacher can design productive learning activities.

Any help a teacher provides is most useful if it builds confidence and independence in the learner. Help that builds dependence on the teacher will not serve the pupil in the situations in which he reads, without the teacher there to guide him. Teachers must help the pupil expand, on his own, language and cognitive resources. Teachers who work *with* children will find that in the process of helping them build strategies for comprehension, they have helped them become efficient and effective readers.

NOTE

1 From Danger in the Deep by Charles Coombs from 'Young Readers Water Sports,' Lantern Press, Inc., Mt Vernon, NY, 1952.

THEORY OF CURRICULUM AND INSTRUCTION

My view of reading instruction I must warn you is built on a strong theoretical base which has been continually tempered by plunging it into the reality of real people reading real language.

I am convinced that, to build effective reading methods and materials, we must (a) understand the reading process; (b) know what it is that proficient readers do; (c) get clear in our minds what reading is for; (d) understand how people become proficient readers: that is, how reading is learned.

Here Goodman suggests that reading instruction must be organized 'totally around advancing comprehension. Each instructional activity should in fact be screened on the basis of whether it contributes to comprehension. Any skills or strategies should be developed within the quest for meaning in which the reader should be continuously engaged.'

This reading provides valuable theoretical and practical insights.

8 COMPREHENSION-CENTERED READING INSTRUCTION

Reading is a process by which a person reconstructs a message encoded graphically by a writer. Like all language activities, reading has as its central purpose, effective communication of meaning. In the full sense, comprehension is the only objective of the reader. To the extent that he has this end continuously in view he is reading; to the extent that he loses comprehension as a goal he is doing something other than reading: saying sounds, naming words, manipulating language. This alone would be enough to justify the claim that instruction in reading must center on comprehension.

But there is an even more basic reason why reading instruction must be comprehension centered. Language does not exist apart from its relationship to meaning. Now this meaning is not a property of language - the sounds or ink blotches have no intrinsic meaning. Meaning is supplied by the reader himself as he processes the symbolic system of language. As a user of the language he relates language sequences to experiences and conceptual structures. He cannot get the message unless he can process the language. But neither can he process the language unless he has the relevant experiential-conceptual background to bring to the particular task. I can't read a technical treatise on nuclear physics: I'm disadvantaged; I lack the background. But I do well at reading even highly technical material where I have strong interests and relevant cognitive structures. Meaning, in short, is both output and input, in the reading process. Unless the teaching of reading is comprehension centered the very nature of the task is changed from reading to something other than reading.

That's my basic message. The rest of my discussion will be (1) an attempt to support this view, and (2) an attempt to explore its implications.

BUILDING READING INSTRUCTION ON A SOUND THEORETICAL BASE

My view of reading instruction I must warn you is built on a strong theoretical base which has been continually tempered by plunging it into the reality of real people reading real language.

I am convinced that, to build effective reading methods and materials, we must (1) understand the reading process (2) know what it is that proficient readers do (3) get clear in our minds

what reading is for (4) understand how people become proficient
readers: that is, how reading is learned.

My research has been devoted to describing what readers do
when they read material new to themselves and deriving from
that a theory and model of the reading process which in turn
can be applied back to predicting, categorizing, and describing what people do when they read. I am fully aware that each
day thousands of teachers are confronted with millions of
learners who must be taught *now* and that the educational
assembly line cannot be shut down until basic knowledge is
available on which instruction must be based. But I am convinced that the quest for that basic knowledge must be pursued.

The alternatives are visible in the old and new solutions to
the reading dilemma in current vogue.

At the risk of setting up straw men I'd like to characterize
these approaches.

(1) There's the 'butterfly collector' approach. Most relatively
effective reading teachers and clinicians are butterfly col-
lectors. They have large collections of bits and pieces, and
gimmicks that work with some children some time. And every
so often they add a new butterfly to the collection making a
mental note as they do so that one day they must organize
that collection. But they never do and they are unable to
build on knowledge or put it in a form that can be transmitted
to others.

(2) Some solutions to the reading problem are neat, sequential,
behaviorally stated 'stairways to nowhere.' Assumptions are
made about what readers must do or know or existing materials
are searched for bits and pieces and gimmicks and these are
stated as behavioral objectives. Early results with such
approaches are always impressive since (1) the readers already
could do a lot of the things they're taught and (2) evaluation
is through tests composed of items that are just like the
instructional materials. But the stairways never get the learner
to that glorious behavioral Valhalla in the sky because to complete the stairway the entire reading process would have to be
understood and that process would have to be amenable to
sequencing into neat behavioral steps. And it is not so amenable.

(3) Other programs are derived from diligent and rigorous
'trial and error.' Try method A, book A, system A against
method B, book B, system B, discard the poor and use the
better. Then proceed with C, D, etc. Or keep changing your
procedures until you get better results. While the latter is
practical advice for a teacher the teacher will certainly need
some criteria for determining how to change. How long would
we have waited for a cure to polio if we were depending on
testing any proffered method against any other or making spor-
adic and intuitive modifications in existing treatments? How in
fact can you achieve major innovations in solving any problems
through trial and error, however rigorous?

(4) A rather homey solution to the reading problem is one I call the 'chicken soup approach.' Phonics is liberally served up to all like chicken soup on the assumption that it might help and it couldn't hurt. Unfortunately it can hurt some learners.

(5) Finally there is the 'systems approach,' recommended as a solution for everything (so why not reading). If we are confused let's organize our confusion systematically. This approach was pioneered by the Department of Defense (affectionately known as the DOD) and has demonstrated its utility in the solution of such problems as the Vietnam war. In the aero-space industry problems are solved through systems approaches at no more than three to ten times their original projected cost. There is however an adage which has found its way into even the Pentagon: Garbage in, garbage out. Reading problems will apparently not be solved simply by broadening the scope of the DOD and renaming it the Department of Education and Defense (DEAD).

Fortunately many children have the internal resources to surmount all obstacles we place in their way and to learn to read anyway. For this fact we should be grateful though it confuses research since children can apparently learn in spite of their instruction rather than because of it.

THE READING PROCESS

There *is* a process of reading with certain characteristics regardless of the nature of what is being read or even the language and orthography in which it is printed.

Reading, like listening, *is* a receptive psycholinguistic process. Language in its graphic form is the starting point. The reader brings to the text his knowledge of the language. As he reads there is an interaction between language and thought processes such that the reader moves from a language encoding of meaning to meaning itself.

Though the sensory modality involved is visual, the reading process is only incidentally visual since even what the reader thinks he sees at any point is only partly what he sees and partly what he expects to see. On the basis of the language structures he controls, the reader is constantly predicting what he will see. He samples from the available cues of the graphic display using language strategies he has developed to select only those cues which carry the most information. He arrives at hypothetical, tentative choices (guesses), as he reads, checking them against his predictions and the grammatical and semantic constraints of which he is aware. Then he needs only enough subsequent information to confirm or disconfirm his prediction.

Reading printed words then is a spiral of predict, sample, select, guess, and confirm activities. The reader has strategies for these activities. *The proficient reader uses the least amount of information to make the best possible first guesses.* He also has an effective set of strategies for checking the validity of his guesses. Simply, he asks himself whether (1) they produce language structures as he knows them, and (2) they make sense. Finally he has a set of strategies for correcting when he realizes that he has been unsuccessful.

Reading is *not* an exact precise process of identifying each letter and then each word and then each sequence. Such a process would be not only inefficient since all information need not be processed, but it would be ineffective as well, because readers would be distracted by the excess of graphic and phonic information and would be less able to integrate it with the syntactic and semantic information they must process to deal with the text as language.

No single cue or system of cues in fact is useful in reading unless it is processed in its relationship to all other cues in a natural language setting. Language is *not* a salami which can be sliced as thin as one wishes with each slice retaining all the essential qualities of the whole. When language is broken into sounds, letters, words, or even phrases what results is something other than language. Language must be understood *in process* as it stands in relationship to its use. It must have structure and there must be meaning for it to be language.

A word needs to be said about context in reading. There are in reality two contexts: one is syntactic, the language structure. The other is semantic: the meaning or message. These are interdependent. In fact it is not possible to having meaning without grammar; but readers use both contexts. Let us remember that the reader is not ultimately concerned with naming, recognizing, or identifying words but that his concern is comprehension. Reading programs have been word centered for too long. The reader does not use context simply to identify words, rather he uses all cues in relationship to all others to reconstruct the message.

THE READER AS A USER OF LANGUAGE

Because reading instruction was disconnected from its language base for so long the most important resource children bring to the task of learning to read has been underestimated or ignored. That resource is their highly developed language competence. Beginners in reading are already highly skilled in using language. They are able to communicate their needs, thoughts, and reactions to the world to others by encoding them in language and producing speech. They are able to understand messages from others by processing the surface phonological structures of speech, inducing the underlying language structures and reconstructing the meaning.

Any limitations on the child's ability to function as a listener in his own community are experiential and conceptual and not primarily linguistic.

All of this is of enormous use to the beginner reader. His task is to learn to induce the underlying language structures from *written* language. As long as he is confronted with graphic material which is real and meaningful (as opposed to fragmentary, artificial, and/or non-sensical) he can utilize his language competence. If however the meanings require more semantic input than he can provide then the task becomes nonsense for him. He must in fact be able to know whether the message he is reconstructing makes sense.

To give the child beginning to learn to read his native language full credit we must differentiate between language competence and language performance. Too many studies of child language have equated the two assuming that what children *do* in language is the same as what they are capable of doing. That can be put another way; we have confused behavior with the competence that underlies it and makes it possible. In studying vocabulary, for example, we have assumed that we could judge its breadth by listing the words used by a child in a given situation. Vocabulary, however, is highly contingent on a particular individual's interest *in*, background *for*, and willingness *to discuss*, a particular topic under particular circumstances. We have been quite willing to accept the conclusion that boys are less competent linguistically than girls at school and preschool ages because in fact girls perform better on typical research tasks. It is at least as likely however that under different conditions that favor boys they would perform better than girls.

We must learn to relate linguistic performance to a theoretical understanding of language competence in order to interpret the former and gain insight into the latter.

Frequently we interpret particular language performance as indicative of lack of competence where in fact it indicates quite the opposite.

The preschooler who says 'I taked it' is showing mastery of a basic pattern for indicating past tense, not sloppy speech. Similarly, the beginning reader who reads 'home' for 'house' in 'The dog had a new warm house,' is showing a high degree of reading competence, not a lack of word recognition. A child who says 'horse' for 'house' in the same sentence is not showing a lack of phonics generalizations so much as he is in some difficulty in using them in language context. A key to his competence will be whether he corrects if his reading is not comprehensible.

The goal of reading instruction is not to change reading behavior but to expand the reader's competence in comprehending written language. Behavior, at best, is a shadow image of that competence.

Perception as it functions in language is very much misunderstood. Every language user learns two things as he learns the language: (1) What to pay attention to (2) What not to pay attention to.

Each language uses only a small number of the ways that sounds may differ as significant distinctive features. The user of language must learn to note those significant features. If he did not also learn to ignore non-significant differences he would be constantly distracted. The unitary symbols of any language are perceptual rather than real units. Features may vary widely within the units but language users will ignore the differences. But minor differences *across* the boundaries must be noted. This is true for written as well as oral language. A reader comes to treat 'A' and 'H' as different though they are very similar and A α a α α as the same though they are very different.

We tend to treat performance on 'auditory discrimination' tests as indicative of linguistic incompetence when it really shows how well the child has learned to screen out differences not significant in his own speech (pin, pen for example).

Speakers of low-status dialects are repeatedly misjudged as linguistically deficient by teachers and researchers because their language behavior does not match an expectation model. But difference and deficiency are not the same. All children, normal in the broadest sense of the word, have a high degree of language competency to bring to learning to read.

THE PURPOSES OF READING

There is a romance that surrounds the purposes of reading that obscures its most vital functions and exaggerates others.

Written language develops in human societies when they become so complex that communication must be carried on over time and space and not merely on a face-to-face basis. Writers may seek to communicate messages to people whose ears they can not reach. They may preserve messages for the later use of others as well as themselves.

The basic reason for existence of competence in written language in an individual in a literate society is to cope with the everyday experiences in his culture which employ written language. He must read signs, follow written directions, fill out forms, read his mail.

Written language is the basic (though not exclusive) medium of literature. But one can function in literate society without reading literature. Minimal functioning with no reading competence at all is much harder.

Putting the purposes of reading in proper perspective it would appear that instruction should be built around what I choose to call situational reading, the kind that is so universal in a literate society that it is incidental to life itself. Situational reading, by virtue of its constant impingement on the life of children is self motivating. Many an American five-year-old can recognize five kinds of peanut butter and twice that many cereals by their labels. Four-year-olds quickly learn to know which door says 'Men' and which one says 'Ladies.'

Once it is learned, reading can, of course, be used in pleasure seeking activities as in the reading of comic books or other literary works.

It may even be used in learning. But I must point out that in situational reading the meanings are either well defined by the situational contexts or within the conceptual grasp of the learner because they relate to recurrent experiences. Both the reading of literature and reading to learn move out and away from the learner and his immediate world.

Language grows in direct proportion to the experiences and conceptual growth of the learner. But there are limits on the leaps he can make. To gain new knowledge or concepts in reading requires considerable relevant semantic input. Bormuth's work indicates that unless a reader can score fairly well on a comprehension test over material *before* he reads he will learn little from the reading.

Particularly in the elementary years, where skill in using written language lags well behind oral language competence, reading to learn has severe limitations. That suggests that reading should support or even follow learning in school rather than become its basic medium. A defensible cycle would be first to do, then to discuss, then to read, and then to write.

Textbooks are, by design, difficult reading tasks. They deal with many concepts unlikely to be known to the learners; the lower the level the more superficial they are likely to be. That doesn't necessarily reduce the comprehension problem since instead of treating a few topics in depth they treat many, bouncing along without developing any semantic context well enough to give the struggling reader much to go on. Many teachers have the mistaken notion that the textbook's function is to teach *for* them and that each child should be able to read and learn from a text written for use at his grade level.

If the focus is kept clearly on comprehension teachers can sense some of the inherent difficulties children encounter in reading school texts. Particularly teachers will need to realize that vocabulary, in and of itself, is seldom the key problem but that the profusion of new concepts, the special ways that language is used, the reading tasks that are particular to each area of study are all major sources of problems.

Vocabulary can develop, in any useful sense, only in close relationship to experiences and concepts. It is the ideas that need introduction before reading. New vocabulary is only of value as it is needed to cope with those ideas.

Even the grammar of language used in mathematics texts, science texts, and social studies books varies. Though all are rooted in the same grammatical system the special uses of language in each field require structures which may be unique to the field or uncommon in other areas. Conditional statements in mathematics involve rather unusual structures somewhat different than conditional statements in science.

Recipes are special language forms which require special strategies to adequately comprehend and use them.

Even the reading of literature requires strategies for dealing with language that has special characteristics. In the situational language which is basic, the reader can depend on it to be predictable. Writers of literature tend to avoid common predictable structures, forms, and vocabulary and to seek novel and hence unpredictable ones. Further, each writer establishes a style of language all his own. The language of Hemingway is not that of Steinbeck.

If learners are to develop the competence to comprehend a wide range of reading materials they must then develop general reading competence to handle other kinds of language. They will also have to see purposes for themselves to make the development of such competencies necessary.

Intrinsic motivation in reading is simply a matter of wanting to get the meaning. That is true whether the form is a sign on a wall, a set of directions for assembling a model airplane, a comic strip, a chapter in a text or a short story.

Motivation which is extrinsic, such as grades, rewards, punishments, may lead to acceptable behavior which does not in fact represent the underlying reading competencies sought. Too many readers can answer questions acceptably over reading materials they do not comprehend. If so they have learned not to read but to behave acceptably.

TEACHING AND LEARNING READING

It should be apparent that I am advocating organizing reading instruction totally around advancing comprehension. Each instructional activity should in fact be screened on the basis of whether it contributes to comprehension. Any skills or strategies should be developed within the quest for meaning in which the reader should be continuously engaged.

Relevancy is not a vague proposition in selecting reading materials. Since meaning is both input and output in reading, materials must be closely related to the background, interests, and experiences of particular learners.

To be comprehensible the language *at every stage of instruction* must be real language which is natural to the learners.

With the focus on meaning pupils will be able to move toward the integrated use of all cue systems in reading.

Throughout this discussion reference has been made to comprehension strategies. Strategies are general patterns readers develop for utilizing the varied kinds of cues available to them in reading print. The term 'skills' has come to mean an isolated, or isolatable, bit of knowledge or technique which a reader uses. Such a term is inappropriate for describing what a pro-

ficient reader does (hence what a pupil must learn to do) since
no such skill could be used invariantly in dealing with *actual*
written language. In fact the reader's strategies must be flexible enough to allow for the changing relative importance of
cues and cue systems in relationship to each other in given
tasks.

In reading a recipe, for example, the difference between
'2t baking powder' and '2T baking powder,' is the difference
between success and failure of the recipe's use. But a cook
who understands the function of baking powder and who is
experienced would recognize the improbability of a reading
error almost immediately. Semantic input serves, then, as a
safeguard on graphic or phonic miscuing.

It is only when the focus is on comprehension that the
relative importance of cues becomes clear and useful strategies
may emerge.

Readers need a set of initial strategies for coping with varied
reading tasks. They need a set of related, but somewhat different strategies for testing the acceptability of their reading
as they proceed. And they need still another set of strategies
for correcting and recovering meaning when they recognize that
they have miscued.

Some strategies will be general for all reading tasks. Others
will be utilized for special kinds of reading.

USES AND MISUSES OF READING

With the focus on comprehension certain key misconceptions
about the uses of reading become apparent.

The 'By the third grade' myth is very popularly subscribed
to. Many teachers believe that if a child can't read 'by the
third grade' he is doomed to school failure. This belief comes
from a strong tendency to make written language the main
medium of instruction much too early and much too completely.
No child can read and comprehend material that assumes concepts and experiences that he hasn't had. When this is compounded by a limited control over the reading process (as compared to listening) he is very much at a disadvantage. Reading
to learn must be used much more carefully at all levels of
instruction. It will be most successful after initial learning has
taken place.

Many secondary teachers use a 'here, read and learn'
approach. They assume that the text is the teacher, that the
pupil is fully able to learn through reading and that their own
role is to test, evaluate and grade. Such a view is untenable.
The text can be a component in the learning process only if it
is used in relationship to experience and oral language. Further,
the teachers must work with their pupils on developing and
extending their comprehension strategies to deal with the texts.

Particularly, teachers must ask themselves how much semantic input is necessary to make it possible for the reader to produce semantic output from a reading assignment. The answer to that inquiry will suggest how the pupils may be prepared for the task as well as whether the task is fundamentally appropriate or inappropriate.

Both the acquisition of the reading process and the effective use of that process depend on the reader and his teachers seeing comprehension as the continuous objective at all times.

'A viable theory of reading instruction,' says Goodman, 'has to be based on an articulated theory of the reading process.' The development of such a theory is not an easy task because of the need to consider additional relevant factors such as learning theory, sound pedagogy, child language development, cultural and social backgrounds, and individual differences. Important inputs that need to be considered come from a wide variety of fields including psychology, linguistics, sociology, communication theory, physiology and neurology, but 'it is not sufficient to add everything together, to pile it into one bag, shake it up and pour out an instructional theory. The knowledge must be integrated. Educationists must take on this task.'

With this background in mind, Goodman examines orthography (the use of written symbols) in relation to reading and addresses two questions:

'How is orthography used in reading? And what other kinds of decisions must constantly be played against those involving orthography?'

Important questions are raised for anyone seriously concerned with the theory of reading instruction.

9 ORTHOGRAPHY IN A THEORY OF READING INSTRUCTION

Orthography must be considered in its relation to a theory of reading instruction because the teaching of reading has come to the point now where it must be soundly based on an instructional theory.

The knowledge is available to answer the crucial questions of reading instruction. It cannot continue simply to be based on traditions that have accumulated over the past, or on unexamined theories that are not fully articulated.

Even when people don't state an instructional theory in building programs for teaching reading or materials for teaching reading they are likely to have one. One of the major problems of reading instruction is the failure on the part of people who are developing and promoting such programs to examine their theories of instruction.

REQUISITES FOR AN INSTRUCTIONAL THEORY

A viable theory of reading instruction has to be based on an articulated theory of the reading process. Simply speaking, we have to have some understanding of what it is we're trying to teach people in order to develop an instructional theory that relates to it. There is a remarkable belief among many people who've spent time working on reading that the process is self-evident and easily understood. Linguistic scholars have always been faced with that problem. As knowledge accumulates about how language works people tend to reject it by saying 'But language can't be that complex because I use it all the time.'

There also must be a learning theory built into the reading instruction theory. And that learning theory has to be appropriate to human language learning. Regardless of recent work with chimpanzees and porpoises, no species yet found does, in fact, develop language in any sense like humans do.

Third, there has to be a sound pedagogy built into this instructional theory. It has to assign a practical functional role to the teacher and to any other professionals that are involved. It has to incorporate some rules for the production of materials and it has to begin to produce a methodology which is sound from a pedagogical point of view. As a teacher would put it, it has to be teachable.

It also has to incorporate scientific knowledge of child language development. Considerable knowledge is developing in this area, not all of which has been applied in the teaching of reading. Besides that, flexibility has to be built into the theory to allow for the characteristics of the specific learners involved.

There has to be a differentiation in instructional theory between language competence, what a person is capable of doing, and language behavior, what he, in fact, is observed to do. Those are not the same thing. They must not be confused in building instructional theories.

We have to take into account cultural and social backgrounds in reading instruction. We have to take into account the legitimate differences in interest between children. Boys in general may be interested in adventure stories. That doesn't mean that any particular boy has to be interested. And theories must, of course, allow for the physical and mental variables that exist among children.

Where do the inputs come from for instructional theory? Obviously we've been seeking input for instructional theory in reading from psychology for some time. There are shelves of books on the psychology of reading. Probably one of the best is the one that Huey wrote in 1908.[1] Somehow we got away from some of the things that he and other psychologists were moving toward at that point. Input also has to come from education, from the classroom, from theoretical work, from dealing with teaching-learning issues. It has to come from linguistics because reading, after all, is one of the language processes. It has to come from psycholinguistics, the intersection between psychology and linguistics.

Other important input comes from sociology, social linguistics, and communication theory. Input must come from social-psychology for a number of reasons, not the least of which is that language is, after all, largely a phenomenon of human interaction. Physiology and neurology are also important.

As obvious as these areas are, we have usually failed to touch all the bases, to examine all the questions that are relevant and to seek the answers from all of these relevant inputs. The task is a difficult one because it's not sufficient to add everything, to pile it into one bag, shake it up and pour out an instructional theory. The knowledge must be integrated. Educationists must take on this task.

Dangers of narrow bases

The people providing the input are going to stop short of instructional theory; they're going to say 'This is knowledge that you need. You decide how to use it.' And particularly when every question involves psychological, linguistic, social, child development, and educational input it becomes a complex but vital function to integrate this knowledge and to make decisions that are as sound as possible in all respects. Legitimately a scholar from one of the academic disciplines ought to stop short unless, of course, he's going to make himself an educationist. There are many risks involved in operating on narrow bases which characterize almost all current reading programs and fragmentary instructional theories.

One such risk is a tendency to make leaps from research and from key concepts emerging from research directly to instruction. A good example of that is what Bloomfield and Fries did as linguists. As soon as they got some interesting notions about reading they immediately moved to developing programs for teaching reading. Both took key linguistic concepts, such as minimal contrasts, and built narrow instructional materials on them. They didn't consider appropriate learning theory or even other aspects of linguistics such as grammar and intonation.

There also is a tendency to work backward from output. That's very tempting, particularly with the preoccupation now with behaviorally stated goals. It's tempting to say 'we're going to get this many children to read at this level by this point in time.' Some have suggested that input is unimportant, that the only important thing is output. Such a view says that ends justify means and that desirable products can result even if processes are not understood or have negative, undesirable features.

Too much available knowledge is going to be ignored if there is only concern for output. Too much unplanned incidental learning will result.

One of the problems with operating from narrow bases is that they provide distorted views of the very elements that are looked at most clearly. For instance, take the relationship between letters and sounds. If that's the only thing that is looked at then one may come to the conclusion that the relationship of any letter to any sound is equally important with all others, that it's the same in a list of words as it is in a text, or that it's the same in all contexts. But it's very easy to demonstrate that, in fact, what's vitally important in one situation is quite unimportant in another.

Consider that contrast which distinguishes two entirely different chemical compounds as in 'sulfate' and 'sulfite' in the sentence 'Add 20 grams of calcium sulfate.' The contrast in the 'ite' and 'ate' suffixes is crucial. But if you know something about chemistry (and if you're going to read something about chemistry you're going to have to know something about it) then you operate within a framework which makes it easy to know when you've miscued. That vowel contrast is very unlikely to be of similar importance even in words of the same sentence that it's found in, so that at any point the value of any particular element varies depending on all other available cues. 'Add 20 grims' is not a contextual possibility. When one operates from narrow bases such information is lost. Particular information is exaggerated out of its relative importance and then learning problems are created where they didn't need to exist.

People can think they teach reading without an articulate instructional theory. Some will say 'I teach phonics; never mind

the learning theory that's involved' for example. Since such
practice really has a theory underlying it, the user is constantly making implicit decisions about unconsidered variables.
Every time one decision is made a whole set of other decisions
follow and the fact that the other inputs are ignored doesn't
mean that decisions in relationship to them haven't been made.

ITA pushes one into ignoring dialect differences or making
unknowing decisions about their relative importance in the
reading process. If one shifts to looking at dialect differences
it may cause one to make some different decisions about the use
of the ITA. That is, once one does add additional input it
changes the values of everything else.

So called 'linguistic programs' that emphasize phoneme-grapheme correspondences a la Bloomfield and Fries are still emerging, perhaps five or ten years beyond that point where there
was any justification at all. But even from a linguistic point of
view if they only concentrate on letter-sound relationships they
lose the significance of syntax and also the significance of
semantic context. Furthermore, of course, one tends to violate
psychological principles by ignoring them and making implicit
psychological decisions. In the Southwest lab program this
writer found inadequate the decisions that were implicit in the
ordering of the things that were being taught since no psychological principles were consciously used in determining
sequence.

Word recognition programs, those based on expanding vocabulary as a concept, have tended to ignore all other language
variables, except as they contribute to word recognition.
Sentences are created that are composed of frequent words but
that are hard to read, with extremely complex or unnatural
kinds of syntax and sequence.

Programed learning is another example of what happens with
a narrow base. Programed learning forces everything through
the narrow bottleneck of highly systematic sequencing. It
elevates sequencing to the primary consideration and then says
'Let's find something we can sequence.' It appears that that's
exactly what the Southwest Regional Laboratory has done. They
didn't decide phonics was a good way to teach reading. They
decided it was a good thing for sequencing in order to get the
kind of programing they could control so that they could now
give the teacher daily feedback on the child's progress. Once
that decision is made then a whole series of other decisions
follow that are not really examined since they would require the
developers to go back and look at the initial key decision.

The part-whole relationship is certainly distorted, perhaps
destroyed in that kind of programing. Questions relating to
whether, in fact, language can be learned sequentially are
ignored. That brings one into the position of having to ignore
a whole body of research from the last decade on child language
development.

Concentration on behavioral objectives forces one to abandon

much that can't be measured. One may say 'If you can't measure it, it's not important,' except that there's neither logic
nor substance to the statement. And, unfortunately almost
any teacher knows that most of what's important that's happening any day can't be measured at that point. Results show
at later points in the child's progress.

Now, a hypothesis may be stated: *No program of reading
instruction can be sound if it is not based on consideration of
all areas of decision making, no matter how sound particular
aspects are.*

The worst part of building narrow programs that don't examine all the relevant areas is that it leaves it to the learner to
make up for the deficiencies of the program. It's been obvious
in research, including ours, that much of learning to read at
the present state of the art of teaching reading is learning to
overcome that which is taught. The learner must do things
specifically against the advice of the program that's teaching
him. That learners can do that is obvious. Many children are
going to have the capacity to overcome the deficiencies in
programs and learn anyway. No program, no matter how silly,
didn't wind up with somebody saying in answer to questions,
'But the children learned.' Some learn with the family Bible or
the Sears Roebuck catalogue.

Teachers don't have the right, however, constantly to shift
the burden to the learner and say never mind the deficiencies
of the program, the kids will learn. Obviously some of them
have trouble doing that, precisely because of the programs'
deficiencies. The non-learners are those unable to ignore bad
advice, screen out misconceptions, fill in the gaps and learn
anyway.

Neither is it enough to validate a program simply by field
testing it. Its basic soundness must also be examined theoretically in terms of the knowledge available and the areas of
decision making that go into building a program based on sound
instructional theory. The basis does exist for judging programs now in terms of their validity on a number of grounds.
Educators have a right to evaluate them on those bases even
if they don't have better programs to offer. Maybe in the process of tearing down existing programs the means of building
better ones can be found.

With this background we can examine orthography, in relationship to a number of aspects of reading, and ask two questions: How is orthography used in reading? And what other
kinds of decisions must constantly be played against those
involving orthography?

A series of key concepts have emerged from recent theoretical
research. First, alphabetic systems don't simply operate on
a letter-sound basis. If there are relationships that can be
described between written and oral language they involve looking at patterned relationships. Sequences of sounds seem to
have relationships to sequences of letters, not simply because

of the alphabetic principle on which the system was produced originally, but also because there is a common base underlying both of these. For the user of language, surface oral language and surface written language are related through a common underlying structure. As a language user generates a sentence, his thoughts bring him to a point at which he can apply a set of orthographic rules and write it.

The second key concept is that regularity ought not to be confused with complexity; an orthographic system can be regular and very complex. That shouldn't surprise us because phonology isn't simple either. This regularity can involve many rules and sub-rules and exceptions to rules that kids learn through writing. These rules are learned by considerable exposure to written language. They can not be taught to one who lacks such exposure. But that's a lesson we've learned in many fields of instruction, not just reading. It's always very tempting to take an adult conclusion and plug it into a child and say 'Now you know what I know.' Obviously learning doesn't work that way, particularly language learning.

A third key concept involves the relationship of grapheme and allograph.

A reader has to be able to equate several very different graphic squiggles with the same abstract name or idea. That is, he must be able to say A and a and A̲ and a̲ are the same but A and H are different even though these last two have the most common features as compared to the others. There are perceptual categories that operate and it's the establishment of these perceptual categories that influences the ability to process graphic input. One must use some distinctive features to do so but those distinctive features are going to shift depending on which allographic system is in operation. Differentiating 'All' and 'Hall' does not use the same features as 'all' and 'hall.' Fortunately, of course, we don't mix those systems very often, except for special effects. When we do they cause trouble in reading.

A fourth basic principle is that the spelling system is standardized across dialects. That makes it possible for people who have phonological differences to be unencumbered with them in communicating with each other because they share common spellings. Each may not understand the way the other says a word but when they write it they write it with the same spelling.

Spelling reform has to take into account this positive characteristic of traditional orthography. Different dialects will of course have different homophones though homographs are the same for all.

Those are some key concepts. They're not inclusive but they're ones that have to be dealt with, and they are somewhat at variance to some old commonplace notions about orthography.

Let's look at the question of recognition and identification. Smith builds an incontestable case for the proposition that readers don't identify letters.[2] Rather, they use the minimal distinctive features to get where they're going. He demonstrates that if they're going to work at identifying letters they need a lot more information than if they're going to identify words. And, of course, one must go beyond words to get at meaning. In fact, if the reader is preoccupied with identifying words it not only is an inefficient process because he's using too much information, but it's ineffective as well because it gets in the way of getting at the meaning and clutters up the short-term memory function.

That raises some real questions about our tendency to teach kids to be careful readers, with all that that implies. A careful reader may use entirely wrong strategies. He may use far more information and not develop the kinds of selectivity that he has to develop to read effectively and efficiently.

Smith uses the term 'reduction of uncertainty' to describe how a reader uses a minimal amount of information to reduce uncertainty as he proceeds. How letters get recognized or perceived becomes unimportant. The question now becomes how little is the amount of information that's required to get to the meaning. That requires some very different kinds of decisions in building programs and instructional practices.

The literature is cluttered with studies based on the idea that one could learn something about language learning or reading by studying lists of words or lists of nonsense syllables, or even unpronounceable strings. There may be some interesting things that can be learned from such research but they have to be carefully evaluated before one draws any conclusions at all about their applicability to learning language including reading. Such research treats language as a string of sounds, letters or words; it assumes that language is like a salami that you can slice as thin as you want, each slice still retaining the characteristics of the whole. That simply is not true. Language can't be broken into pieces without qualitatively changing it.

A reader, like a listener, has to get from some surface information to an underlying structure at which point he can assign meaning. A sentence that illustrates this is 'See Spot run.' The understood subject is not present. The reader has to, somehow, induce it. He has to somehow induce a relationship between an imbedded clause 'Spot run' to another, 'You (understood) see (something).' There are a whole set of relationships that he has to get at and through to get from 'See Spot run' to an understanding of what meaning is involved. The task of the reader is to get from surface structure to deep structure to meaning, not to get from written language to oral language to meaning which implies a wholly different direction and one in fact that is quite unproductive.

The reader has to use the graphic input, but he has to constantly process grammatical and semantic information as well. The value of the graphic input, then, is entirely dependent on the amount of syntactic and semantic information that he can process. One can show this in many ways including some rather traditional ones, like how many words can be remembered if they're meaningful and grammatically sequenced as compared to if they're nonsense or simply strings of unrelated letters. Obviously much more information is being processed and therefore much less of the graphic information must be used when the other information is available.

Readers are able to make predictions. A prediction is based on minimal kinds of information and the linguistic competence that the reader brings to the task. As soon as he recognizes a graphic display as a written language form that has some kind of familiarity to him he starts to predict its patterns. Punctuation appears to be an unimportant part of the reader's cues because it comes at the wrong end of the sentence. The reader has to predict a question pattern long before he gets to the question mark. The exclamation point only confirms what he already should have known if he's going to read successfully. So at the best punctuation is a system of checks against the reader's predictions. Intonation is largely a function of syntax in oral reading. Once the reader has a pattern, he assigns an intonation. He doesn't use the intonation to predict the pattern.

Readers can leap over steps. The writer must go completely through a generative process resulting in a more complete product than oral language requires. But the reader can sample from that and make leaps to his own underlying structure and then to meaning. What becomes important is that he samples just enough additional graphic information that he can confirm or contradict what he has predicted. The reader samples, guesses and then tests. The tests are primarily semantic and syntactic. If those don't work then the reader takes another look at the graphic information so he may have a double cycle where he samples certain graphic information and then comes back for more if he needs it. He uses the most useful cues the first time. The second time through he needs to use some cues that are normally less useful or reprocess the same cues and try it another way.

The reader is selecting (even in the beginning) the graphic information he uses on the basis of what he expects to be there. An efficient reader then uses the minimum amount of information that he needs.

There are a series of strategies the reader must develop. Let's examine them and ask what the significance of orthographic input is in each.

Prediction is largely based on the syntactic competence of the learner and the experiential-conceptual background that he brings to the particular task. If he's reading something where he lacks background he has a hard time predicting its meaning or handling it, for that matter, when he gets through to it. In terms of sampling strategies the graphic input is very important. But what is most important is what the reader knows about the relative amount of information that particular graphic cues carry and therefore which distinctive features he ought to be looking for. It's this search for cues that is missing from many earlier notions of the use of graphic information. It's commonly assumed that the reader must pull in all graphic information, stir it around and then start to process it. But the processing actually starts before he has used any input and influences what he collects, how he perceives it, and how he uses it.

In the testing strategies there is a sequence in which the reader decides whether his guesses are right by asking a series of questions of himself. First he uses meaning asking, 'Does it make sense?' Second he uses syntactic information: Is that something that really fits there? Only then does he say, 'How does it start? How does it end? What do I think the word might be?', using graphic information. For confirmation graphic cues only become important after he's already made a decision that there's something wrong. Then, he may take a second look. Readers may of course have been taught to be very careful and to read accurately. Then they may be operating in a very ineffective reverse sequence, processing too much graphic information with accuracy, not comprehension, the goal. Correction, of course, is vital. Correction strategies provide the ability to do something about it when a reader realizes that he's gone wrong. That does depend on some rather sophisticated ability to reprocess graphic input and to get at some of the graphic input that gives less reliable information.

The significance of semantic input in reading must be understood. Every person is functionally illiterate to some extent. No one can possibly read and understand everything that is written in his native language. The ability to read and understand is totally a function, beyond a certain minimal point, of the amount of background the particular reader brings to each task. That contradicts a widespread commonsense notion built into many achievement tests that there is some kind of reading achievement level that cuts across everything within a single individual no matter what he's asked to read.

Phonics isn't necessary to the reading process. In fact, in a proficient reader any kind of going from print to oral language to meaning is an extremely ineffective and inefficient strategy. By inefficient is meant that it's not the best way to do it and by ineffective is meant that the reader doesn't get the results that he's after.

The question, of course, is whether in beginning stages of acquisition phonics has any function. This writer believes that excessive concern for phonics induces short circuits in reading. Instead of teaching the processing of language to get to meaning, phonics instruction teaches the processing of language to get to sounds or to get to words. Such instruction at best introduces many strategies that either have to be subsequently unlearned or which will interfere with the effectiveness of the reading process. Maybe the success of speed reading courses is simply that they force people to abandon these ineffective processes that they've learned in school and to move to a more rational, more productive way of reading. Those short circuits are evident in a number of ways. But the most alarming evidence is the lack of comprehension in upper grade and secondary pupils who score well on skill tests.

In current reading miscue studies at Wayne State, using four different ability groups of tenth-graders, all but the lowest group could read, for research purposes, the same story. Such readers vary in the kinds of miscues and the extent to which they correct more than they do in the number of miscues. But most particularly, what varies is their comprehension. Schools may be teaching kids not to comprehend. They may be teaching them to match oral language with written language, which is very different from comprehending.

Reading materials used in instruction must be relevant. Irrelevant materials are not only bad from a humanistic point of view but they're bad instructional materials since background determines comprehension. Some Hawaiian kids reading a story about the first robin of spring are having an irrelevant experience but it is also impossible for them to know whether they have understood. They lack the background experience to know whether they have understood. They lack the background experience to know what the heck a robin is and what's spring and what a robin has to do with spring. Teaching must be directed toward developing ability to sample for distinctive features.

Perhaps all this discussion has provided is a new set of questions to ask, a new focus. If so, the most crucial concept is that language is always a means and never an end. And teaching kids to match letters to sounds is not related to the end that is comprehension. Teaching them to read nonsense is as bad because they can't tell, when they're done, whether they've been successful since what they read makes no sense. The orientation toward meaning is intrinsic in the process that the child has to master and basic to the mastery of the reading process. It isn't something that comes later. It isn't possible to break reading into code and meaning because the code has no existence and certainly no use apart from meaning.

NOTES

1 E.B. Huey, 'The Psychology and Pedagogy of Reading.' First published in 1908. Republished 1968, MIT Press, Cambridge, Mass.
2 Frank Smith, 'Understanding Reading,' Holt, Rinehart and Winston, New York, 1971.

There is no simple breakthrough in reading just around the corner which will change instruction to a foolproof science. As more is understood about reading and learning to read, it becomes ever clearer how complex these processes are. No simple antitoxin can be injected in non-readers to make them readers. But progress will come as misconceptions disappear in favor of sound understanding. Materials and curricula based on scientific insights will replace those built on tradition, trial-and-error and expediency. And a reading curriculum will evolve tied to an effective theory of reading instruction.

This article presents a comprehensive treatment of many aspects of reading and the other language processes as they apply to curriculum and to all levels of instruction. This is a key article for all who already have some familiarity with the subject.

10 BEHIND THE EYE:
What Happens in Reading

with Olive Niles

A child, eyebrows knit, haltingly, speaks as he stares intently at the small book he is holding, 'See Tom. See Tom...' He stops, apparently unable to continue. 'We haven't had that next word yet,' he states in a troubled voice to his teacher.

'Mary is only seven, but she can read anything,' says the doting mother to her friend. 'Read us that article from the "Times",' she says to the little girl. The child reads an article on national politics, with great speed and animation, while the friend listens appreciatively. She stumbles occasionally, as the going gets rough now and then, but is apparently untroubled by the task. 'Did you understand all that dear?' her awed listener asks, 'She has a little difficulty putting it into words, but I'm sure she understands,' interposes the mother.

'I give up,' the weary graduate student mutters to himself as he sits at the small table in the library stacks. He's just finished his third reading of the article his professor has assigned. He forces himself to formulate, out of the conceptual jumble he finds himself lost in, a few questions to raise in class. 'Maybe the class is too advanced for me,' he wonders. 'Why don't these guys write so people can understand?'

'I can't make head or tail out of this damn thing.' A best-selling writer is speaking long-distance to his attorney. 'It's some kind of release I'm supposed to sign giving this producer the film rights to my latest book. But it's full of all kinds of parties of the first part and whereas's.'

'Read it to me,' says the lawyer. The author begins, 'The undersigned, who shall be known as ...' The attorney listens, interrupts a few times to ask for repetition, and is ready by the time his caller has finished to offer his legal advice. He clarifies the meaning of the document to the author, restates the legal terminology in phrases his client finds meaningful, dictates a clause to be added to protect the author's rights.

Reading is obviously involved in each of these episodes. But, at what point does it become reading and at what point does it cease to be reading and become something else, thinking perhaps, or concept formation, or the acquisition of knowledge?

Is the child who is limited to calling the names of word shapes he has been taught in any sense a reader? If he is not, at what point does he become one? Is it when he has a larger sight-word repertoire? How large? Is it when he has learned how to 'attack' new words? If, like the hypothetical Mary above, he can 'read' things he can't understand, is he reading?

To what extent must a reader arrive at the meaning the writer intended? If he must fully *comprehend*, then our graduate student is a non-reader. Even if a moderate level of comprehension is required he has fallen short of the mark. Are all readers then only semiliterate?

Who has read the legal document? The lawyer who is hundreds of miles away from it and who cannot even see it, or his client who holds it in his hand? Or did reading require both of their contributions? Shall we call what the author did reading, and his attorney's contribution interpretation? Or shall we say that the author was word-calling and the lawyer comprehending?

The issues that are raised in these episodes are neither simple nor easily answered. To a certain extent, of course, we can be arbitrary. We can define reading to be anything we choose. But if our definition is to be useful, it must be one we can use consistently; it must be inclusive of that which is relevant and exclusive of that which is not. It must also be productive. Definitions which are too narrow or too broad or too vague or too specific tend to cut off or dissipate inquiry rather than promote it. Further, a definition must be consistent with reality.

To move us toward a definition of reading, it may help to list certain evident aspects of the process:

* Reading begins with graphic language in some form: print, script, etc.
* The purpose of reading is the reconstruction of meaning. Meaning is not in print, but it is meaning that the author begins with when he writes. Somehow the reader strives to *reconstruct* this meaning as he reads.
* In alphabetic writing systems there is a direct relationship between oral language and written language.
* Visual perception must be involved in reading.
* Nothing intrinsic in the writing system or its symbols has meaning. There is nothing in the shape or sequence of any letters or grouping of letters which in itself is meaning.
* Meaning is in the mind of the writer and the mind of the reader.
* Yet readers are capable through reading of reconstructing a message which agrees with the writer's intended message.

A DEFINITION OF READING

At this point, we're ready to state a definition of reading: 'Reading is a complex process by which a reader reconstructs, to some degree, a message encoded by a writer in graphic language.'

In this definition it is no more significant that the reader
starts with graphic input[1] than that he ends with meaning. To
understand this process, we must understand the nature of the
graphic input. We must understand how language works and
how language is used by the reader. We must understand how
much meaning depends on the reader's prior learning and
experience in the reconstruction of meaning. We must understand the perceptual system involved in reading. As we come
to see the reader as a user of language, we will understand
that reading is a psycholinguistic process, an interaction
between thought and language.

WRITTEN LANGUAGE: THE NATURE OF THE GRAPHIC INPUT

Written English is, of course, an alphabetic system. It uses
a set of letters almost directly adapted from the Latin. The
Latin alphabet in turn was derived from the Greek. Most modern
languages are written with alphabets derived from the same
group of ancient, related alphabets. Alphabetic writing differs
from other systems in that the system is a representation not of
meaning directly, but of oral language. In original intent, the
units of written language (letters) represented the sound units
of speech rather than meanings as in pictographic and other
systems.

Oral language is produced in a time sequence, but written
language must be arranged spatially. Though various arrangements are possible, and used in other systems, in English print
is arranged from left to right and top to bottom in successive
lines. While space separates patterns of letters just as oral
patterns are marked by intonation contours, pauses, pitch
sequences, and relative stressing. Larger patterns require
markings, punctuation, to set them off from other patterns.
Again, intonational features are replaced to some degree in
print by periods, commas, and other graphic signals. In this
feature, as in a number of others, there is no one-to-one
correspondence between oral and written language. The intonation pattern of a question like 'Do you understand?' is distri-
buted over the whole oral sentence, while graphically it is
represented only by a capital letter at the beginning and a
question mark at the end. It is marked as different from the
statement form only at the end. (Contrast Spanish which puts
a question mark at both ends.)

RELATIONSHIPS BETWEEN ORAL AND WRITTEN ENGLISH

While written language is a secondary form, both historically
and in the personal history of any individual, it must be seen
as a different but parallel form to oral language, since both for
the literate user are fully capable of meeting the complex needs

of communication. Written language has the advantage, only recently made possible for oral language, of being perfectable and preservable. Oral language on the other hand is more easily and more rapidly produced in a wider range of circumstances.

Having said that English uses an alphabetic writing system, we must now caution that the set of relationships between oral and written English is not a simple small set of letter-to-sound correspondences (or phoneme-to-grapheme ones, to use linguistic terms). For several reasons, to be accurate, we must say that the relationships are between patterns of sounds and patterns of letters. The most significant of these reasons is that spelling patterns are basically standard and stable while oral language changes over time and space.

Spellings are standard.   Standard spellings were developed by printers in the early years of the development of printing and the spread of literacy. Though Americans may differ from the British in the spellings of a very few words like 'labor' (labour), there is a great agreement on word spellings among speakers of all English dialects. 'Pumpkin' is the spelling whether one says 'punkin,' 'ponkin,' 'pumpkin' or whatever. This is, of course, a considerable advantage, since written communication between speakers of diverse English dialects is made more effective. Any other arrangement would require establishment of a standard dialect upon which to base spelling. Subsequently either the dialect would need to be protected from change or periodical updating of the spelling system to catch up with the changes would be required. If this could be accomplished, the spelling system would be highly suited for the one dialect's speakers, but increasingly dysfunctional for all others. Change is always going on in language. It cannot in any case be closed off. No lesser man than Napoleon tried and failed to keep language from changing.

Oral language sequences.   Another factor in making the relationships between oral and written English complex has to do with the nature of oral language sound sequences. For example, note these related words: 'site,' 'situate,' and 'situation.' In 'site,' we have a well-known pattern with a vowel-consonant-e (V-C-e). The 'e' serves as a pattern marker. Notice that the relationship of the prior vowel to a sound is not clear without the rest of the spelling pattern. But when, through affixes, the word 'situate' is formed, a sound sequence occurs after the /t/ which requires a shift in the oral form to a 'ch' sound /č/. The same shift occurs in the word sequence 'don't you.' We must either change the spelling to 'ch' or retain the 't' and lose the close letter-sound correspondence. Similar shifting is required in moving to 'situation' where the sound becomes 'sh' /š/. The spelling system has alternatives. It may retain the close correspondence of sounds and letters and thus change

spellings as the sounds shift. Or it may retain the letters even
when the sound shifts and thus preserve the derivational
character of the word relationships. The system tends to do
the latter perhaps because speakers of the language seem to
shift as required so automatically that they are not bothered
by the spelling discrepancy. It simply sounds too strange to
his ears for a speaker of English to say 'situation' differently.
This may be illustrated with this nonsense word offered in
three alternate spellings: 'boft,' 'boffed,' 'bofd.' The final
consonant cluster is pronounced the same by native speakers
of English. Because /f/ precedes the final consonant, the latter
is produced as /t/; spelling cannot induce a speaker to abandon
that pronunciation.

Much has been written about regular and irregular relationships between oral and written English. The distinction loses
its meaning if we understand that the patterns of correspondence are complex, but systematic. Some examples above have
already illustrated this complex-regularity. Here is another:
's' may not frequently represent the sound 'sh' /s/, but when
it does, as in 'sure' and 'sugar,' the circumstances are consistent ones and it is thus every bit as regular in its representation as it is in 'sister.' 'Hymn,' 'damn,' 'bomb,' 'sign,' appear
irregularly spelled, but they are not so if we consider the
'silent letters' relate to derived forms such as 'hymnal,'
'damnation,' 'bombard,' 'signal.'

A number of early applications to reading materials that
stressed linguistics tended to apply a rather narrow view of
regular letter-sound correspondence. The Bloomfield-Barnhart
materials, the SRA Linguistic Readers, and the Harper-Row
Linguistic Science Readers are examples. The Merrill Linguistic
Readers, based on the work of C.C. Fries, had a somewhat
broader view of regularity as represented in spelling patterns.

THE NATURE OF LANGUAGE

If we are to define and understand reading, we must understand the nature of language itself. Paradoxically, language
is learned so early and so well that we tend to take its functioning for granted.

How language works

Language is always a means and only rarely an end in itself.
We are so distracted, as we use it, by meaning (the end for
which language is the means), that we are quite unaware of
how language works to convey meaning. Consider, for example,
a simple statement: 'John hit Bill.' In either oral or written
form, it is not the symbols, phonemes, or letters but the
systematic structuring of these symbols that makes comprehension of meaning possible.

The listener or reader must recognize the patterns 'John,'

'hit,' and 'Bill' and he must also recognize the pattern of patterns which makes a statement of relationships possible. The difference between 'John hit Bill' and 'Bill hit John' is in the sentence patterns or syntax. Nothing else tells the listener or reader whether Bill or John hit John or Bill. Grammar, the system of language, makes it possible for language to convey the most complex relationships humans conceive.

All language is patterned: the patterns are the sequences in which the elements may occur. In 'John hit Bill,' it is pattern alone that tells the listener who was hitting and who was being hit.

In English, pattern is itself the single most important aspect of grammar. Other languages make more use of word changes (inflections) such as affixes to carry extensive portions of the grammatical system. In such languages the nominative and accusative endings might have differentiated the aggressor from the victim in the example above. English preserves such a system in its pronouns. 'I hit him' and 'He hit me' use different forms in grammatical cases. But notice that we still would not say 'Him hit I.' Pattern is still preserved.

Certain English words and word parts serve as pattern markers. In a statement like 'A man was feeding his dogs,' we have a pattern: A — was —ing his —s. The pattern markers, function words like 'A,' 'his,' and 'was,' and inflectional endings like 'ing,' and 's' set the pattern up. In themselves none of these elements carry meaning. But without the grammatical pattern they create, we cannot express even the simplest relationship between the words that do carry meaning.

How language is used

When a child undertakes to learn to read at the age of five or six, he is already a skilled user of language. He has somehow learned to generate language to communicate his thoughts, emotions, and needs to his family and peers. Further, he is able to comprehend what other people say to him. To state that he has learned by imitation does not accurately represent the case. He has, in fact, devised language for himself which moves toward the norms of adult language because the more it does, the more effective he is in communication.

Moreover, he has not simply acquired a collection of words or sentences to use when the occasion is appropriate. He has learned the rules by which language is produced. Language is rule-governed. As long as a child can only produce language he has already heard, his language capability is severely limited. Infinite numbers of sentences are possible in a language. If a child had to hear them and learn them before he could use them, language learning would be a much slower process than it is. But a small number of rules govern language production. These are the rules that tell the child which noun to put before and which after a transitive verb when he runs up to a teacher on the playground and says, 'John hit Bill.' They are the rules that make it possible for him to say, 'When I hit him, he hits me back,' getting 'hit' and 'hits' in the right position and making one clause subordinate to another. They are the rules that make it possible for him to say things he has never heard anyone say before and be sure that other speakers of the language will understand.

Generating language. In speaking or in writing, meaning in the mind of the originator creates a deep language structure (a set of base forms) and activates a set of rules which transform that structure and generate a signal, either graphic or oral. This process must be a complete one. The signal must have a surface structure that is complete. All essential elements must be present, and extraneous ones must not be. We might describe this whole process as 'encoding.' A structured code signal has been produced. The user of a language has so well learned this encoding procedure that it is virtually automatic. Meaning, as a language user formulates it, literally creates an automatic chain of events which results in language code. A model of speech, quite simplified, is reprinted in Figure 10.1.

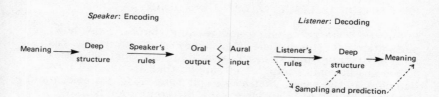

Figure 10.1 Spoken language

Note in this model that the speaker's output is not the same as the listener's input. What is said is not precisely what is heard, just as in reading what is written is not precisely what is read. This relationship might be compared to the relationship of fetus and mother. Her bloodstream nourishes the uterine wall from which the fetus draws its nourishment, through its own bloodstream. But, the two bloodstreams are not connected.

Note also that meaning is not in the oral output or the aural input. Meaning is only in the minds of the speaker and the listener. The listener (like the reader) must recreate meaning for himself from the input he has obtained.

Language has been learned by the listener in the context of experience as it was used in those situations by people around him. His ability to recreate meaning depends on his ability to associate those experiences and the concepts he has formed through them with the language.

The speaker in generating language must produce a sound

sequence which is decodable by the listener. In this oral language signal, the sounds must be sufficiently well articulated and the structure sufficiently complete that the listener has all the information he needs.

At first appearances, it would seem that listening would be a kind of mirror image of speech with the process simply reversed to get from surface structure of aural language to meaning.

In fact, however, the listener may, through a process that combines sampling and prediction, leap to the deep structure and meaning without using all the information available to him. He acquires strategies as a language user that enable him to select only the most productive cues. His user's knowledge of language structure and the redundancy[2] of that structure make it possible for him to predict and anticipate the grammatical pattern on the basis of identifying a few elements in it. The context in which the language occurs, created by the previous meanings he has gathered, allows him to predict the meaning of what will follow. All these combine to make listening related to but a very different process from speaking.

PERCEPTION IN LISTENING AND READING

Before we compare listening and reading, let's explore how perception operates in listening. Every language uses a small number of sound units, which some linguists label phonemes. These are in reality bundles of sounds that are treated by listeners as the same. Just as we call many different colors and shades of colors red, we hear many different sounds as /t/. Two colors could be quite similar, but one would be called red and the other orange, while two other more dissimilar colors might be both called red. In the same way the phoneme is a perceptual category. As a language is learned these categories become functional. The child learns to treat certain differences as significant and others as insignificant. In short, he not only learns what to pay attention to, but, equally important, what not to pay attention to. So the native speaker of Japanese learning English does not distinguish 'late' from 'rate' because he has learned to ignore a difference which isn't significant in Japanese. Similarly, a speaker of English has difficulty differentiating the Spanish 'pero' (but) from 'perro' (dog).[3]

Perception in language is and must be both selective and anticipatory. To be aware of what is significant in language one must ignore what is not. Perception, to be functional in listening, must be augmented by anticipation. The sounds are so fleeting and follow each other so rapidly that time does not allow for each to be fully perceived and identified. Mastery of the phonological system, however, and of the grammatical system as well, enables the listener to use partial perceptions and sample the input. Under some circumstances, of course, the partial perceptions may be too fragmentary or distorted and the listener may have to ask for repetition. But, to be quite blunt, what we think we hear is as much what we expect to hear as it is what we do hear.

Contrast the task of repeating even a short sequence in a foreign language with a comparable or longer one in a known language. The foreign language simply doesn't correspond to available perceptual categories, nor can we fit what we do catch into any system that would aid prediction.

Perception in language use cannot be viewed, then, as a simple series of sound perceptions or word perceptions. It must be understood in relation to the grammatical structure of the language, and to the structure of the meaning that is being communicated.

All that has been said in comparing speaking and listening basically applies to the parallel language processes, writing and reading.

The writer generates his signal in exactly the same way that the speaker does. In the last stage, these generative processes differ. In speech, a series of phonological rules determines the exact sound sequences which will be uttered. In writing, instead of phonological rules a set of graphotactic rules (spelling if you prefer) produces the exact grapheme sequences.

As we have indicated earlier, though both speaking and writing must produce complete signals, writing is usually polished and perfected to a greater degree than speech through editing by the author. Furthermore, the reader works from a more or less permanent graphic input while the listener must contend with input that in most cases perishes as it is produced. Rereading is possible. Relistening requires that the speaker cooperate in repeating what he has said.

But reading, like listening, is a sampling, predicting, guessing process. Proficient readers, in fact, learn to use the reading process much more rapidly than they normally use the listening process. Listening is held pretty much to the rate at which speech is produced. That, of course, is much slower than the processing of average proficient readers.

In the guessing game which is reading, three types of information are used. Each has several subtypes. They are used in reading simultaneously and not sequentially.

INFORMATION USED DURING THE READING PROCESS

  I *Grapho-phonic information*
    A Graphic Information: The letters, spelling patterns and patterns of patterns created through white space and punctuation. A word or suffix represents a graphic pattern; a phrase or sentence is a pattern of patterns.
    B Phonological Information: The sounds, sound patterns and patterns of patterns created through intonation

(pitch, stress, pause). Read any line on this page and note how these work.

C Phonic Information: The complex set of relationships between the graphic and phonological representations of the language. Notice here we are speaking of the relationships and not an instructional program for teaching them.

II *Syntactic information*

A Sentence Patterns: The grammatical sequences and interrelationships of language. The —s —ed the —s, is an example of a sentence pattern common in English.

B Pattern Markers: The markers that outline the patterns.
1 Function Words: Those very frequent words that though themselves relatively without definable meaning, signal the grammatical function of the other elements. Examples: 'the,' 'was,' 'not,' 'do,' 'in,' 'very,' 'why,' 'but.'
2 Inflections: Those bound morphemes (affixes) which convey basically grammatical information. Examples: 'ing,' 'ed,' 's.'
3 Punctuation-Intonation: The system of markings and space distribution and the related intonation patterns. Pitch and stress variations and variable pauses in speech are represented to some extent by the punctuation in writing.

C Transformational Rules: These are not characteristic of the graphic input itself, but are supplied by the reader in response to what he perceives as its surface structure. They carry him to the deep structure and meaning. If he is to recognize and derive meaning from a graphic pattern, he must bring these grammatical rules into the process.

III *Semantic information*

A Experience: The reader brings *his* prior experiences into play in response to the graphic input.

B Concepts: The reader organizes the meaning he is reconstructing according to his existing concepts and reorganizes experience into concepts as he reads.

C Vocabulary is largely a term for the ability of the child to sort out his experiences and concepts in relation to words and phrases in the context of what he is reading.

All of these kinds of information are available to the reader at the same time in graphic language. In the sampling process, they support each other much as they do in listening. Particular cues take on strategic importance in relation to the full array of information in the input which they could not have in isolation. In a list a word like 'the,' for example, is a word with little or no referential meaning. It summons forth, from the reader's stockpile of information, no experiences or concepts. But put 'the' into a sentence and it becomes a grammatical cue of some importance. In these sequences: 'He hurried to farm' (his land) and 'he hurried to the farm,' 'farm' is marked as a noun in the second sequence by 'the,' whereas in the first, 'farm' is a verb and the reader will expect an object to follow.

The relationship between oral and written language is of more significance in reading than in listening. Particularly in learning to read the language he speaks, a child may draw on his oral language competence as he develops control over written language. The alphabetic character of the writing system makes it possible to match sound sequences already known with less familiar graphic sequences.

A possible simplified model for reading in early stages might look like that in Figure 10.2.

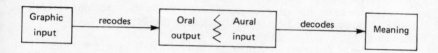

Figure 10.2 Early reading[4]

The child here recodes graphic input as speech (either out-loud or internally) and then, utilizing his own speech as aural input, decodes as he does in listening. Notice the model assumes some direct decoding from print to meaning, even at early stages.

Some writers on the topic of reading have assumed that for instructional purposes these two aspects, recoding and decoding, are separable. And indeed, materials and methods have been built on that assumption. As a prereading program, instruction is provided to the child in matching letters and sounds (i.e. synthetic phonics, Sullivan's programed reading) or in matching spelling patterns and sound patterns (e.g. Fries Linguistic Readers) or in matching oral names with graphic shapes (sight vocabulary). But in all of these types of recoding instruction, the reader is confined to words or word parts and may not sample the syntactic or semantic information that would be available in full language. What's more, the process is one in which meaning cannot result. Thus by our tentative definition (see p. 100) recoding in itself is not reading.

In any case, a second instructional phase would be needed to help the learner adapt his recoding strategies and techniques to the full language situation in which all information is available and decoding may result.

Reading does eventually become a parallel process to listening which then would have this appearance.

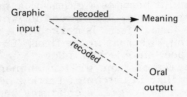

Figure 10.3 Proficient reading

In this model, recoding has at best a supplementary role. The basic decoding is directly from print to meaning, though there is some echo of speech involved as the reader proceeds even in silent reading. At times, the reader may find it helpful to recode print as speech and then decode. (The reverse may also be true for literate speakers. They may occasionally 'write it down,' recoding speech as graphic input and then decoding.)

When silent reading becomes proficient, it becomes a very different process from oral reading. It is much more rapid and not tied to encoding what is being read as speech. In silent reading, the reader sweeps ahead sampling from the graphic input, predicting structures, leaping to quick conclusions about the meaning and only slowing down or regressing when subsequent sampling fails to confirm what he expects to find.

Oral reading which is fluent and accurate may involve simultaneous recoding and decoding. But for most proficient silent readers, who don't have much occasion for oral reading, oral reading apparently follows this model:

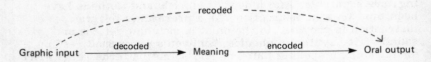

Figure 10.4 Oral reading

Primarily oral output is produced *after* meaning has been decoded and hence, though comprehension may be high, the oral output is often a poor match for the graphic input. The reader sounds clumsy and makes numerous errors.

Figure 10.5 illustrates in some detail the psycholinguistic process which is silent reading. This model represents the *proficient* reader, but it also represents the competence which is the goal of reading instruction.

Reading is an active process in which the reader selects the fewest cues possible from those available to him and makes the best choices possible. If he is highly proficient, he will have good speed and high comprehension; reading will be a smooth process. If he is less proficient or if he is encountering unusually difficult material (as in the case of the graduate student in our early examples), reading will be less smooth and will involve considerable cycling back to gather more cues and make better choices.

Meaning is the constant goal of the proficient reader and he continually tests his choices against the developing meaning by asking himself if what he is reading makes sense. The process does not require that he perceive and identify every cue. In fact that would be both unnecessary and inefficient. But it does require that the reader monitor his choices so he can recognize his errors and gather more cues when needed.

Such traditional terms as 'word recognition,' 'sounding out,' and 'word attack' stem from a view of reading as a succession of accurate perceptions or word identifications. Such a view is not consistent with the actual performance of proficient readers.

THE APPLICATION OF READING

Reading, if it is successful, is, as we have shown, not a passive process. The reader is a language user who interacts with the graphic input. Successful reading yields meaning that becomes the means to further ends. The reader may follow directions, respond to questions, read further. The extent and direction of application depend on the nature and purpose of what is read. Literary materials, because of their aesthetic, stylistic qualities, yield a kind of pleasure and satisfaction which creates further appetite for literature. Plot and story line in literature propel the reader forward. 'I just couldn't put it down,' he may say.

Informational materials may have a similar effect; new knowledge leads to a desire for more knowledge. Or such material may meet a small but immediate need, as for example when the reader needs to clarify a particular fact in the encyclopedia.

Language and thought are interactive in reading, but at some point thought processes leap out and away from the message of the writer.

In this interaction a reader may be involved in cycles of reading, reflective thinking, flights of fancy and then more reading. In certain kinds of materials, recipes for example, the reader may follow a 'read' and 'do' cycle. He reads and then gathers his ingredients; then he reads again and performs step one and so forth.

Though reading and the application of the fruits of reading are separable, it must always be remembered that reading is never pursued for its own sake, even in literature. If the reader finds no 'payoff,' he will not continue to read. This is as true in the stages in which reading is being acquired as it is in the stages of proficient reading.

Materials used in the teaching of reading at all stages must necessarily be meaningful. Children with different purposes and interests will need a variety of materials to keep them reading. Ironically, development of reading competence is best achieved when the learner's focus is on the content of materials and not on reading itself. Social studies, science, mathematics, literature and other materials contribute well to the child's reading development while serving other curricular ends, if their conceptual load is not too heavy.

ADAPTATION IN READING

By the time he undertakes to become literate in his native language every child has acquired considerable competence[5] in its basic communicative use. The basic form of his language, that used in common discourse and conversation, is his means of communication, expression, thinking, and learning. It makes sense to start with this common discursive language in reading. Experience stories, directions, labels, signs are examples of early reading materials that use common language.

Children have not necessarily acquired the same kind of competence in dealing with other specialized forms of language. Literature utilizes one such special form. The language of literature has its own special set of rules and contingencies. Poetic license makes it possible for the poet to reverse some key language priorities for the sake of meter, rhyme, or mood. Similarly, literary prose employs structures and language devices differently from common language.

The strategies that the child has learned in listening transfer well to reading common language. To deal with literary language he will need to modify his strategies and perhaps acquire some new ones.

A good deal of prereading experience with literature will help the child build a strong base for reading literature for himself. Some children grow up in a world of literature: they are surrounded by books; their parents read to them; they acquire favorites which they soon know by heart. By the time such children come to school, they have a feel for the peculiarities of literary language and a sense of what to expect from it. They can predict in literary language as they can in more common language. For the large number of children who lack such background, teachers can begin to build it through oral reading to the children and other devices while the more basic literacy ability is being built.

Subsequently, children can begin to read literary language. As they do so, they will necessarily modify the techniques and strategies they use in reading to accommodate the structure of literary language. Even then, it will probably make the most sense to start with literary forms and themes which are most like common language and move to literary forms that deviate more. Folk and fairy tales may be pleasurable to the child because of their familiarity. But the archaic language, the unusual structure, and the allegorical nature of their plots may combine to make them unsuitable for early literature reading. One possibility, of course, is to rewrite them for young children in order to eliminate these problems. A criticism of that approach is that in the process their qualities as literature may be lost and they may become dull and lacking in color and characterization. In a similar sense, adaptations of great works of literature for children too young to handle the original may make them more readable but destroy their essential merits. In both cases, such critics conclude it might be better to postpone reading such materials until the child's reading competence has reached a point where he is ready to learn to cope with the special demands they make on him.

Research into literary style is beginning to suggest that writers employ less common language structures frequently to achieve a sense of individuality and distinction. If this is true, then some specific assistance to children in recognizing and predicting these structures may greatly enhance their ability to read particular authors.

In the past several decades, a large and varied literature especially written for children of various ages has been produced. Such literature makes it possible to guide youngsters through material that they can select to suit their own interests and levels of ability. In the process, they will build their ability to deal with more sophisticated literature. A number of publishers have organized better selections in kits with multiple copies of each title and teacher guide material.

Schools present the learners with the need for dealing with a number of other special forms of language. Textbooks, in general, use language in special ways which vary from common language use. They tend, particularly in elementary and secondary schools, to present a very large number of topics, facts, and concepts rapidly and superficially. Reading to learn may well stimulate learning to read, but only if the concept load (roughly the number of new ideas presented) is not so heavy as to cause the reader to lose any sense of meaning. Textbook reading, through the elementary years at least, probably requires considerable introductory, preparatory work on the part of the teacher. Concepts and ideas can be introduced through demonstration, experimentation, concrete illustration. Vocabulary can be developed orally in relationship to these experiences. Then, and only then, is the child ready for the task of reading about the same concepts in the text. He reads them not so much to gain new concepts as to reinforce them. In the process, he learns to handle the unusual language uses of textbooks. If textbooks are well written and handled well in elementary schools, he may, by the time he is in high school, be able to initiate study at times through a textbook with the teacher following up and reteaching the concepts he meets in the books.

Another alternative is to change our thinking about how textbooks are used in elementary and junior high schools. Part of the problem with textbooks is that they move rapidly from topic to topic, a fact inherent in the nature of the task they undertake. Consequently, they present a large vocabulary of terms not well developed in context. Perhaps multimedia approaches would help; kits and coordinated packages containing film loops, audio and video tapes, transparencies, and other materials as well as reading materials could replace the single text. The texts could become elements in resource kits to provide more specific focus on single concepts or depth treatment of groups of related concepts.

Children will encounter problems in learning to deal with other kinds of reference books too. The need for reference skills, use of index, contents and glossary is obvious. Less obvious problems involve strategies for dealing with specialized vocabulary and language structures. Encyclopedias, for example, employ distinctive writing styles. There are also key problems for the reader in learning to modify his whole reading style to reference reading. Even graduate students do not always have effective techniques for selecting and reading from reference works only those portions germane to their needs. Skimming is one of several gross sampling strategies needed for specific use in some kinds of reference work.

Science, mathematics, social studies, music, art, industrial arts, home economics, in fact all school subjects, require learners to handle special kinds of language. It cannot be assumed that general reading competence leads automatically to these special abilities. Using a recipe, following a set of plans, interpreting a contour map, following a laboratory procedure - all present special reading problems. The abilities required must of course be developed in the context of the tasks. To pick an example, a reader can't learn how to read a recipe unless he is really making something. And the best test of the effectiveness of the reading will be the way the final product tastes. The implication is apparent. Every teacher of whatever subject and level must be prepared to help children to meet new demands on their reading competence and to develop the special strategies which these demands require.[6]

A special word needs to be said about vocabulary. Every time a learner pushes into a new field or into a new subject area within an old one, he encounters new vocabulary or new uses for old terms. That problem is a by-product of his quest for knowledge. The vocabulary is unfamiliar because the ideas and concepts it expresses are unfamiliar. Like new concepts, new vocabulary learned in relationship to the new knowledge must be built on the base of pre-existing vocabulary. If the new vocabulary is more effective in manipulating the new ideas

it will be absorbed, and old language may be modified or set
aside. Vocabulary development outside of the context of new
ideas and pre-existing language is not possible.

What we commonly call a vocabulary problem is never simply
a matter of putting a verbal label on an object. In reality, it
may represent a variety of different problems.

1 The reader encounters a printed form he does not recognize for a word in his oral vocabulary. This is the simplest
vocabulary problem since he has experiences and concepts
to relate to his oral vocabulary.

2 The reader encounters a printed form that is not familiar
and not in his oral vocabulary. But the concept is a known
one. He has other language forms to express it. In this
case the problem is to associate new language with old.

3 The reader encounters a printed form that is unfamiliar,
has no oral counterpart for him, and represents a concept
which is new to him. He may in fact lack relevant experience on which to base such a concept. This is the case in
which vocabulary must follow conceptual development.
Otherwise, we have a fourth possibility.

4 A written form is familiar and may even have an oral
equivalent, but the reader has no meaning for it. Within
narrow limits he may even use it to answer test questions
correctly without understanding what he is reading.

5 The final possibility exists as readers become proficient.
They may encounter printed forms and come to attach concepts to them without ever encountering them in oral
speech. One does not have to be able to pronounce a
word to understand it.

OBJECTIVES OF THE READING CURRICULUM

Once we have defined reading and discussed it as a process,
a next step in considering reading curricula is to restate this
process as a series of objectives. First, however, an important
distinction must be made. That is the distinction between language competence and language performance.

Competence and performance

Much has been said in curricular literature about behavioral
objectives. In this view, the ultimate objective of instruction is
always to change behavior (which we treat as a synonym for
performance). But this view fails to take into account the concept that there is underlying all performance a basic competence.
It is this underlying competence, and not the behavior itself,
that we seek to build through education.

Above we delineated some variations involved in vocabulary.
To use this as an example, in expanding vocabulary we must not
mistake performance, the uttering of words, for competence,

the understanding that must underlie the effective use of words. Too often school lessons change performance (behavior) but only superficially get at competence, and thus a change is a temporary or meaningless one.

While we must seek evidence in performance of the competence that learners have achieved, we must be very cautious of either equating performance and competence or of interpreting performance too directly and simplistically.

In language and reading this distinction is particularly important. Vocabulary, to continue the example, is going to develop in direct ratio to the experience and interest that a learner has. Low vocabulary yield in the performance of children in certain task situations cannot be directly interpreted to mean that the child has a small vocabulary. It may mean only that the topic or topics were not ones that interested him; it might also mean that for various reasons such as fear, unfamiliarity of the situation or the interviewers, or disdain for the task or teacher, the child simply did not perform in any way representative of his competence.

Here is another example: There are periods in the development of reading competence when oral reading becomes very awkward.[7] Readers who have recently become rapid, relatively effective, silent readers seem to be distracted and disrupted by the necessity of encoding oral output while they are decoding meaning. Ironically, then 'poor' oral reading performance *may* reflect a high degree of reading competence rather than a lack of such competence.

Relevance

The language user, though he may be a beginner as far as literacy is concerned, brings to the task of learning to read the sum total of his life's experiences and the language competence he has already acquired. He has learned language well no matter what rung on the socioeconomic ladder his dialect occupies. To make it possible for each learner to capitalize fully on these resources the reading curriculum must be relevant to him. It must make it possible for him to build on his strengths, not put him at a disadvantage by focusing on his weaknesses.

All learners have had experiences. A learner is only disadvantaged if the school rejects his experiences as unsuitable to build learnings on while accepting those of other children. Similarly language difference is not a disadvantage unless the school rejects certain dialects and insists that a child must speak and read in a dialect in which he is not competent.

Remedial reading classes and clinics invariably have more boys than girls, more blacks than whites, more minority group youngsters than is proportional in the population these programs serve. This is not so much an indication of real weakness in these groups as it is of the failure of school reading programs to adequately reach them.

Too much time has been spent trying to find weaknesses and

deficiencies in children which might explain their lack of success in learning to read. A flexible, relevant reading curriculum would capitalize on the strengths of children of both sexes and of all shapes, sizes, colors, ethnic and cultural backgrounds, dispositions, energy levels, and physical attributes. Every objective in reading must be relevant to the pupils we are teaching.

Comprehension: the prime objective in reading

Essentially, the only objective in reading is comprehension. All else is either a skill to be used in achieving comprehension (for example, selecting key graphic cues), a subcategory of comprehension (for example, critical reading) or a use to be made of comprehension (e.g. appreciation of literature).

Comprehension depends on the successful processing of three kinds of information: graphophonic, syntactic, and semantic. A series of abilities is necessary to make this process successful. How these abilities operate within this process is illustrated in the tentative Model of Reading (Figure 10.5).[8]

Reading instruction has as its subsidiary objectives development of these skills and strategies:

Scanning: The ability to move from left to right and down a page line by line.

Fixing: The ability to focus the eye on the line of print.

Selecting: The ability to select from graphic input those key cues which will be most productive in the information processing. For example, initial consonants are the most useful letters in words.

Predicting: The ability to predict input on the basis of grammar and growing sense of meaning from prior decoding. (Prediction and selection operate together since each is dependent on the other.)

Forming: The ability to form perceptual images on the basis of selection and prediction. The reader must combine what he sees with what he expects to see to form a perceptual image.

Searching: The ability to search memory for phonological cues and related syntactic and semantic information associated with perceptual images. The reader brings to bear his language knowledge and his experiential and conceptual background as he reads.

Tentative choosing: The ability to make tentative choices (guesses) on the basis of minimal cues and related syntactic and semantic input. It is crucial that the reader use the least amount of information possible to make the best guess possible. To do so, he will need well developed strategies that become almost automatic.

Testing - semantic and syntactic: The ability to test choices against the screens of meaning and grammar. Literally the reader says to himself: 'Does that make sense?' 'Does that sound like language to me?' This involves the crucial ability to

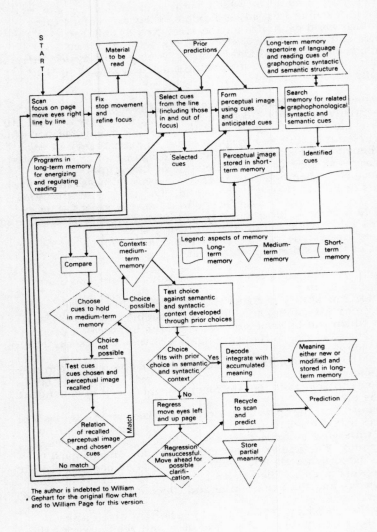

Figure 10.5 The Goodman model of reading

recognize his own errors when they are significant. Readers
who do not use these two screens will tend to have low comprehension and will make little effective progress in reading,
though they may become good word callers (recoders in the
sense defined above).

Testing - graphophonic: The ability to test the tentative choice,
if it has failed the prior test, against the recalled perceptual
image and to gather more graphic information if needed. Note
that it is only when the choice has been rejected on semantic
or syntactic grounds that there is any need to resort to further
graphophonic information. A miscalled word is most likely to be
recognized as a mistake if it doesn't fit the meaning and grammar screens.

Regressing: The ability to scan right to left and up the page
line by line if a choice is found unacceptable on prior tests.
This involves the reader's recognizing that an anomaly or incon-
sistency exists in his processing to date and attempting to
locate the source or point of error and then reprocessing.
This is the device by which the reader corrects the errors he
has recognized. A great deal of learning takes place through
correction. The reader teaches himself new strategies and new
insights as well as new words.

Decoding: When a successful, acceptable choice has been made,
the reader integrates the information gained with the meaning
that has been forming. This may involve assimilation of new
meaning or accommodation of meaning previously decoded, or
both.

Each of these abilities involves a set of strategies and techniques. Though phonic generalizations and sight words are
learned and used in the reading process, it is the acquisition
of key strategies which makes this knowledge develop and
which makes it useful to the reader. In early reading instruction children will form associations between oral and written
language (phonics generalizations). But only in the selection
strategies, the perceptual image forming techniques, the
graphophonic testing, and the semantic and syntactic contexts
does this knowledge take on its true importance.

Some of the techniques we have tended to label word attack
skills are useful. But, if we raise our sights from words to the
whole reading process, these techniques will change their relative importance. Consider this short sequence:

The boys stumbled into the house after their long hike.
Mother said, 'You must really be *fatigued*. Sit here and
rest while I get lunch ready.'
When she returned with the food, Mother discovered they
were so fatigued that they had fallen asleep.

Now, if we assume that 'fatigued' is an unknown word to be
'attacked,' we will tend to employ phonics, structural analysis

and other techniques that can work within the context of the word to achieve its recognition. This will be a problem, if, as is likely, the reader has not heard the word and therefore cannot match it with an equivalent.

If, on the other hand, we are concerned about the same problem as it actually is encountered in the reading process, we will see that the meaning of the passage can come through rather clearly without the identification of this word. In fact, it is quite likely that in this short sequence the reader had become aware that the word must mean something like 'tired.' Should he assume another definition, 'hungry' for example, subsequent reading might cause a correction. All of the syntactic and semantic information that the reader has going for him makes him relatively independent of the graphophonic information.

DEVELOPING SOPHISTICATION IN READING

Adequate functioning of the reading process depends on development in a number of areas, both mechanical and intellectual. A deficiency in any one of these can affect the quality of the child's reading and lessen its meaning for him.

Techniques and strategies

If a reader does not develop independence in the use of the strategies and techniques required for adequate functioning of the reading process, then special attention may be required. Cycles of skill instruction could be planned which would move the learner from language to a focus on the technique of knowledge which he needs and then back to language so that he can test the technique as he attempts to read.

To pick a simple example, suppose that a child is not aware that initial consonants are the most useful graphic cues. Instruction might help him by selecting from reading material words that start in various ways. Then the reader would return to the reading material to utilize the technique of selecting initial consonant cues.

If on the other hand children become overdependent on specific techniques, then again they can be guided within the full scope of reading materials to put the techniques in proper perspective in relationship to other techniques and available information. Suppose a child had become too reliant on initial consonants and was using neither meaning and syntax nor other graphic cues well. He could be helped to move away from his overdependence while the weak strategies were being developed at the same time.

Sequencing of skill instruction in reading has often been strongly advocated by publishers and curriculum workers. But the reading process requires that a multitude of skills be used simultaneously. As we have indicated, many of these skills are already employed by the learner in listening. Any sequence will necessarily be arbitrary.

Flexibility

In discussing adaptation, we indicated the need for developing general reading strategies and special reading strategies for literature, science, social studies and other language uses. The key to this development is experience of the learner with a wide variety of materials, and guidance from the teacher as it is needed to help develop specific strategies to handle the requirements of these special reading materials. This is only one kind of flexibility needed. A second kind of flexibility has to do with reading purpose. The reader needs to gain flexibility in the way his reading process functions in relation to the outcome he desires.

If he desires a high degree of comprehension with great detail then he will be more demanding of himself and more painstaking. If at the opposite extreme he is only concerned with getting a quick notion of the general drift of what he is reading, he will use test processes more freely, sample more widely, and not bother to worry about errors as he reads. If speed reading courses have any validity it must be in their ability to get readers to break out of a single inflexible reading style and into a more variable one.

A sense of the significance of reading

A child who was a beginning reader was once asked why she thought it was important to know how to read. 'You might park some place,' she said, 'and there might be a No Parking sign there. And a man might come out and say, "Can't you read?"'

The story illustrates a small child's view of the great importance of being able to read in a literate society. An individual in a literate society has many, many encounters every day that require the comprehension of written language. Success with adult illiterates in building literacy has been achieved by building the instructional program around their most pressing needs: signs, applications, labels, directions, and other mundane things that readers take for granted.

A lesser, but still important motivation for the acquisition of reading comes from the pleasure and satisfaction it provides. This is not to say that simply by telling children how much fun reading is they can be motivated to learn. Rather, they can be led to discover this for themselves. The enjoyment of a good story will whet the appetite for more. The satisfaction of getting the information needed from a reference work will stimulate the reader to make greater use of reading as a source of information.

In aiding children to see the significance of reading, we should avoid the temptation of preselecting all the material for them. Children, like adults, have varied tastes and interests.

What most children like or profit from may be totally uninterest-
ing to one child. If a child is to find himself in reading, a wide
range of topics, formats, and even quality must be represented
in the material available to him.

In the multimedia world in which today's children become
literate, reading need not be isolated from or exalted above
other media. Television, movies, radio can and do actually
stimulate reading. Today's readers have seen and heard events
that their parents and grandparents encountered only through
their newspapers. They bring a much broader background and
range of interests to reading than any earlier generations.
Above all, motivation for reading requires that schools make
themselves relevant to today's children.

Critical sense
To read critically is to read skeptically. The reader asks himself not only, 'Do I understand what this means?' but 'Do I
buy it?' Implicit in critical reading is a set of values and
criteria which is constantly brought into play throughout the
process.

Three things are requisite to developing critical reading
competence. First, the reader must develop a set of appropriate criteria to judge what he is reading, or at least he must
have general criteria that will help him deal with matters such
as plausibility, credibility, ulterior motives of the writer or
publisher, and so forth. Second, he must see critical reading
as necessary and possible for himself. Third, he must be aware
of the devices which writers use to appeal emotionally and
subtly to him as a means of influencing him.

Much of the reading required of children in school deters
rather than promotes critical reading. If there is always one
right answer to a question, if the teacher settles an argument
by pointing out that the book has given the information on
page 38 (implying that books are never wrong), if children are
led to believe that they are not competent to judge the merits
of their social studies or science books, then the teacher cannot turn around and ask children to read an essay in their
reading text critically. One either reads critically or one does
not. The strategies required to read critically must be developed for all reading tasks and not just for special ones
designed for instruction.

Some of the most effective users of language in our country
are paid high salaries by Madison Avenue agencies to convince
the public that they cannot possibly exist without their clients'
products. The same tactics have been used with remarkable
success to sell political candidates. Only a truly critical reader
or listener can hope to ferret out fact from propaganda.

CONCLUSION

Everyone agrees that reading is a critical area in education. Everyone agrees that methods must be found and curricula developed to teach all children to read effectively. Energy and money are expended for materials, clinics, special teachers by school systems and by parents. That private clinics flourish and that schools are increasing their efforts are mute evidence that the problems of reading instruction have not been solved.

The state of reading instruction today is that of an art. Skilled teachers and specialists have the know-how to help *most*, but not all, of their pupils.

There is no simple breakthrough in reading just around the corner which will change instruction to a foolproof science. As more is understood about reading and learning to read, it becomes ever clearer how complex these processes are. No simple antitoxin can be injected in nonreaders to make them readers. But progress will come as misconceptions disappear in favor of sound understanding. Materials and curricula based on scientific insights will replace those built on tradition, trial-and-error and expediency. And a reading curriculum will evolve tied to an effective theory of reading instruction.

The basis for such progress now exists. If parents, teachers and administrators can resist simplistic panaceas and keep up sustained efforts to achieve more effective reading instruction then the next decade can be the one in which the major problems are solved.

NOTES

1 As we think of reading as an information seeking process, it will help to think of the graphic material as input and meaning as output. Oral reading produces speech as a second output.

2 Redundancy means, here, that each bit of information may be conveyed by several cues in the language. For example, notice in this sentence how many cues indicate the plural nature of the subject: 'Two boys are eating their sandwiches.'

3 If you don't hear the difference, then you don't know Spanish phonemes, which is the point here.

4 In this diagram, 'recode' is used to mean going from code to code (aural to graphic); 'decode' is reserved for processes that go from code (in either form) to meaning. In this sense, comprehension and 'decoding' are virtual synonyms while word-calling and sounding-out are 'recoding' processes. A third term, 'encode,' is used to mean going from meaning to code (again either written or oral). In our early example of the writer and his attorney, the writer could only 'recode' printed language as oral language.

But the lawyer could 'decode' from language to meaning. Then he could 'encode' meaning in an oral language form his client could 'decode' (comprehend).

5 We use 'competence' here, as some linguists do, to represent the basic, developed capacity for using language. 'Performance' is a behavioral indicator of that 'competence' but behavior should not be confused with the abilities that make performance possible. (Further elaboration is offered on pp. 115–16).

6 Of course it will also help to assure that materials children are asked to read are written well. Poor writing is not likely to be easily read.

7 Kenneth S. Goodman and Carolyn L. Burke, 'Study of Children's Behavior While Reading Orally,' Final Report, Project S 425, USOE, March 1968.

8 The author is indebted to William Gephart for the original flow chart for this model and to William Page for the current version.

'Language must be the core of the curriculum and in the same sense it must be a major concern of teacher education.' Here Goodman and his colleagues provide important and practical suggestions for a variety of programs relevant to pre-service and in-service teacher education. A colleague once called this 'a "should" list' because its objectives are stated not as behavior but as things that should *happen*: 'students should examine their own belief system...' 'Secondary teachers should examine and appreciate the language competence of secondary school-age pupils.'

What this emphasizes is the author's view that education should be rooted in theory, values, and substantive knowledge and not based on simplistic, prescriptive behavior change objectives.

11 LANGUAGE IN TEACHER EDUCATION

with Yetta M. Goodman and Carolyn L. Burke

Language is the most uniquely human of all human attributes. It not only makes human communication possible at a level which is in no sense within the reach of any other species, but it is also the medium of thought and of learning. Language makes possible the manipulation and reorganization of experiences into hierarchical generalizations and concepts. Further, language makes it possible for people to express their developing insights to others for response and criticism. This presentation phase is a vital part of human learning. It is central to the interaction of teacher and pupil.

Effective teacher education programs must be based on and be concerned for understanding of linguistic and psycholinguistic concepts for the following reasons:

1 Language is the medium of learning.

2 Language is the basic medium of instruction.

3 Effective teachers must build on the existing language competence of learners in order to achieve communication with the pupils and in order to plan and carry through instruction in all areas of learning.

4 Success in learning both in and out of school is dependent on increasing effectiveness and flexibility in language use both productive and receptive.

5 Literacy, normally acquired after formal education has begun, is an extension of the learner's language competence and of natural language learning. Effective teachers of literacy must appreciate and know how to use the language competence of learners. They must also understand how reading works as a process by which meaning is constructed from language.

Language must be the core of the curriculum and in the same sense it must be a major concern of teacher education.

Common sense beliefs about language, language learning, language processes, and language differences have derived from limited scholarship in past eras, from superficial observation and from received cultural traditions strongly influenced by social prejudices and attitudes that confused social, economic, cultural, political, and linguistic factors. Ironically, teachers in general and those particularly charged with dealing directly with aspects of language such as reading, speech and 'English' have been more likely to hold unsound non-productive views of language phenomena than the general public. The effect has been to create classes that were dull and irrelevant, which attempted to teach concepts about language which contradicted a reality available to every pupil, which isolated and dissected language processes and by so doing destroyed them, and which ignored the central importance of language in learning.

An initial goal, then, of a teacher education program, must be to confront prospective teachers with linguistic reality, to cause them to test their common sense beliefs and attitudes, and to help them find and accommodate to new scientifically based insights. This can not be accomplished through university classes only. Neither can it be achieved through immersing students in primary classrooms. Rather there must be guidance by informed instructors who can help them organize their belief systems and test them against reality and who can make available to them techniques and resources for coping with reality. We can't assume that pre-service teachers will discover on their own that 'sloppy language' is systematic, that non-verbal kids are 'so hard to understand' because the teacher has been ignoring the speech of some children as unworthy of consideration.

As crucial as this change of basic attitude toward language is, it is only the beginning in moving from non-productive (or counter productive) common sense to the base of knowledge and insight that can make effective teaching possible. All teachers need to understand how language works and how it's used in communicating, thinking and learning. Teachers of reading, language arts, English, speech and foreign languages need particularly strong backgrounds. To them such knowledge is as important as human anatomy is to the medical practitioner.

Such knowledge is available from recent research on child language development, and from recent research and theoretical work in linguistics and the related cross disciplinary fields of sociolinguistics and psycholinguistics. It can not, of course, become available for application to students simply through lectures or books. Nor is such knowledge easily or directly translatable into curriculum or classroom activity. Again students need skilled guidance from instructors who can help them focus concepts on educational problems and who can help them to use scientific knowledge to understand teaching and learning phenomena. Whether this competence is acquired through methods classes, or content classes, or field assignments is not important. Most likely students will require some combination of all three. What is crucial is the guidance they get and the competence of the staff they work with.

STAFF DEVELOPMENT

There is a peculiar situation in the development of teacher educators with background in language and language learning, at the present time. While programs in linguistics, sociolinguistics and psycholinguistics have mushroomed to the point where they are producing more master's and doctoral level graduates than there are jobs, no programs have emerged in applied fields related to education with the exception of TESOL (teaching English to speakers of other languages). Though the need for linguistically sophisticated educators is widely recognized and demand for such people is extremely high, no structures in colleges of education exist to produce them.

To provide the input necessary for the pre-service teacher education program described above staff would have to be recruited from education and developed in terms of language insights or staff would have to be recruited from linguistics and related fields and developed in terms of educational insights. It is clear that the success of an undergraduate program would be dependent upon a strong graduate program and in fact a by-product of such a program would be the development of teacher educators capable of replicating such a program elsewhere.

IN-SERVICE EDUCATION AS RELATED TO PRE-SERVICE

The same imperatives apply to the in-service teacher that apply to the pre-service teacher. It's particularly important that teachers working directly with pre-service teachers acquire the same insights and the same change in basic attitudes toward language that are being developed in the undergraduates. If this does not take place the student teacher will be in a conflict situation. Furthermore changes in curriculum and materials and methods will be of little effect if on-the-job teachers are not prepared to evaluate and use them intelligently. Staff development must include in-service as well as pre-service experience. There must be particular concern for cooperating teachers who work with pre-service teachers.

PROPOSAL FOR AN INTER-DISCIPLINARY TEACHER EDUCATION PROGRAM

This program will be described as a series of experiences designed to develop competences, attitudes, and knowledge rather than a series of courses. Since language is never an end in itself but always a means to an end (communication, concepts, information) such experiences should be related to other experiences and with classroom situations.

Students should observe, record, study and analyze the natural language of one or more children (at levels relevant to teaching goals).

Students should examine their own belief system and become aware of other systems for interpreting linguistic behavior to determine underlying linguistic competence. This should be done in direct relationship to the natural language observation.

Students should become aware of the theoretical positions and research to support them on child language development. They should examine, directly or through protocol materials, particular children's language at varying stages of development.

Students should engage in directed introspective activities designed to make it possible for them to understand their own linguistic competence. They should become aware of their own idiolect and dialect features.

Students should engage in basic study of the English language in terms of two or more of its dialects in order to develop insights into differences and similarities in English and into how English functions. They should apply grammars such as descriptive or transformational to actual language corpora.

Students should examine the relationships between thought and language and thought and learning through a series of experiences with individual children, in small groups, and in classes. They should examine research and theory on the acquisition of knowledge through listening and reading and conduct activities designed to apply and test such ideas.

Students should examine the social, political, economic, and cultural aspects of language and the effects toward language. This can be accomplished through introspective devices, surveys, and examination of research literature.

Students should acquire systems for describing phonological, orthographic, morphological and syntactic phenomena in language and should have experience in their application.

Students should examine all areas of knowledge and learning which are directly involved in their own career plans in terms of how language and language learning are involved in each. They should study curricula, texts and other materials, as well as common methodology to understand how linguistic and conceptual interrelationships are treated and developed.

Students should demonstrate, with learners, their knowledge and competence to deal with linguistic and conceptual development in relevant classroom activities.

Prospective elementary teachers: should examine the language competence of pupils at school entrance ages. They should demonstrate the knowledge and competence necessary to build pride and confidence in pupils.

They should have sufficient direct experience with children's language to develop proper appreciation for their linguistic competence.

They should become familiar with the range of dialects found in their communities and demonstrate ability to understand and communicate with all groups.

They should analyze the oral reading of pupils at various levels of proficiency in order to gain basic insights into reading as a process and into the strengths and weaknesses of readers at various levels of proficiency.

They should become familiar with a theoretical model of the reading process and be able to relate it to the reality they find in children's reading.

They should examine relating learning to oral and written language development in the range of subjects found in elementary curricula.

They should examine common materials, methods, and curricula in classroom situations on the basis of knowledge of the reading process and reading learning.

They should plan and carry out instructional programs in reading, writing and other literacy related language aspects.

Secondary teachers: should examine and appreciate the language competence of secondary school age pupils. They should come to appreciate, value, and respect the full range of diversity and learn to avoid confusing linguistic difference with deficiency.

They should understand reading and writing sufficiently well as linguistic processes that they can help learners to become more effective in using them in learning and expression.

They should understand the relationship between oral and written language through experience in relating each to learning experiences in classrooms of appropriate level and subject concentration.

They should become able to communicate with and understand pupils who speak the full range of dialects found in their communities.

They should become aware of the language characteristics of adolescents including their propensity for linguistic innovation and be able to understand and respond to current teen-age language.

English teachers: should acquire a strong understanding of the grammar, phonology, morphology and lexicon of English in its many dialects and be able to relate this knowledge to planning curriculum and instruction.

They should become able to plan and carry through programs designed to help a full range of pupils become more effective users of language in speaking, listening, reading and writing.

They should become able to separate learning activities designed to provide pupils with knowledge about how language works from those designed to help them use it more effectively.

They should themselves become models of flexible, varied, effective language use and shed any tendencies toward narrow up-tight linguistic performance.

They should acquire through direct experience the ability to build on the linguistic competence of learners.

Foreign language teachers: should become confident and fluent in the language they teach and aware of its diversity.

They should understand the basic mechanisms by which first and second languages are acquired and be able to apply this understanding in planning curriculum methodology and instructional techniques.

They should learn, through basic classroom experience, how to build instruction around developing competence as a receptive and productive user of language.

HOW TO IMPLEMENT A PROGRAM FOR FILLING THE LANGUAGE GAP IN TEACHER EDUCATION

1 Entering students in education should have a basic scientific knowledge of language or acquire one immediately after entering. This may require a course. If so, it should be foundational but oriented to relating language and learning; it should *not* be the first course in linguistics for linguistics majors.

2 The undergraduate faculty for preparation of teachers should include staff members who have a substantial understanding of language and learning. Such staff should either be educationists who are linguistically aware or linguists with a deep interest in education.

3 There should be a unit, institute, or cross-disciplinary committee on language and learning in every college of education. This committee (unit) would offer advanced degree programs and coordinate language aspects of pre-service and in-service programs. It should include other university units outside the college who share interests in language and learning, such as departments of English, linguistics, psycholinguistics, anthropology, and foreign languages.

4 The committee (unit) should foster research related to instructional and dissemination aspects with the same pupil populations as the teacher education program serves.

5 Programs for in-service teachers should be developed with particular emphasis on those most closely involved with undergraduate students.

6 Language should be considered a major strand in the teacher education program for all teachers at all phases of development.

7 Special strength in language should be built for teachers whose special emphasis involves language most directly.

8 Advanced degree programs should involve students in linguistic and psycholinguistic study and application in research, in-service and pre-service education.

The need for bringing more linguistic and psycholinguistic sophistication into teacher education is increasingly being recognized. What is needed now is for some forward-looking colleges of education to create the forms and structures to make this input possible.

LINGUISTIC APPLICATIONS

In this brief, simple paper, Goodman presents four basic concepts about language that teachers need to understand and
apply in the classroom. They are as much fundamental, foundational beliefs as they are cognitive concepts.

12 LINGUISTIC INSIGHTS WHICH TEACHERS MAY APPLY

While the basic application of linguistic and psycholinguistic insights to reading materials and methodology has yet to be made, there are some key concepts about language and how it is used to convey meaning that can make a difference in the teaching of reading now. If a teacher understands and applies these concepts, regardless of the texts or the method she is now using, the results should be better reading by more children.

It is the belief of this writer that, in teaching reading, linguistic knowledge must be integrated with other knowledge from psychology, child development, and classroom practice; the new must be merged with the old. Present materials with linguistic labels do not achieve this new synthesis. But teachers themselves can begin the process where it is most important: in the classroom with the learner.

The purpose of this paper is to present some of these key concepts and to suggest some of the applications classroom teachers can make.

THE LANGUAGE COMPETENCE OF CHILDREN

Concept 1. Children by the time they come to school have already achieved a virtual mastery over the oral language of their community.

We have for years permitted ourselves to be distracted by the immaturities in children's speech from the basic control that they have achieved over their language *before* we start to teach them to read. The language competence that the beginner brings to the task of learning to read his native language is an enormous resource for him if the teacher recognizes and takes advantage of it. He has learned to use the systems in language to comprehend aural language. He makes the necessary discriminations and organizes the stream of sound that is aural language into decodable units. All of this he can and does use in reading - unless he is prevented or distracted from it.

This means that the child can use himself as his own language resource. He can ask himself two questions as he reads and trust his own judgment about the answers: (1) Does what I'm reading make sense (can I decode meaning from it)? (2) Does what I'm reading sound right (is it grammatically acceptable)?

In language-experience approaches, or in the use of experience charts in other methods, new importance must be attached by the teacher to preserving the language of the child. We have understood the importance of using the learner's own experiences in making charts for early reading. We have not sufficiently understood the importance of using the child's own grammar, phrasing, and vocabulary. If the language is altered or transformed into the teacher's language or, worse, the language of the pre-primer, then it is no longer his and he cannot use his power over language to the same degree.

THE NATURE OF LANGUAGE

Concept 2. Language is systematic.

Language is acquired so early and so well that, though we use it constantly, we are unaware of its basic characteristics on any conscious level. We tend to think of language as composed of sounds and words and of its written form as composed of letters and sounds. But neither words nor letters nor sounds are capable of carrying meaning unless they are arranged in some acceptable pattern within a language system. Morse code uses dots and dashes, but when these two symbols are interspersed with long and short spaces and arranged in patterns they can begin to carry meaning.

Language by its nature, then, is systematic. The system of language is grammar. Grammar is not a characteristic of 'good' language or 'proper' language, or language learned in school. All language that functions in communication has a grammar. In comprehending language grammatical information is constantly being processed by the listener or reader, just as in generating language grammatical information is indispensable to the speaker or writer.

A teacher does not have to be trained in linguistics to grasp the significance of the systematic nature of language and apply it. Children must be aided in applying to reading the strategies for use of grammatical information they already use in listening. They can only do this when the material they are reading is language. Word lists, flash cards, phonic charts all isolate elements from the grammatical contexts in which they have reality. Too long we have kept the focus in reading on words and phonic relationships. We must put language back together and present learners with reading materials and exercises in which the system of language is intact and in which they have all the information at their disposal which they have learned to use in comprehending language.

There are, in reality, two contexts in language. One is the semantic, or meaning, context. It is the total message of the sentence and of the sequence of sentences in which any particular element occurs. But there is also the grammatical context, the syntactical pattern and its markers, which underlies the semantic context and makes it possible for meaning to be conveyed. One could not deny that in a nonsense sentence like, 'A marlup *was* pov*ing his* kump,' there is a grammatical context so strong that it makes us feel as if the sentence *ought* to mean something.

Again let us remember that the child does not need to be taught grammar. He knows, deep inside him, the grammar of *his* language. The fact that he can not verbalize this knowledge is quite unimportant. He can *use* it. And his teacher can help him use it even with materials that are not designed to take advantage of this great resource. She can avoid presenting words in isolation. She can put 'skill exercises' into whole grammatical, meaningful contexts. She can encourage the learner to draw on his knowledge to recognize and correct his own miscues. She can encourage him to go beyond basal materials and to read broadly materials that are within the scope of his understanding.

DIALECTS

Concept 3. A language is a family of mutually understood dialects. Each speaker of a language speaks one or more of these dialects.

Linguists studying languages and comparing them have found that all languages are in reality bundles of dialects. Each dialect is systematic in its own right, as we have indicated all language must be. And each dialect differs from all other dialects in consistent ways. These dialect differences develop whenever speakers of a language are separated over time, space, age, class, or interest.

Speakers of different dialects of a language will be able to understand each other, though not as well as they understand speakers of their own dialect. When differences between dialects become so great that their speakers cannot communicate then they have become different languages. Just as language and culture are related, dialects are integrally involved with their subcultures.

Dialects can and do differ in sounds (phonemes), inflections (mostly word endings), grammar, intonation, vocabulary, and idioms. Furthermore the units of one dialect do not directly correspond to those of another dialect. A frying pan may be a generic term to one dialect group but exclude heavy cast iron pans for another group that calls those skillets. A speaker of one English dialect carries his friend to work and totes his books while another drives his friends and carries his books.

ALL LANGUAGES CHANGE

Concept 4. Language is constantly changing.

A closely related concept to the dialect concept is that a characteristic feature of all language is change. What is true today of
language is not necessarily true tomorrow. Some aspects such
as vowel phonemes and word meanings change rapidly, others
more slowly, but all change. Perhaps the simplest explanation
of why language changes is that it is man-made, a social invention that is constantly being recreated and which responds
to the needs of the culture that creates it.

 The important thing for the teacher of reading to keep in
mind is that every child speaks, relatively well, the mother
tongue, the native language of his community. We must not
confuse difference in a child's language with deficiency. What
complicates matters is that dialects take on the social status of
the group that speaks them. In turn the dialect marks the
social status of a speaker in the eyes of others in his general
society. What is often called 'standard' English is nothing more
than the speech of the group with highest social status in the
region.

 The questions of whether or if schools have a responsibility
to replace a low-status dialect with a high-status one or add a
second dialect for speakers of low-status dialects are important
but not germane to the teaching of reading. In fact it is most
important that reading teachers keep separate the tasks of
learning to read and changing language. A speaker of a low-
status dialect has the same kind of language resources as any
other speaker. He can draw on these if the teacher does not
confuse him by 'correcting' him when what he has read is
consistent with his own dialect. His confidence in himself as a
language user must not be undermined at the point at which he
is learning to read.

 Fortunately spellings are constant in English across dialects.
The teacher can encourage the child to read in an oral language
which is natural for *him*. She can teach herself to differentiate
between reading errors and dialect differences and comfort herself with the knowledge that the more a child's oral reading
sounds like his native speech the more likely he is to be understanding and developing proficiency in reading.

THE RELATIONSHIP BETWEEN ORAL AND WRITTEN LANGUAGE

Concept 5. Though English uses an alphabetic writing system,
the oral and written system relate through the representation of
patterns of sounds by spelling patterns.

Modern research on the relationship of speech to print has made
clear that there are no simple letter-sound or phoneme-grapheme

correspondences in English. Rather the letter must be seen as part of a pattern representing a pattern of sounds. Rules that govern these relationships can be stated, but they are profuse and complex. The term regularity in these relationships must be seen as relative to the pattern in which a relationship occurs. Thus 'chew' is regularly spelled and so is 'situation' in which the same sound sequence occurs.

All this should lead teachers to the realization that phonic relationships (those between spelling and speech) must be developed within language contexts.

Furthermore, since speech varies among dialect groups no one set of phonic relationships can be applicable to all dialects. In fact each dialect has its own set of phonic relationships. A high status speaker from Maine who says 'meteor' sounds as if he is saying 'media' to a midwestern speaker. There are four pronunciations of 'almond' accepted in different parts of the country. In two, the 'l' is 'silent'; in two, it can be heard.

This realization of the variability of phonics ought to convince teachers that every reading program must be personalized to make it relevant to the learner and group of learners. That means hard work on the part of teachers but it is the only justifiable alternative to irrelevance.

CONCLUSION

This paper has stated just a few key concepts concerning language and has hardly scratched the surface of their applications, but it is hoped that teachers will let these ideas permeate their teaching and make the changes in their teaching and in their use of present materials that they come to see are needed.

Linguistics is input for curriculum making, but like all such input, it may be used in varying ways and it may be misused. As a discipline it is concerned with the scientific study of language and not with language instruction, (but) a language curriculum cannot be built without dealing with linguistic matters.

Here Goodman highlights the kinds of input that linguistics provides for the building of elementary language curricula and examines relevant goals of school language programs.

13 LINGUISTICS IN A RELEVANT CURRICULUM

When you start out on a trip, the first decision you need to make is where you're going. Everything else, all the other decisions involved in planning the trip, flow from the decision about the destination. Furthermore, the means of conveyance, the route, the time required to get there, cannot be determined unless the destination is continuously kept in mind.

So it is with the elementary language curriculum. First you must decide on objectives, the purposes of the curriculum, before any other decisions are possible or meaningful. The wise choice of objectives will require many kinds of input, not the least of which is values. What does the school, and the community that has chartered the school, want for its children? What should it want for them? There are other sources of input; the children themselves and basic discipline like psychology, sociology, and linguistics.

If there is a single test that all objectives and the curricula built to achieve them should meet, it is the test of relevancy. A curriculum must be relevant to the society, to the times, but most of all, it must be relevant to the learners. This is true in every area of education, but it is most vital in the area of language, because language is central to all communication, learning, and thought.

But language programs have often been the least relevant aspects of the curriculum. Frequently children are asked to learn things that are neither useful to them in any sense nor true in relation to their own language.

To be relevant, a language program must be consistent with the prior language of the learners. It must offer them insights into language as it really is or it must make it possible for them to use language more effectively. It must expand and facilitate language use and not put artificial restrictions on its use.

THE NEED FOR LINGUISTICS

Linguistics makes no promises in this endeavor and thus need keep no promises. Linguistics is input for curriculum making, but like all such input, it may be used in varying ways and it may be misused. As a discipline, it is concerned with the scientific study of language and not with language instruction. A language curriculum cannot be built without dealing with

linguistic matters, just as a bridge cannot be built by engineers
without dealing with the laws of physics. But knowing the laws
of physics does not determine how the bridge may be built, or
where, or when, or in fact whether it should be built at all.
Similarly, linguistics does not directly answer the key curricular
questions.

Three kinds of input are provided by linguistics for use in
building elementary curricula in language:

1 Concepts to be used and dealt with in making decisions
about method, scope, sequence, procedures.
2 Knowledge to enlighten teachers and to form the base of
language content for the learners.
3 New vantage points for looking at language and language
users. One such useful vantage point comes from descriptive linguistics: language is viewed as the product of human
activity. Another different and useful vantage point comes
from generative-transformational linguistics that views language as human process.

Such input neither can nor should be ignored in building
elementary language curriculum. It cannot be ignored, either,
in evaluating existing curricula and methodology. But new
decisions do not come from substituting new input for old. The
new and the old must be accommodated so that what emerges
is consistent with that which is valid from both. Language
programs can be linguistically valid; they cannot simply be
linguistic, for that would imply that linguistics as such is
capable of generating language programs with no assistance
from philosophy, learning theory, child development, sociology,
or pedagogy. What makes a program linguistically valid is that
it utilizes linguistic input when dealing with linguistic matters.
But that does not guarantee that it is consistent within itself or
relevant.

THE GOALS OF SCHOOL LANGUAGE PROGRAMS

It is in the context of relevancy that I would like to examine the
objectives of the elementary language program and the linguistic
input which will prove useful in building a relevant program.
This is an era in which educators had better be able to answer
when parents, community groups, and the learners themselves,
ask us why.

School language programs have three basic purposes:

1 *They seek to help learners become more effective users of
language.* Since this is a direction in which the learners have
constantly been moving since they began as infants to acquire
language, it is a key objective and one easily made relevant to
the learners. It is most important, however, that we do not

presume that certain kinds of instruction or learning activities
lead to more effective language use when in fact they do not.
To take a simple example, handwriting becomes more effective
as it becomes more legible. Beauty or conformity to a model of
perfection may either not contribute to effectiveness or may in
fact reduce it.

2 *They seek to provide the learners with knowledge about
language.* A distinction always needs to be made in building
school curricula between 'knowing that' and 'knowing how.'
Language is an exciting and important aspect of human activity.
It is worth studying, in order to understand *that* it works in
certain ways. But, such knowledge has little to do with the
knowledge of *how to use language.* Studying grammar, whether
conventional school grammar or one of the new linguistic grammars, has little effect on actual language used by the learner.
Fortunately, he has already learned the grammatical system
of his language. He is his own resource on language when he
examines it. Inquiry and discovery techniques can help him
to examine his own language in relevant ways. It does not matter what social status his language enjoys, it still has the
characteristics of language that the school wants him to understand. Language study, to be relevant, must deal with language 'like it is.'

3 *School language programs seek to expand the language of
learners.* Often, misunderstanding the nature of language
difference, we have sought to change children's language to
eliminate bad language and substitute good language. Now we
are coming to understand that language difference is legitimate
and expected. We are coming to understand that it is neither
necessary nor desirable to demand that a child give up his
native dialect in order to learn a dialect with higher social
status. We are coming to understand that the goal is to help
the learner achieve the linguistic flexibility that will serve his
communicative needs at all stages of his life. We are coming
also to understand that the learner must be a willing partner
in this enterprise (not cajoled, threatened, or conditioned into
cooperation) and that it must at all stages be relevant to his
current needs.

Language moves at all stages toward more effective use. Less
effective forms tend to give way to more effective ones. This is
the essential motivational force behind language learning. When
it comes to expanding language there is a direct relationship
between motivation to learn and the communicative needs of the
learner. Relevancy is critical.

In planning activities and curricula to achieve these three
ends, we have often confused them and confused ourselves
about the reason why we engage in certain activities. Here we
are very much entangled in old misconceptions. Perhaps the
deepest rooted of these and one of the most destructive is that
we teach children language in school. We have tended to ignore
the tremendous language resources that children have already

acquired and flattered ourselves that when we are teaching grammar lessons, we are teaching children how to use their language. At best, if our grammar lessons are well conceived, we are providing children with insights into the ways that language works - and that has little or nothing to do with their effectiveness as users of language.

Time and time again research has confirmed the intuitive discovery of many teachers: the way to improve language effectiveness both in oral and written forms is to stimulate children to use language, frequently, freely, and confidently.

A related error comes from the elitist view that dialects can be arranged hierarchically, which leads teachers and material writers to assume that children who don't speak standard English are speaking a corrupt or sloppy form of it, or at least a lesser form. They confuse difference with deficiency and thereby create a wholly irrelevant curriculum. They insist to the learner that what sounds right to him is wrong and what sounds wrong is right. Instead of expanding his language, the curriculum they create has the effect of putting it into a linguistic strait jacket.

LINGUISTICS AS INPUT

If we remember that linguistics is a source of input in the curricular and teaching decisions, we must make it a method or a set of materials; if we remember that this input must be synthesized with input from many other disciplines to aid in solving our problems, then we are ready to consider the specific ways that this input can help to build a more relevant curriculum.

1 Linguistics can help us - the educators - to understand how language works and to appreciate its functions in communication, thought, learning.
2 Linguistics can help us to understand the language of the children we teach and to appreciate its form, system, and legitimacy.
3 Linguistics can help us to see the child as an expert language user and eliminate our illusions about where language is learned.
4 Linguistics can be a source of content when we build curriculum about language.
5 Linguistics can be a source of insight to the teacher in dealing with all language areas: reading, spelling, composition, literature, oral expression.

We must always strive in our schools for more effective, more relevant methods and materials. But no New English program, no new language arts series, no programed learning materials can fully exploit the applications of linguistics to building a relevant curriculum. This can only be accomplished by enlightened teachers who work in direct contact with the readers for whom the curriculum must be relevant.

Schools treat language as if it is the private preserve of teachers....Language is not a strait-jacket that teachers apply. It is not something to constrain one's ability to express. Language should be a tool. As long as teachers have an elitist, absolutist - perhaps racist - attitude toward language, they are going to be listening to children in class and not hearing them.

In this powerful article Goodman clearly shows the importance in education of respecting the background and the language of the learner. He contrasts two models of school language development, 'the uptight model' and 'the expansion model,' arguing convincingly of the need for the latter. Once again the child is the central concern. The curriculum, he believes, should be built on the premise that expansion on the existing language strengths of learners is both the most legitimate goal and the soundest pedagogical strategy for schools to develop.

14 LET'S DUMP THE UPTIGHT
MODEL IN ENGLISH

A popular Country and Western song a few years back had the title 'Don't Put the Shuck on Me.' The gist of the message was, 'Just because I talk differently, don't think I'm stupid.'

People who move from place to place are sometimes stereotyped by their speech. People assume that newcomers who speak differently are less bright or less 'cultured.' But all dialects are legitimate; language is a family of dialects. Dialects cannot be arranged on a ladder in order of quality.

In England, the idea that some dialects are superior to others grew out of the class structure. The dialect that had the highest status was the King's English. Had the King spoken some other dialect, it would have become the King's English.

In 'My Fair Lady,' Professor Higgins says that he is going to teach Eliza to talk like a duchess - no, better than that. He would teach her to talk like a saleslady in a fancy women's dress shop. A duchess is not quite so careful about her speech as a saleslady trying to sound like a duchess.

Dialects differ in every aspect - in phonology (sound), vocabulary, syntax, idioms. But if a speaker of one dialect cannot understand a speaker of another dialect, separate languages are involved. Dialects by definition can be understood by speakers of other dialects of the same language.

If anyone is culturally disadvantaged, then everyone is. Whenever someone is among people who share an unfamiliar culture and dialect, he is handicapped. He has difficulty in getting some of the good jokes; he is not in on some of the in-group things that people say. Not everyone has the background to appreciate classical music, but then not everyone can appreciate soul music, either.

Each of us speaks a dialect - several, perhaps. We are familiar with dialects we hear spoken frequently. We are less familiar with dialects we do not hear often. Americans are more familiar with some American English dialects than they are with Australian or South African or British English dialects.

Urban areas, which attract newcomers from different parts of the country, are a patchwork of dialects. Sometimes a social class in an area is made up of people who came from a certain part of the country and speak the dialect of that section. In Chicago, many workers and skilled tradesmen come from southern Illinois and southern Indiana. Many of the earlier comers who were in more favored economic status came from the East. The newcomers and the long-time residents hear one another's

dialects and become familiar with them and better at understanding them, but they do not always understand each other
fully. In a graduate seminar, the subject of soul food came
up, and a student from Iowa - in all seriousness - said, 'There's
a store on the corner that sells chitterlings, but I haven't had
the guts to try them.' She was too disadvantaged to realize
she was making a pun. (If you don't get the pun, it's a sign
that you are culturally disadvantaged.)

LANGUAGE: SUPERIOR AND INFERIOR?

Dialect differences can be described. The different ways in
which language is used can be described. But as soon as a
value system is imposed - as soon as one dialect is labeled
superior to another, or more literate, or more advanced - racist,
elitist views take over and linguistic reality is left behind. The
speakers of some dialects may reach a higher level of literacy
than the speakers of others, but we had better be careful not
to say that some speakers are culturally superior because they
have reached a higher level of literacy.

LANGUAGE: HOW IT IS

Literature is not the sole (soul) possession of high-status dialects. We tend to think of literature as something in books. We
forget that there is an oral tradition, too, that is more vital in
some groups than in others. Kids in the inner city in Detroit
play games and chant rope-skipping rhymes that have a direct
tie to Elizabethan ones. The kids sometimes vary the rhythm or
change words to bring in local place names and personalities,
but the continuity is evident. Bobby Burns, Paul Lawrence
Dunbar, James Whitcomb Riley, Bret Harte, Mark Twain, and
Langston Hughes, all created literature in low-status dialects.
A brief look at some of the American English dialects demonstrates that difference is not the same as deficiency.
  Phonological differences are most apparent to the general
public. Noticing that some people say 'Ah' and that some people
say 'I' is about as far as many people go in understanding that
there are differences in dialects. The vowel sounds are among
the most actively changing in the language: it is not surprising
that people notice differences in vowel sounds from dialect to
dialect. But there are other differences - vocabulary differences. In some places, people say 'bucket'; in other places,
people prefer 'pail.' In one locality, people say 'soda'; in
another, 'pop' or 'tonic.' Sometimes people are charmed by the
quaint idioms that others use but are unaware of their own
idioms. It is natural to them to say, 'Let's take a walk.' The
expression is an idiom, even though they do not think of it as
an idiom. 'Don't Put the Shuck on Me' will strike you as being

either charming or peculiar if it is someone else's idiom.

Dialects differ in syntax, in their grammatical system. Fortunately, these differences are minor, but they probably contribute most to misunderstanding or differences in interpretation. If an inner-city child answers the roll with 'I here' instead of 'I am here,' he is not using an incomplete sentence. He is saying something complete in his own dialect. Differences in grammatical systems of various dialects cause a bit of cultural disadvantage one way or the other in communication.

Differences in intonation throw us off when we hear somebody else's dialect. We have difficulty getting what they are saying. Travelers in unfamiliar parts of the country who have difficulty understanding a dialect they cannot quite tune in on are probably miscued by intonation. The pitch or stress patterns are unfamiliar.

Add all this up, and you have communication problems. But they stem from differences, not deficiencies.

LANGUAGE: WHERE IT'S AT

'Start where the child is,' an adage advises. To use contemporary terms, the school must take the child's language 'where it's at.' The school must look at basic competence and examine it in terms of differences and the proposition that differences and deficiencies are not the same thing.

Language is a unique human capability. Man alone can share his experience through language, organize his experience into concepts, and discuss it with other people. No porpoise ever swam to a microphone and generated a sentence he never heard before, discussing some experience of his. Parakeets and parrots and dolphins can be taught to talk in the sense that they can produce, on cue, certain recognizable phrases, but that is not using language in the sense that human beings use it: as a medium of thought, as a means of communicating, a way of expressing needs and emotions.

LANGUAGE IS FOR MESSAGES

The unique role of human language must be emphasized. Teachers have to be careful what they do to the language a child brings to school, not simply because of his self-image and his self-respect and his attitude toward who he is and the group to which he belongs - they are important enough - but because his language makes it possible for him to communicate with the world. If teachers attack the child's language, they cut him off from the world.

Language as the child has learned it is not simply a set of sounds or words. That notion must be abandoned. Baby books have their slot for Baby's first word. But what goes into baby

books are first utterances or first globs of language. What
should go into the baby book is the first intentional use of
language. A child who responds to a cue by waving his arms
and mumbling something that sounds like 'bye-bye' is going
to continue to wave and mumble on cue if he gets a big response. The difference between that performance and standing
in his crib, shaking the sides, and saying 'want cat' is most
significant. In the bye-bye situation, Baby is making a simple
stimulus-response reaction, but when he shakes the crib and
calls for food, he is using language with purpose. He can control a linguistic string only about one syllable long. This limits
his performance but conceals the competence he has developed
in the language. Research shows that between twenty-seven
and thirty months – a very short period – a child who had been
talking in nouns and verbs suddenly blossomed forth with
prepositions, pronouns, and all the function words he had not
used before. Though the child's performance changed remark-
ably, the competence that was involved had developed earlier.
All that happened at that point was that the child stopped talking in his telegraphic language, 'want eat,' and started saying,
'I want something to eat.' He had the competence and now his
articulation and co-ordination made it possible for him to match
his competence with performance.

HOW LANGUAGE HAPPENS

As the child learns language, he acquires not just words, not
just sounds, but the grammar of the language as well, and as
he acquires the grammar, he begins to induce rules that govern
this language. The very mistakes a child makes are clues to the
kind of competence he has developed. When a child says 'I taked
it' instead of 'I took it,' he is demonstrating that he is general-
izing a rule for forming the past tense but has not learned the
limits for applying that rule. By making mistakes and by discovering what is effective and what is not, he polishes and
refines the rules and adds subrules. By the time he comes to
school, he is able to perform a unique human trick. He is able to
say something he has never heard or said before, and be understood by other people in his language community.

LANGUAGE HAPPENS BEFORE SCHOOL

In the beginning, his language community may be simply the
family, but his language community expands rapidly. He moves
from an individual idiolect into the community dialect. The force
behind this growth is the child's need to communicate effectively. A child continues to do what he finds effective and stops
doing what he finds ineffective. The more he speaks like the
people around him, the more effective he is. The less he speaks

like them, the less effective he is. So he tends to move toward their rules, their patterns, their phonology, their words, their idioms.

This all happens well before the child comes to school, though some of it is still being polished later. Much of the early study of children's language development has drawn unwise conclusions. Immaturity in language has been confused with differences in dialects. All children move toward the language norms of their community. They are learning a dialect. But as in all learning, there are leaps and bounds and plateaus and backsliding. In learning a language children do not move from one stage of perfection to another. Kids make mistakes in using language. That's one of the charming things about having a growing child around the house. By responding to a child (not correcting him), we help his language become more effective.

ARE RESEARCHERS WITH IT?

When a child comes to school, he has learned to speak his language. He may have some phonological immaturities. 'Won' and 'run' may sound the same when he says them. He may say 'taked' instead of 'took,' or he may have difficulty combining sentences. These are minor shortcomings compared with what he has learned. Researchers studying children's language have confused these immaturities with differences between dialects. Highly respectable studies misinterpret their findings that some children use shorter sentences than other children do. The children who use shorter sentences speak a dialect that does not use the present tense forms of 'to be.' The child who says 'He home' has a shorter sentence than the child who says 'He's home.' 'I going' is shorter than 'I'm going.' But 'I going' is no less mature or less complete than 'I am going.' If one is incomplete, the other has an unnecessary word in it. In reality, there are two grammatical systems, and one can judge only mature and immature forms within each system. Since researchers have not carefully separated immaturity from differences in dialects, they do not really know whether some groups of children develop more slowly in language than others and whether some are truly less mature than others.

In the USA research tends to show that black children develop language more slowly than white children because the studies are based on this misconception. Basil Bernstein says anybody can do a study comparing working-class children and middle-class children in England and get predictable results that upper-class children are more mature in language development.[1] But researchers get these results simply because of the way the studies are done and because of the assumptions that are made. If a researcher cannot differentiate between differences in dialects and immaturity, he is going to make some tragic mistakes that will be carried over into curriculum and teaching. A lot of children will be confused and will come to think that teachers are hypocrites who make their pupils say funny things that do not really fit in with the world.

'DIGGING AND BEING DUG'

The phrase 'digging and being dug' comes from Langston Hughes:

> I play it cool and dig all jive,
> That's the way I stay alive;
> My motto as I live and learn,
> Is dig and be dug in return.[2]

This is what children are doing with language: they are trying to 'dig' and to be 'dug.' That's what language is for. In using it for communication children acquire language forms and categories rooted in the cultural experience. Language becomes a marvelously effective tool for thinking. Children can use language to mull things over. They can use language to manipulate their thoughts and experiences and come up with a new idea. They can use language to try the idea on the world to see whether their language is effective. If it is not effective, they can try another way. If it is effective, they can hold on to it. Since they are trying to be 'dug' by people who mean the most to them and who are trying to 'dig' them, they learn the language that is closest to them - their community dialect. It is the same for all children. There is no difference in the language-process in Grosse Pointe or in Detroit's inner city. Children all learn their own language about equally well. If they do not all show their language competence in school, that is the school's fault, not the kids'.

THE ONLY LANGUAGE A CHILD HAS

It is important to understand the role that language plays in the child's life by the time he gets to school, whatever form he brings with him. Emily Dickinson has called her poems her 'letters to the world.'[3] A child mails his letter to the world in a language that is available to him. If, when he comes up to a teacher and says something that is important to him, she smiles and says, 'No, dear, we don't say it that way,' he is not going to mail her any more letters until he figures out what is going on. He may figure out that it is a game he does not know the rules of. The disadvantage is one the school created. His language identifies him with his culture; it is part of him. If it is rejected, he is rejected. But what is most crucial is that his language is his medium of learning. That is what he has been using to organize his experiences, to think with, to talk over his needs, his reactions to the world, his emotions. When in nice ways or not nice ways schools undermine a child's language, they are undermining his ability to learn. The school-imposed disadvantage comes from rejecting the language of some children and welcoming the language of others (with some minor restrictions even on that). The issue is simple and basic: do schools accept language and build on it? Or do they reject it and try to teach the child the preferred form and meantime deprive him of the means for learning he already has?

TELLING IT LIKE IT IS

It is necessary to differentiate social aspects of language from linguistic aspects and then consider when schools can 'tell it like it is.' When can schools help children face the social realities of language? What is the optimum age?

WHO TALKS HOW?

People who have been studying dialects have identified a phenomenon that should not surprise many teachers. In a community like New York, or Los Angeles, or Milwaukee, where there may be three or four ways of saying something, there will be high agreement on what might be called a socially preferred form. Some expressions are identified as low-status language even by many who use them. Whether this is brain-washing or a general attitude in the community, some expressions are markers. Saying 'ain't' is a social marker that puts someone who uses the word in a lower status than someone who does not. These are not linguistic realities, they are social realities.

Language has social status because the social status assigned to different groups of people is carried over to their language. The language gets the status of the speaker, and the speaker gets the status of the language. Americans do not face this fact as well as people in countries that are less democratically oriented. Americans do not like to admit that what is correct is a class phenomenon or that what is proper is the way proper people speak and that other people are classified as not proper or vulgar.

Social awareness is different from the linguistic awareness that most children have at an early age. Children know that people speak differently, but they do not understand the subtle kinds of values that grown-ups get involved with. Children do not know why something is better than something else. Children do not know why the way somebody who wears a business suit talks is better than the way somebody else who wears a blue shirt talks. Children do not know why somebody with a white skin is assumed to talk better than somebody with a black skin. These are social facts of life that kids are not ready for until they develop the social awareness that comes in early adolescence, in junior high school. Walking right, talking right, dressing right - adolescence is the time when these are important.

If teachers are going to deal with realities, they must deal with them honestly and let the kids make their own decisions about how these realities affect them. But if the teacher 'tells it like it is' and then says, 'Now, you see what's wrong with you, so I'm going to change you for your own good,' he may force children into a situation of defending their differences as the teacher tries to change them.

The only person who can ever make any kind of change in language is the person who is motivated to change. Social awareness needs to come, but change will result only from the learner's own decisions.

CONFRONTATION WITH A MYTH

Before leaving this topic, let's face squarely the social mobility myth. Teachers deceive themselves and their pupils when they say that if a black man changes how he talks he can be assured that he is not going to be discriminated against by somebody who does not like Negroes. The myth says that when a black man applies for a job he is qualified for, he will not get the job if he does not speak the way the personnel man thinks he ought to. The fact is if the personnel man is prejudiced, the black man is not likely to get the job because of the color of his skin and it is not going to matter much how he talks. It is possible in the realities of today's politics that if he makes himself acceptable in speech and dress, he may become the one house Negro a firm hires to satisfy the federal inspector who comes through to see that the firm is complying with regulations. But that does not mean that all Negroes who are qualified are going to be employed or that they will be employed to their full capacity no matter how they talk. Schools have let this myth cloud the issue. They try to change the language of kids who are six years old, because fifteen years later, when they are twenty-one, they may be applying for a job. That is not sound educational practice in any case. Children live in a here-and-now world.

The whole question of whether our schools have either the right or the charge from society to change people so that they become more alike is one that has to be examined carefully. The role of the school is not to make everybody talk the same way and act the same way and be interested in the same things, and all live on the hillside in boxes made of ticky-tacky. Equal opportunity does not mean schools that require everyone to conform to a narrow model of correctness.

Do schools have the right to say to kids, 'You can make it, and we will help you make it as long as you agree to stop being what you are and become what we want you to be'? The school's role is to help all kids become more effective in whatever they are interested in. That requires a very different kind of curriculum. A relevant one.

UPTIGHT AIN'T RIGHT

In Figure 14.1, the left-hand diagram looks like an upside-down funnel; that is the curriculum model that schools have tended to use. They systematically force the language of children into the narrow channel labeled 'correct,' 'proper,' or 'standard.'

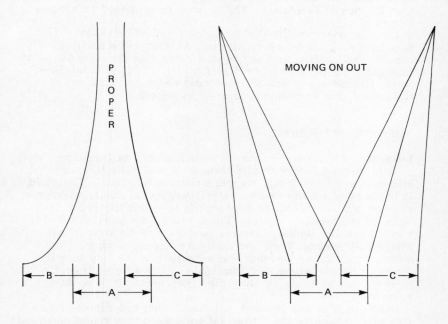

Figure 14.1 Two models of school language development

There is only one right way to talk. That becomes school language, and the kids who can make it are fine and the kids who cannot are out of luck. If a child's language begins just below the narrow column, he is in the area representing culturally advantaged children. His normal direction of growth is straight up the funnel. He may be hemmed in a bit, but he is moving in the direction in which his home language takes him.

But look at the area on both sides. The children there must move sideways or not at all. If they cannot move sideways, they can sit there until they are old enough to drop out of school, or they can get to be so out of it in a couple of years that by the time they do tune in to the language in school it is too late. The model, because of its narrowness, is not even a good one for the advantaged child. School should be an expanding experience.

The other model is an expansion model. It starts wherever the child is. The role of the school is not to funnel him into a narrow channel, but to expand outward with him, to help him, not to become something different, but to become something more. What he is, is good. What he brings to school is good. It is useful. It is a medium of learning. He can expand outward from that. As a child expands his language, language differences become less significant in terms of handling the complexities of new ideas. That's what is supposed to happen in school.

The narrow funnel is the 'uptight' model of education. The popular phrase is an excellent one. As kids move along in school, they get so hemmed in with rules that they are literally 'uptight.' To move away from this model, teachers must disabuse themselves of one of their most cherished illusions – the notion that language is learned in school.

TURNING OFF SCHOOL

Little that happens in school has much effect on language. Most of it is learned before pupils come to school. The bulk of what else happens to language happens outside of school. The child is bombarded by the media. Television, radio, films, billboards envelop him. In school he may simply tune out the droning voice of the teacher saying, 'Don't say it this way, say it that way.' Even the Madison Avenue people have discovered language differences. Ford had Louis Armstrong saying, 'You ahead in a Ford aw de way,' because that is the way to sell Fords to people who speak that dialect. If you give them the message in the language they dig, they are a lot more likely to be receptive.

If language is not learned in school, what are schools doing and why? Recently the writer sat with some young acid-tongued leaders of the Black Student Association at an urban university. They were talking about the teaching of reading to black children. These students speak in interesting ways. They say that there is racism in our school curriculum. They say that forcing black children to change their language is chauvinistic. To these young men the fact that schools do not succeed with many black children is proof enough that there is an irrelevancy here, that schools are putting children at a disadvantage. To this writer more elitism than racism is involved.

Schools treat language as if it is the private preserve of teachers. Teachers assume the right to decide when something can be used or cannot be used (oops - may not be used). This absolutism makes them the custodians of the language.

ARE TEACHERS WITH IT?

Language is not a strait-jacket that teachers apply. It is not something to constrain one's ability to express. Language should be a tool. As long as teachers have an elitist, absolutist - perhaps racist - attitude toward language, they are going to be listening to children in class and not hearing them. When children say something that is perfectly meaningful, teachers are going to continue to treat it as a wrong answer, because they have not taken time to understand it. Teachers often say they have children who do not talk. If these teachers listened they would discover that not only do children talk, but they talk reasonably well and they have interesting things to say. Sometimes the things are not in keeping with the teacher's culture; sometimes he cannot quite believe what the kids have experienced. But they do have things to say.

Teachers tend to believe that changing language can make it more effective. Nothing could be further from the truth. Even if the learner wants to learn to talk the way the man does, he still will have to face the fact that for a long learning period he is going to be considerably less effective in this new dialect than in his old familiar one. The proof of this is beautifully demonstrated every day in school. The inarticulate child leaves the classroom, steps across the threshold, and suddenly becomes articulate; words gush out of his mouth as he discusses with his playmates how to choose sides for the game they are going to play.

WORDS TO TUNE IN WITH

If there are ways (and the second model in Figure 14.1 suggests one) of building effectiveness without depriving a child of the language he has, schools ought to use those ways in preference to anything, at any stage, that will for a long period deprive him of his language effectiveness or reduce it. There is a fine program for high-school students, called 'Upward Bound.' This writer would like to see the name changed to 'Outward Bound.' Upward implies that the kids are now 'low,' and the goal is to raise them. Implicit is a view of sympathy for those who are inferior. As long as schools perpetuate that attitude, their pro- grams reflect it and they justify changing children because they are making them something better. But if one substitutes 'Out- ward' for 'Upward,' the school can move to a view that truly accents language and is directed toward expanding outward from it. Education can help kids increase their efficiency, effectiveness, and ability to communicate, but it should never undermine what they already have.

Language and experience and concepts are linked together. Schools cannot ignore the experiences a child has had outside of school that already have language related to them. Schools can help a child build more language, but they cannot build it in a vacuum.

Here is one example of the kind of thing that makes language real and relevant. The word 'cowardice' came up in a reading lesson in fifth grade. The teacher asked: 'Who knows what "cowardice" means?' There was some mumbling in the group. Several children produced 'wrong' answers. Finally one boy who knew the game looked in the back of the book in the glossary, read the definition, and then said, 'Cowardice is showing fear in the face of danger.' That did not mean any more to him than the original word, but the teacher was happy. During the hubbub, three or four kids were saying 'chicken.' That is their language, their word for cowardice. They have the concept. What kid in the fifth grade would not have the concept of 'cowardice'? If the teacher is going to help language grow, he had better build bridges to the existing language and not say, 'Those poor unfortunate children, they don't even have a simple concept of cowardice, because they don't have the right words to express it.'

WORD BRIDGES CHILDREN USE

Consider a proposition that flies in the face of some things that are being said about language and learning: If somebody can think a thought, he can find the language to express it. A marvelous vehicle is available for doing that when the speaker lacks the precise terms. It is called 'simile.' When a simile occurs in literature, teachers think it is beautiful, but when they ask a pupil for a definition and he says, 'Well, it's like a —' and then uses a simile, they say, 'But definitions are not like a.' But that is the way we use language. A teenager said he had painted his new hot rod 'candy apple green.' A candy apple that is red is iridescent, but this car was iridescent green, so it was candy apple green. A seven-year-old told a researcher that a tuning fork 'be shimmering.' 'Shimmering' applies to jello, not to tuning forks; but he gets the point across very well.

Generally, the most important people to communicate with are one's immediate peers. Think of a group of kids tinkering around a hot rod, discussing all the parts and how they work. The kids may not use the language the engineer uses, but their language is effective and when they say 'this do hickey' they do not mean 'that do hickey.' They may eventually learn the engineering terms if they go on to make a career of mechanics or automotive engineering. Meantime they develop the language just as a group of space scientists do when they are discovering concepts nobody ever thought of before.

MOVING ON OUT

Here, in barest outline, is a program designed to accept the language of all learners, to build on it, and to help children 'move on out.'

Schools must start by cherishing – not simply tolerating or accepting – the language of all children. There must be as much respect for children's language as there is for Shakespeare's, or Hemingway's, or Madison Avenue's. It's all language and all beautiful.

The schools must build the pride and confidence of every child in his own language. Each early school experience must contribute to his confidence. At no time must an experience make a child ashamed or confused about his language. Nothing can be built on a base of shame and confusion.

The school must put children at ease in using familiar language in new situations with small groups, with larger groups, and occasionally with whole classes. Children must come to feel that they can use their language to express their own views of the world.

As children encounter new ideas and experiences in school, they should be encouraged to express them in their own language, using simile and metaphor when existing forms are lacking.

At the same time children should be exposed to a wide variety of language. They need to acquire familiarity with and appreciation for other dialects of English. They need to hear highly effective speakers of a variety of dialects (not only teachers and television announcers, but also sports announcers, preachers, poets, soul-singers).

Schools can then assist children as they try out new language to deal with new situations, ideas, and concepts.

As children reach adolescence, they can be helped to cope with the social insight they develop.

Schools can help pupils acquire linguistic flexibility. Usually pupils go through a series of stages:

awareness and understanding of alternate forms
trying alternate forms in appropriate settings
using old and new forms with equal ease
letting old forms sink into disuse as pupil's needs change.

At all stages and levels schools must see language as creative. Schools should never close children in with taboos and restraints.

The ultimate goal is to make language a supple, fully flexible tool of thought, learning, and communication.

NOTES

1 Basil Bernstein, presentation at Michigan State University, East Lansing, November 1968.
2 Langston Hughes, 'Montage of a Dream Deferred,' New York: Holt, 1951, p. 19.
3 Emily Dickinson, 'Poems by Emily Dickinson,' ed. by Martha Dickinson Bianchi and Alfred Leete Hampson, Boston: Little, Brown & Co., 1957, p. 2.

Language in its ordered flow is the medium of communication...not words or morphemes. In receptive phrases of language, reading and listening, we work backward from the surface structure deriving the rules and subsequently the deep structure. But we cannot and do not treat words in print or morphemes in speech as independent entities. We must discover the grammatical relations in order to determine the semantic interpretation.

In this article the history and the features of words and morphemes are traced in relation to reading and the lack of one-to-one correspondence between them is amply illustrated. The article shows the continued development of Goodman's model subsequent to the preceding article, and concludes with implications for reading instruction.

15 WORDS AND MORPHEMES IN READING

As written language developed and the alphabetic principle evolved, graphic displays shifted from direct representation of meaning to representation of oral language. Letter sequences were designed to represent sound sequences. Much later the device of using extra space at appropriate intervals in written language to create segmental units was introduced and the already existent term 'word' was applied to these units.[1] Like spelling patterns, word boundaries stabilized and conventions grew up that were in fact much more resistant to change than comparable phenomena in oral language. As language analysis developed, particularly in the form of dictionary making, written language and not oral language became its vehicle. The word was indeed a useful unit. Its range of meanings could be recorded, its grammatical functions listed, its relationships to other words induced. Just as spelling was intended to reflect phonology so written words were intended to correspond to actual segments of speech (even the term 'parts of speech' suggests this). But initial inadequacies in understanding and transcribing the segmental units of oral language created a gap. As the word concept in written language codified and oral language continued to change the lack of fit between oral and written language on this segmental level widened.

When linguists began to study segmental units in speech they found the need for a new term, 'morpheme,' to describe these units. Words, those conventional units of written language separated by white space, do not really exist in speech. The word has become a unit of written language.

All this of course would be of only academic interest, if it were not that much of the research on language and the teaching of language has been based on the assumption that (1) words are natural units of language (2) words in print correspond to words in speech. In reading in particular the focus on words has grown in great part from the mistaken assumption that they were the gestalts of language. Thus when Gray and others recognized that reading instruction had to deal with something more than matching letters and sounds they moved to a word focus. They took for granted that words were perceptible units even to beginning readers. Reading came to be closely tied to the acquisition of an expanding sight vocabulary, a repertoire of learned wholes. Though this is of course an oversimplification of what its detractors called the 'look-say' approach to reading, the best proof of how word centered it was is in the evidence from research that in reading tests based on this approach simple word recognition tests correlate quite highly with total scores. Such correlations have been interpreted as proving the validity of word recognition focus in reading instruction. On the contrary, all that they prove is that children tend to learn what they are taught. Ironically, if we test the ability to recognize words as evidenced by our ability to match their printed form with an oral equivalent, children given phonics training tend to do somewhat better than their sight word peers in the stages when the repertoires of the latter group are limited. Chall and others have taken this as evidence that phonics, as such, is a necessary base for early reading instruction. If one could equate language with words and reading was only a matter of finding the oral equivalent for the written form then this perhaps would be true. The question would be simply whether to use a method in which words were taught and the phonic relationships induced or discovered by the learners (word centered) or a method in which phonic relationships were taught and words were acquired through phonic attacks (phonics centered). In her recent comparison of studies of reading methods Chall used seven basic criteria.[2] Four of them involve word recognition in some sense, one is letter-sound correspondences, one involves speed and only one involved comprehension. The obvious focus was on the word as an end in itself. Thus 'the great debate' is caught within the confines of the word. If we can clarify the relationships of words to written language and to comparable (but not corresponding) units of oral language we may not only shed light on the phonics-word controversy but perhaps demonstrate that the debate is quite obsolete: a relic of the history of reading instruction.

Modern insight into the relationships between oral and written English on the letter-sound level has already shown that these relationships are much more complex than letters having sounds, or letters representing sounds or phonemes corresponding to graphemes. This complexity is not simply a case of regularities and irregularities as has been commonly assumed even by many linguists who turned their attention to reading. What appears as irregularity to the casual observer results actually from the different ways that phonemes (oral symbols) relate to oral language and graphemes (written symbols) relate to written language. As Venezky has indicated, we find regularity if we treat the symbols as part of separate systems each with a set of rules governing their patterning.[3] The relationships are between these patterned systems rather than between the unitary symbols themselves. Thus the common sounds in 'church,' 'situation,' and 'watch' are irregularly represented if we match one unit of speech to one of writing but quite regularly represented if we match patterns with patterns. Phonics, then, must be more broadly redefined if it is to have any meaning at all. We must see it as the complex set of relationships between the phonological system of oral language and the graphic system of written language. Such a definition will also help us to see what variations in the phonological system among dialects of English are accompanied by variations in the phonics relationships since the graphic system tends to be stable across dialects.

We must view words and morphemes also as segmental units which relate through rules to the patterned systems of which they are part. Both words and morphemes tend to take on a reality in our minds they do not quite deserve because of their apparent stability in a variety of linguistic settings. Instead of regarding them as useful constructs for dividing longer units of language (sentences, utterances, sequences of discourse) into segmental units we begin to regard the longer units as accumulations of words or morphemes.

In actuality, of course, these molecular segments have no existence apart from language structures. What we call their meaning is in reality the portion of the meaning of a larger unit that may be assigned to one segment. What we write in dictionaries is the range of possible meanings assignable to a given word in the sentences in which it may occur. As many entries are made in the dictionary for a word as there are ranges of meaning for the word. The meaning of a sentence depends on the words or morphemes that compose it but it is always more than the sum of their meanings. Similarly one may speak of the grammatical functions of words or morphemes but these are only the portions of the syntax of a sentence assignable to the segmental unit.

In Chomsky's view the syntactic component of language begins with a base consisting of context-free rules, the function of which is 'to define a certain system of grammatical relations that determine semantic interpretation and to specify an abstract underlying order of elements that makes possible the functioning of the transformational rules.'[4]

The end of the generative process results in choice of specific forms of specific morphemes in specific sequences that fulfill the grammar-meaning-phonology constraints that have been imposed by the rules.

Here is a simple discourse that illustrates how this works:

Mother: Mary, will you ask Jimmy to hang up his jacket.
Mary: Hey Jim, hang your stuff up.
Jim: I did.

Here each speaker is conveying essentially the same information concerning the hanging up of the jacket. The situation in which the discourse is occurring and its sequence evoke a set of rules that result in varying actual utterances. Jim, in fact, need only use a pro-noun and a pro-verb to represent the entire sequence: James hung up his jacket. He is able to communicate his response effectively with no resort to meaningful

terms. Literally he cites an underlying grammatical pattern.
Alternate responses could have been similarly communicated:
'Yes, I will'; 'No, I won't'; 'I don't have to' (pronounced
hafta). This last could elicit the following repartee:

Mary: You got to (gotta).
Jim: I don't either.
Mary: You do too.
Jim: Why?
Mary: Mom said so.

Only in the last do we get any new meaningful element and even
there 'so' represents 'that James should hang up his jacket.'

It could serve no useful function to describe in detail the
sequence of rules required to produce these utterances. The
important point is that language in its ordered flow is the
medium of communication and not words or morphemes.

In receptive phases of language, reading and listening we
work backward from the surface structure deriving the rules
and subsequently the deep structure. But we cannot and do
not treat words in print or morphemes in speech as independent
entities. We must discover the grammatical relations in order
to determine the semantic interpretation.

Educated, literate speakers of language have learned to think
of words as self-evident entities, and to impose the characteristics of written words on oral language. Their perception of
language is influenced but this should not be confused with
reality.

The remainder of this paper will explore morphemes and words
as segmental units, the lack of one-to-one correspondence
between them and the implications for reading instruction.

MORPHEMES, ORAL LANGUAGE MOLECULES

Like the molecule the morpheme is the smallest segment which
has all the basic characteristics of the larger system. The
morpheme's capability of carrying syntactic and/or semantic
information distinguishes it from smaller segmental units,
phonemes, that must be integrated into morphemes before they
can really be considered linguistic units (actually a few morphemes are only one phoneme ions).

It is useful to treat morphemes as being divided into two
classes, free and bound. Free morphemes occur in a variety
of settings with relative freedom from accompaniment of other
specific morphemes. Bound morphemes occur in more limited
settings and always in precise relationship to another relatively limited set of morphemes, usually free morphemes.

In 'walked,' 'walk' is a free morpheme and 'ed' is a bound
morpheme, one of a small number of bound morphemes in
English that carry primarily grammatical information. This

bound morpheme ('ed') always occurs as a suffix of certain
verbs. It has three basic variants (allomorphs); they occur in
complementary distribution with the choice made on phonological
grounds; the final consonant in the base determines the particular allomorph. This type of inflectional suffix is a remnant of
what was once a more general aspect of English grammar.

Other bound morphemes serve derivational functions and carry
more semantic information. The 'er' in 'worker' makes a noun
of the verb 'work' and adds the 'someone who' meaning. Other
bound morphemes take the form of semantic prefixes. The problem with these is that they range from old dead Latin bound
morphemes to current more active ones. These dead forms have
lost their ability to combine freely with all appropriate morphemes. In a sense they have lost their separateness. In verb
formations English speakers seem to prefer to use common verbs
with particles to produce discontinuous verbs rather than use
older forms with prefixes. We don't 'dissect' we 'cut up.' We
would rather 'eat up' than 'consume.' It's easier for us to 'tear
down' than 'demolish.' Or at least it seems easier because this
verb-particle system is a live one that can be used flexibly to
handle meanings. There is even a tendency in English to supply
redundantly another carrier of the same meaning as the prefix.
Thus we say 'combine with,' 'reflect back,' 'attach to,' 'enter
into,' 'descend from,' 'eject from,' 'provide for,' 'submerge
under.' The bases that prefixes attach to are frequently not
free English morphemes but also old Latin ones which only occur
in such combinations and hence must be regarded as bound
morphemes themselves. In a sequence like 'combinations' one
can find five bound morphemes but no free morphemes.

The degree that particular bound morphemes will be apparent
segmental units to any given speaker of the language and that
he will be able to separate a given bound morpheme from a base
form is variable. Most speakers treat words like 'descend' as
single units.

Intonation, particularly relative stress, is very much involved
in relating morphemes, and influences some phonological options.
Verb-noun pairs such as 'produce/produce,' 'contract/contract,'
'record/record' are examples of how the relationship between
morphemes produced by intonation affects meaning. In the sentence 'All blackboards aren't black boards' we can distinguish,
by the relative stress, boards that are black from those that are
for use with chalk. The closer relationship between the two morphemes in 'blackboard' than in 'black board' results in what we
have called compounds (two free morphemes united). And of
course we do represent that relationship in print by an absence
of white space or a hyphen in place of the white space. But
neither device consistently represents this compounding. 'Blood
test' is a compound but it is not joined when used as a noun
('He took a blood test') and hyphenated when used as a verb
('We blood-tested our chicks'). We have 'eye doctor,' 'eyebrow,'
'eyelid,' 'eye-catching.' All have the stress pattern of com-

pounds. The conventions of print do not directly correspond to the intonational devices of oral language.

One phase of intonation used to relate morphemes more or less closely is juncture; the length of pause between morphemes can be varied. 'Nitrate' has a different kind of juncture than 'night rate.' However these junctures are only relatively different and in the flow of speech it is often quite difficult to discern any difference. A speaker can of course intentionally exaggerate the juncture to be sure ambiguity is avoided. But is a certain toothpaste 'proved effective' or 'proved defective'?

What further complicates things is that morphophonemic rules cut across morpheme boundaries in the flow of speech. The same rule that operates in 'situation' applies to 'can't you' (cancha). We find 'education' and 'don't you' (doncha). Certain sequences involving these morphophonemic rules are so common that their constituents are apparently not distinguished by young speakers. 'Have to' (hafta), 'going to' (gonna), 'with them' (with'm), 'with him' (with'm), 'must have' (must'v), 'should have' (should'v) are examples. Only the meager set of contractions recognized in print represent this phenomenon, and even those are avoided in some situations. One unit in speech is represented by two in print. The resulting problems affect both reading and spelling. The problem does not confine itself to children. Adults often have difficulty distinguishing segmental units in idiomatic or archaic expressions. Recently an undergraduate used this spelling in a paper I received: 'anotherwords' (in other words). Teachers are quite familiar with what happens when children are asked to write the Pledge to the flag or the national anthem. I must confess for many years I was saying 'in the visible' (indivisable).

Jones has indicated that the difficulty in determining junctures is not confined to the uninitiated. Phoneticians employed in her research study frequently could not find expected differences in pause length. Prepositions and articles on the basis of their limited privilege of occurrence and the junctures that separated them from the next morpheme behaved very much like prefixes.[5]

Any one can confirm the difficulty of using purely intonational cues in segmenting the flow of speech into free and bound morphemes by listening to a brief statement in an unfamiliar language and trying to guess how many units are heard by a speaker of the language. Native speakers do of course bring their user's knowledge of the language to bear on the same task. Stable units are perceived by them as segments of wholes.

Recent research on child language development has demonstrated that children at early ages do produce language that can be segmented into morphemes.[6] Berko has also demonstrated that children have mastered rules relating to inflectional suffixes, as demonstrated by their ability to produce the expected allomorph for nonsense bases she supplied.[7] It's obvious that parallel to their mastery of grammatical and phonological rules

children are also acquiring a sense of language units. Parents
are well aware of a stage when children begin to ask such questions as 'What does — mean?', selecting a unit from language
they have heard. Some of the funny sounding language children
produce consisting of unsuccessful efforts at interchanging
units are assumed to be equivalent by the child. It must be
reiterated, however, that children speak in language, not
words, and that the sense of morphemes does not precede their
use of sentences. The whole is not a combining of parts; the
part is differentiated out of the whole.

WORDS, WRITTEN LANGUAGE MOLECULES

Words, unlike morphemes, are very easy to identify as units.
One can pick up a page written in an unfamiliar language that
employs words as graphic units and easily count the number of
words. In producing written language identifying word units
creates a more difficult problem; ultimately the producer of
written language must remember what is and what is not a word.

To the literate, words are familiar units in language sequences
and in non-linguistic settings. Words occur in lists, dictionaries, and in fact anywhere that we choose to put them. Of
course one can recite a list of morphemes too. But that's not
very common. The trouble is, again, that words are not the
real entities that they appear to be. They retain their physical
appearance as entities but they lose much of their semantic and
syntactic quality as language units. A list of five words is not
at all comparable to a five-word sentence. This confusion of
words as entities and as units of written language has been
evident in a great deal of reading research and practice. It
has also been evident in much of the research on so-called
verbal learning. Sometimes such research has even dealt with
lists of word-like nonsense assuming that the ability to deal
with such nonsense could be directly interpreted as language
ability.

ONE-TO-ONE RELATIONSHIPS

In the previous sections, some aspects of the lack of correspondence between words and morphemes have been pointed
out. Problems with compounds, affixes and intonation were
discussed. The illusion of a one-to-one correspondence
between oral language units and written language units appears
to stem from the treatment of words as entities. The oral name
for the written word (in isolation from language) is assumed
to be a unit of oral language.

In a sentence such as the following this illusion of one-to-one
correspondence is illustrated: 'I'm going to have to find a way
to get away tomorrow.' One word 'away' and two words 'a way'

sound very much the same. Morphophonemic rules cut across morpheme boundaries in 'going to,' 'have to,' and 'to get.' The literate reader is not bothered by this lack of close correspondence, in fact he will, in general, not be aware of it. He thinks that he reads every word, one at a time.

But for one learning to read this lack of correspondence will cause problems. If he matches oral names with graphic word shapes he becomes a word caller and may lose the meaning. He is dealing with print arranged in words but he must make his associations on higher language levels if he is to comprehend.

WORDS IN READING

It is no great revelation to first grade teachers that children frequently don't have any idea what words are. Perhaps what has been said here will begin to explain why they don't. The implications of this understanding should lead in two directions: (1) Less word-centeredness in reading materials and instruction. (2) More careful development of word sense in beginners where it is necessary and possible.

Several simple steps can help to move the teaching of reading away from word focus. Essentially they involve shifting focus to comprehension; the goal of reading instruction becomes more effective reading for more complete comprehension. Instead of word attack skills, sight vocabularies, and word perception the program must be designed to build comprehension strategies. The presentation of words in isolation should be avoided wherever possible. Words are harder to read in isolation than in context and the isolation of words makes them ends in themselves.[8] Children learning to read should see words always as units of larger, meaningful units. In that way they can use the correspondences between oral and written English within the semantic and syntactic contexts. As children induce these correspondences they will develop the strategies for using them in actual reading. They will be spared the need for transferring the correspondences from non-reading to reading.

As proficiency develops in reading, silent reading should predominate so that written language will become parallel to oral language; the child will then learn to go from print directly to meaning with no need to resort to oral language.

The development of word sense is something that must be nurtured as reading progresses. Children will differentiate words from graphic language wholes just as they have learned to differentiate morphemes in oral language. First a learner knows a graphic sentence; then he knows familiar words in new sentences; finally he knows words anywhere including lists. Teachers can assist children by helping them to see phrases as subdivisions of sentences and words as recurrent elements within them.

Word meanings are also differentiated out of varied contexts.

As the reader meets a word in various sentences he begins to form an idea of the part of the meaning assignable to that word. He then tests his definition in subsequent encounters. A dictionary can confirm his definition or sharpen it but it cannot supply a definition.

CONCLUSION

There will always be some problems in learning to read that result from the lack of close correspondence between the units of oral and written language. Instruction based on an understanding of language and language units can help to minimize these problems.

NOTES

1 Introduction of white space to separate words did not take place until about the eleventh century. E.B. Huey, 'The Psychology and Pedagogy of Reading,' Macmillan, 1908, reprinted Cambridge, Mass.: MIT Press, 1968.
2 Jeanne Chall, 'Learning to Read: The Great Debate,' New York: McGraw-Hill, 1967.
3 Richard Venezky, English Orthography: Its Graphical Structure and Its Relation to Sound, 'Reading Research Quarterly,' vol. II, no. 3.
4 Noam Chomsky, 'Aspects of the Theory of Syntax,' Cambridge, Mass.: MIT Press, 1965, p. 141.
5 Margaret Hubbard Jones, Some Thoughts on Perceptual Units in Language Processing, in 'The Psycholinguistic Nature of the Reading Process,' Goodman, ed., Wayne State University Press, in press.
6 David McNeil, Developmental Psycholinguistics, in 'The Genesis of Language,' Smith and Miller (eds), MIT Press, 1966.
7 Jean Berko, The Child's Learning of English Morphology, 'Word,' vol. XIV, 1958, pp. 150-77.
8 Kenneth S. Goodman, A Linguistic Study of Cues and Miscues in Reading, 'Elementary English,' October 1965, pp. 639-43.

LANGUAGE DIFFERENCES

The legitimate goal of education is to assist each learner to become all that he is capable of being. The goal is not to force him to become something he is not. For too long we have defined equal education as the equal opportunity to become carbon copies of ourselves. It is time that we understood that we can help children to grow without forcing them into a mold of conformity.

We begin this section with this clear, simple account of the importance of language and the value of seeing dialect difference as a rich diversity rather than a deficiency.

16 ON VALUING DIVERSITY IN LANGUAGE: Overview

Language, in its many, many forms, is man's most useful and most marvelous possession. It is uniquely his. He alone among the animals has achieved the ability to represent in a symbolic encoding the experiences he has and his reflections upon these experiences. He alone has achieved a medium of communication with others of his species so flexible and so effective that he may not only make them aware of his needs, feelings and insights but may actually transmit knowledge to them and influence their behavior and attitudes.

Man alone has a fully functioning medium of thought that makes it possible to multiply the effectiveness of his intellectual capacity as thought is captured and manipulated through language.

What is perhaps even more remarkable is that every human society has developed language. Stone-age man is no less a user of language than atomic-age man. Each group has a language that is suitable for dealing with the experiences and communicative needs of its members. Furthermore, each language is open-ended - dynamic, changing constantly as indeed it must to perform its changing functions.

Each child creates language for himself, moving toward the language forms of his community, as he strives for effective communication. His success is so obvious that it is taken for granted by most adults. By the time a child is five or six, regardless of the culture into which he is born, he is fully competent to use his mother tongue to meet his own needs in communication, thought and learning. And he has the ability to continue developing language as he grows and learns and as his needs become more complex.

The language he comes to control is that of his family and, as such, is closely interrelated with the culture of the community. It has developed categories and structures that represent well the community's mores, beliefs, values - not only for the child to communicate with those around him but for him to discuss and react to his experiences on their terms. As the life-view of a group or a subgroup or individual within it changes, language in turn changes. Hippies offer the most recent example, but adolescents in general find it necessary to change, alter or invert language as they reject adult values. Scientists are another group that must create language as it gains new insights and develops new theories to explain our experiences with each other and the universe in which we live.

Language is not the private property of any one culture society, nation, race, ethnic group or socio-economic class. Nor is the language of any group superior to that of any other group. Each group's language is best for its needs. Most people will agree that French, German, English, Chinese and Russian are equally useful to their users and that Navaho, Ashanti and Hawaiian are admirably suited to the communicative needs of their respective users.

But when it comes to comparing dialects of a single widely used language such as English, many of us, including some educators, are reluctant to extend the concept. We find that our views of correct English, proper English or standard English conflict - leaving us with the inconsistent conclusion that black speakers of Ashanti in West Africa have adequate language but black speakers of English in Chicago's ghetto do not.

Superimposed on our perceptions of differences in the way English is spoken is our perception of the status of speakers. In England that perception would make the King's English better than anyone else's since the class system makes royalty better than anyone else. An inferior speaker speaks poorly, then, because he's inferior; and he's inferior because he speaks poorly. This circular logic has led us away from seeing the social basis for attitudes toward language difference. It has led us to consider low-status dialects as corruptions of high-status ones, though in fact the historical facts do not support such conclusions.

Educators for generations have assumed that getting a pupil to speak more 'properly' automatically made him more effective. The language of low-status groups has been characterized as sloppy, incomplete, ineffective and inadequate. The confusion between language difference and language deficiency permeates texts, tests and curricula in wide use today.

Educators have fallen prey to the elitist notion that they speak a superior form of the language and in fact the only form suitable for learning. Armed with righteousness, they have sought to make their pupils over in their own linguistic image. They have exhorted their pupils to learn the language of the teacher while disdaining to listen carefully themselves to the language of the learners.

The effect of this confusion has been to create learning disadvantages where none need exist. The impact has been hardest on the poor, on ethnic minorities, on the culturally divergent. Even those who have succeeded in school have frequently done so by rejecting themselves, their cultures, their people, as well as their language.

The disadvantages need not exist because the alternatives are basic and simple once we have purged ourselves as educators of our elitism. What has been treated as weakness emerges then as strength. The children we are teaching are found to have language. They have learned the language of their communities in the same manner as any other children. They have a language medium that, regardless of its social status, is the flexible tool of communication, thought and learning.

As we listen we discover that their language is systematic, that they can communicate with each other effectively, that once confident we will listen and accept their language they can discuss their experiences with us and can deal with new concepts using the language they bring to school.

If we can accept without prejudice – not just tolerate – dialects divergent from our own, then we can truly 'start where the child is.' We can help the learner to build on a base of pride and confidence instead of negating his language competence in a cloud of shame and confusion.

We must accept his experience as legitimate too because only then can we build a curriculum that is relevant. No child is devoid of experiences. From the time of his birth his world is bombarding him with sensory input. A ghetto child or a migrant worker's child clearly has experiences useful to him in building concepts and offering a base for further learning, however different from the experiences of more economically privileged children.

Building on the language and experience of all learners, we will find that we are working with them in the natural direction of growth because new experience creates the need for language growth and expanded language makes it possible for learners to cope with new experiences. The irony is that we may even achieve the goal of making it possible for learners to control a second dialect of English as they expand outward (not upward) on the base of their own dialect and encounter situations in which they are likely to be more effective in an increasingly familiar alternate form. They will acquire this ability to shift if and when it is useful for them to do so.

The legitimate goal of education is to assist each learner to become all that he is capable of being. The goal is not to force him to become something he is not. For too long we have defined equal education as the equal opportunity to become carbon copies of ourselves. It is time that we understood that we can help children to grow without forcing them into a mold of conformity. Indeed, if we learn this lesson we will experience success where previously we have had repeated failure.

Science has brought us to the understanding the poets always had: all language has system, utility and beauty.

Here Goodman highlights key insights provided by our new understanding of language, language differences and reading and shows how they apply to children's literature and the need for real language in good books in the lives of our children. This article is a plea to free ourselves, the authors of children's books, and our pupils to celebrate fully language in its true diversity in children's books.

17 UP-TIGHT AIN'T RIGHT!

I play it cool and dig all jive,
That's the reason I stay alive.
My motto, as I live and learn,
Is dig, and be dug in return.

Langston Hughes,
'Montage of a Dream Deferred'

Poets can be expected to have an intuition about language and language difference because it's the medium in which they work, the clay that holds the shape of the ideas, emotions, and feelings that the artist is expressing. Langston Hughes expresses the essential truth that all language varieties have a particular suitability to maximize communication among the individuals who share a common interest, experience, culture, or way of life. Each dialect, a language variant developed in a community of language users, is the one best form of communication for dealing with the common experiences of its users. Hughes's poetry and prose reflect this understanding as do the works of other poets: Burns with his Scottish dialect and Paul Lawrence Dunbar, an earlier black poet whose critics never seemed to grasp the importance of the choice of dialect to the success of his poems.

Modern linguistic theory and research has only recently caught up with the linguistic intuition of the poet. A new, scientifically based view of language has emerged which must be understood and applied in creating and evaluating books for children so that they might utilize the full rich potential of language as children interact with literature.

This new full view of language has provided a number of key insights.

1 Every language such as English, is in fact a family of related dialects. These vary to some extent from each other in every aspect: grammar, phonology, vocabulary, but they are not so different that speakers of one dialect can not understand speakers of another dialect. Differences are great enough to impede communication but not prevent it. When differences become great enough that dialects are not mutually understandable, then separate languages have evolved (as is the case between Spanish and Portuguese). No one dialect is the language from which all others have derived or wandered. Dialect differences emerge among people separated by time and space, age, or interest.

179

2 Difference in language is not deficiency. Language cannot be divided into two forms: right and wrong. My dialect is not a funny way of speaking yours. All dialects are fully formed. They are rule governed, systematic, and capable of expressing any experience common in the culture from which they stem. Furthermore they are flexible enough to deal with any new experience or view that the speakers of the dialect may encounter. One reason why linguistic change is so common and rapid is this ability of language to adapt to the needs of its users. Dialects may vary in the social prestige that they carry but this is a reflection of the social status of the people who use them. Low-status people speak low-status language because that is the status the general society assigns to all aspects of their culture.

3 Children and youth play a particularly important role in linguistic change. Their experiences and the way they view them are likely to differ from their parents. Furthermore, use of the language of their parents seems to require an implicit acceptance of the life view of an older generation. Rejection of the values of the dominant groups in society leads to linguistic change. Sometimes this even means inversion of language with positive terms becoming negative and vice versa. So about the best thing about a car some 16-year-olds can say is that it's 'super-bad.' All dissident groups (hippies are a recent example) develop language forms to replace those of the culture or system they reject.

4 Thought, learning, literature are not the monopoly of those who speak high status language. Oral literature existed long before any written literature appeared. Furthermore, it flourishes most among low-status groups who are less influenced by the mass culture of the larger society. The play party game, a folk song-dance combination, is found among poor black and Appalachian white children even when they are transplanted to Northern ghettos. Lorenz Graham found Bible stories such as that of David and Goliath which were first, of course, a part of the oral tradition of the ancient Hebrews, transformed back into the oral tradition as African converts translated them into an idiom which brought them into harmony with their own culture and experience:

> The giant say, 'Ho! Small boy done
>   come to say how-do.'
> David say, 'I come for fight!'
> Giant say, 'Do you mommy know
>   you out?'
> David say, 'Now I kill you!'
> Giant say, 'Go from my face less I
>   eat you?'

David stand,
He put rock in him sling,
He turn it all about and round and
    round,
The giant coming close,
The sling leggo,
Hmmmmmmmmm.................bop!

The giant holler out,
He hold him head,
He turn,
He try to walk,
He fall,
He roll,
He twist about,
He die.

Then David's brothers come and say,
'You fool!
The war palaver be for men,
Go home!
Go home and mind the sheep!'

And David say, 'Now I go.'

Lorenz Graham,
'David, He No Fear,' Crowell, 1971

Science, then, has brought us to the understanding the poets
always had: all language has system, utility, and beauty.
    A decade of highly productive research on children's language
development has made clear that all children learn the language
form first which is most useful in communication within their
families and their immediate communities. This is true for all
human societies. Even deaf children who are born to deaf
parents will learn sign easily and well if that is the language
of their homes. Though individuals will differ in their linguistic
effectiveness, language development is not slower in one group
than in another regardless of social, cultural, economic, or
racial differences.
    Receptive language, the ability to understand others, moves
ahead of productive language in children's development of linguistic competence. They can understand more than they can
express. This is true in first language acquisition but it is also
true in learning second languages or second forms of the same
language. Ironically this accounts for an advantage urban poor
children have over their middle-class peers. Children who
speak, as their mother tongue, a low-status dialect of the ghetto
will also acquire receptive control, the ability to hear and
understand, the other dialects with which they come in contact.
So they will be able, eventually, to understand the policeman,

teacher, grocer, as well as those who speak their own dialect. This does not mean they will ever drop their own dialect for productive use or learn to use both productively but it is an advantage over the more privileged child growing up in a community where all the 'worthwhile people' speak the way he does. Even if the suburban child sometimes hears low-status speakers he has no need to tune them in.

Modern linguistic science and the related interdisciplinary fields of sociolinguistics and psycholinguistics have also made possible a better understanding of the reading process and how it is acquired. Reading can be viewed as a receptive language process. The reader, a user of language, constructs a meaning from language which he hopes agrees substantially with that of the writer. Reading is not a matter of learning to match letters to sounds or name words. Rather the reader uses his language competence to get to the underlying language structures and the meaning. A key element in his success is that he must, as in listening, focus on meaning. He must ask himself as he proceeds whether he is getting sense from the print. As long as he does that he can use all the linguistic competence that he has built in listening to succeed in reading since the underlying grammar of both written and oral language is the same. The more natural the language, that is the more like language as he knows it, the easier will be this task. The more relevant the content is to his experience and his conceptual background, the more he is likely to read and understand. For all readers the ability to get meaning from a particularly written text depends very much on the meaning which the particular reader brings to the task. This is true for adults reading a Russian novel or a recipe for baking a cake. It is even more true for children just acquiring reading competence. Less proficient readers need more relevant, natural materials. The lower the proficiency of the reader, the more important is the level of background knowledge he brings to the reading.

Motivation in learning to read is the same as it is in all language learning. There is a need to communicate, to understand and be understood, or as Hughes put it 'to dig and be dug,' which is a powerful force behind language learning. Reading materials that kids really need to understand are going to be most useful in helping them acquire literacy. Fiction is probably not a particularly good vehicle for beginning reading since its language has different grammatical constraints than conversational discourse and it is less universally familiar than other language forms.

Uptight, conservative notions of what is acceptable and suitable in children's books need to give way to freer criteria designed to achieve more acceptable, more natural, more varied, more realistic materials. Such books can be of tremendous help in making the acquisition of literacy a natural extension of the language learning that produces oral language competence. Authors and editors of children's books can base language decisions on a single pervasive principle: it must be real language as people really use it. It has taken black people more than a decade to realize fully that if black is beautiful so is the way black people talk. There is nothing demeaning about presenting the language of any group as they use it in coping with every day's experience and in communicating with each other. Purifying, standardizing, or homogenizing language not only misrepresents it and the people who use it, but is likely to result in a loss of some of the beauty and strength the more suitable language could express.

There has been, of course, a tendency in literature of earlier times to overdraw language just as there has been to overdraw characters: to create a kind of linguistic caricature like that of the minstrel show, of Amos and Andy or L'il Abner. Minority group members who have struggled for upward social mobility have worked hard to rid themselves of the stigmatizing lower class dialects and in the process have sometimes come to equate them with the sterotypes. They too must make peace with their cultural heritage so that they and other members of their groups may achieve the full ethnic self-respect so necessary in a pluralistic society.

There was a tendency in recent years for publishers to respond to indignant minority groups by replacing the caricature dialect in their books with a fumigated form of English no one speaks. As a character in 'Purlie' comments, 'That ain't it either, Charley.'

There is no need to create special phonic spellings for the sounds of varied dialects. English spelling is standard across dialects, which in reality is a major advantage. Pumpkin is the spelling regardless of how it's pronounced. There are at least four ways Americans say 'almond,' some with an 'L' sound and some without, but the spelling is shared by all. Artificial spellings in fact complicate the reading particularly for those unfamiliar with the dialect the writer is trying to represent.

It is not just the black child or the Chicano child or the Appalachian who needs books portraying real people telling it like they do. All children need to encounter the richness in language, culture, and experience which is America. The illusion that many youngsters grow up with that everybody is like them except a few people who are either peculiar or quaint can only break down with exposure to reality.

Perhaps the best sign that Americans are becoming comfortable with their differences is the growing ability of groups to laugh at themselves and to enjoy the sorts of humor that linguistic diversity makes possible. This has finally found its way into books for children. An example is 'The Dragon Takes a Wife' (Walter Dean Myers, Bobbs, 1972). Harry, a dragon, wants to beat the knight who always beats him, so he can win a wife. He seeks help from Mabel May Jones, a sweet and kind fairy. 'I can dig where you're coming from,' she sympathizes. She incants a spell to help him:

> Fire, be hotter
> And hotter than that
> Turn Harry on
> So he can burn that cat!

But this doesn't help. Harry keeps losing.

'Well, don't get uptight, honey: ain't nobody perfect!' she says. Finally, after several more failures. Mabel May thinks she knows what the problem is, 'My magic thing ain't working because you got your mind set on losing. You got that losing stuff in your system and you can't move right.' So Mabel changes herself into a dragon to show Harry how to move. He not only learns and wins, but falls in love with Mabel May. Mabel May, who 'never did dig fairying too much,' marries Harry. Harry gets a good job in the post office and they live happily ever after.

Language is not a strait-jacket for human expression. It is rather a tool as flexible as we choose to let it be, if we can take the advice Mabel May Jones gave to Harry the Dragon and 'learn to move' with it.

The following two articles are inseparable. The first should not be read or quoted without the reader at least being familiar with the second for here is one occasion where a Goodman hypothesis was shown by the miscue research data to be untrue.

In Dialect Barriers to Reading Comprehension (1965), which contains an excellent and thoughtful discussion of the effects that differences in dialect might have on children in the classroom, Goodman hypothesized that the more divergence there is between the dialect of the learner and the dialect of learning, the more difficult will be the task of learning to read.

In Dialect Barriers to Reading Comprehension: Revisited (1973), Goodman concludes that the evidence does not support that hypothesis and replaces it with the following:

> The only special disadvantage which speakers of low-status dialects suffer in learning to read is one imposed by teachers and schools. Rejection of their dialects and educators' confusion of linguistic deficiency interferes with the natural process by which reading is acquired and undermines the linguistic self-confidence of divergent speakers.

The remainder of the article supplies convincing evidence in support of the new hypothesis.

18 DIALECT BARRIERS TO READING COMPREHENSION

The task of learning to read is not an easy one. But it's a lot easier to learn to read one's mother tongue than to learn to read a foreign language, one which the learner does not speak. Actually each of us speaks a particular dialect of a language. Each dialect is distinguished from all other dialects by certain features as: some of its sounds, some of its grammar, some of its vocabulary. The dialect that the child learns in the intimacy of his own home is his mother tongue. All physically normal children learn to speak a dialect. Whatever happens to his language during his life, however fluent and multilingual he may become, this native dialect is his most deeply and permanently rooted means of communication.

Since it is true that learning to read a foreign language is a more difficult task than learning to read a native language, it must follow that it is harder for a child to learn to read a dialect which is not his own than to learn to read his own dialect.

This leads to an important hypothesis: The more divergence there is between the dialect of the learner and the dialect of learning, the more difficult will be the task of learning to read.

This is a general hypothesis. It applies to all learners. If the language of the reading materials or the language of the teacher differs to any degree from the native speech of the learners some reading difficulty will result. To some extent also there is divergence between the immature speech of the young learner and adult language norms in the speech community. Children have mastered most but not all of the sounds and syntax of adult speech. A further divergence reflects the fact that older members of any language community are less influenced by language change than are the youth. Thus the teacher may cling to language which is obsolescent in form or meaning. Books particularly lag behind language change since they freeze language at the date of composition. Though this paper is mainly concerned with gross dialect differences it must be remembered, then, that the reading problems discussed apply to some extent to all learners because minor dialect differences are features of even homogeneous speech communities.

THE DIVERGENT SPEAKER

For purposes of discussion we'll call the child who speaks a dialect different from that which the school, text, or teacher treats as standard, 'the divergent speaker.' Divergence, of course, is relative and there is by no means agreement on what standard American English is. Divergent is a good term, however, because it is neutral as a value term and it is important, perhaps critical, in considering the problems of the divergent speaker to avoid labeling his language as bad, sloppy, or substandard. We need to keep clear that, though some dialects may carry more social prestige than others, they are not necessarily more effective in communication. Gleason has said, 'It is a safe generalization to say that all languages are approximately equally adequate for the needs of the culture of which they are a part.' Dialects represent subcultures. Therefore it can similarly be said that all dialects are equally adequate for the needs of the subculture of which they are a part.

Every child brings to school, when he comes, five or six years of language and of experience. His language is closely intertwined with the culture of his community; it embodies the cultural values and structures the way in which he may perceive his world and communicate his reactions to others.

His language is so well learned and so deeply embossed on his subconscious that little conscious effort is involved for him in its use. It is as much a part of him as his skin. Ironically, well-meaning adults, including teachers who would never intentionally reject a child or any important characteristic of a child, such as the clothes he wears or the color of his skin, will immediately and emphatically reject his language. This hurts him far more than other kinds of rejection because it endangers the means which he depends on for communication and self-expression.

Things that other people say sound right or funny to a child depending on whether they fit within the language norms of his dialect. He has become exceedingly proficient in detecting slight, subtle differences in speech sounds which are significant in his dialect and he's learned to ignore other differences in speech sounds that are not significant. He uses rhythm and pitch patterns of his language with great subtlety. He enjoys puns on language which employ very slight variations in relative pitch and stress. By the time divergent speakers are in the middle grades they have learned to get pleasure from the fact that an in-group pun based on their common divergent dialect is unfunny to an outsider like their teacher who doesn't share the dialect.

All children develop vocabulary that falls generally within the vocabulary pool of their speech community. Through repeated experience common for their culture they have begun to develop complex concepts and express them in their mother tongue.

In every respect the process of language development of the divergent speaker is exactly the same as that of the standard speaker. His language when he enters school is just as systematic, just as grammatical within the norms of his dialect, just as much a part of him as any other child's is. Most important it is a vital link with those important to him and to the world of men.

There are some differences between the problems of the divergent speaker in an isolated rural community where a single dialect is the common speech and has been for several generations and the problems of the divergent speaker in the center of one of our great cities. This latter child may live in a virtual ghetto, but his friends and neighbors represent a variety of language backgrounds. Transplanted regional dialects become social class dialects. As the city-dweller grows older he comes into increasing contact with the general culture and its language. In the home community the idiolects, the personal languages of individuals, will cluster closely around a dialect prototype. But the dialects of urban divergent speakers are much more varied and shade off from distinct divergent dialects to standard speech. Variables such as family origin, recency of migration, degree of isolation from influences outside the subculture, attitudes toward self, personal and parental goals are some of the factors that may determine idiolect.

DIVERGENT LANGUAGES OR DIALECTS

Language diversity among divergent speakers complicates the task of understanding the literacy problems which they have. The basic problems will be the same but the specific form and degree will vary among individuals.

Teachers need to give careful consideration to the separate characteristics of several kinds of language divergence. They need first to differentiate immature language from dialect-based divergence. Language that is immature is always in transition toward adult norms. Teachers need not worry too much about immaturity in language since desired change is virtually inevitable. On the other hand whatever the teacher does to speed this change is in the direction the child is moving. He can confirm the teacher's advice in the speech of his parents. But if the teacher 'corrects' the dialect-based divergent language, this is at cross purposes with the direction of growth of the child. All his past and present language experience contradicts what the teacher tells him. School becomes a place where people talk funny and teachers tell you things about your language that aren't true.

Another point that needs to be clarified is the difference between standard regional speech and some imaginary national standard which is correct everywhere and always. No dialect of American English ever has achieved this status; instead we have a series of standard regional dialects, the speech of the cultured people in each area.

It's obvious that a teacher in Atlanta, Georgia, is foolish to try to get her children to speak like cultured people in Detroit

or Chicago, just as it's foolish for any teacher to impose universal standard pronunciations which are not even present in the
teacher's own speech. I'm referring to such hypocrisies as
insisting that 'u' before 'e' must always say its own name and
therefore 'Tuesday' is /Tyuzdey/. Cultured speech, socially
preferred, is not the same in Boston, New York, Philadelphia,
Miami, Baltimore, Atlanta, or Chicago. The problem, if any,
comes when the Bostonian moves to Chicago, the New Yorker
to Los Angeles, the Atlantan to Detroit. Americans are ethnocentric in regard to most cultural traits but they are doubly
so with regard to language. Anybody who doesn't speak the
way I do is wrong. A 'green onion' is not a 'scallion.' I live
in Detròit not Détroit. I can carry my books to work but not
my friends. 'Fear' ends with an 'r' and 'Cuba' does not. Such
ethnocentrisms are unfortunate among the general public. They
may be tragic among educators. Too often we send children off
to speech correction classes not because their speech needs
correction but because it isn't like ours. Pity the poor child
who finds himself transplanted to a new and strange environment and then must handle the additional complication of learning to talk all over again. And, of course, if the child is a
migrant from the rural South to the urban North, his speech
marks him not only as different but socially inferior. He is told
not just that he is wrong but sloppy, careless, vulgar, crude.
His best defense is to be silent.

In his classroom the divergent speaker finds several kinds of
language being used. First is the language or bundle of idiolects within dialects which he and his classmates bring with
them as individuals. Represented in their language or dialect
is the language or dialect of their parents and their speech
community. Next there is the language of the teacher which
will exist in at least two forms. There will be the teacher's
informal, unguarded idiolect and his version of correct standard
speech; the way he says things off guard; the way he strives
to speak as a cultivated person. Another version of the standard
language will be the literary form or forms the child encounters
in books. To this we must add the artificial language of the
basal reader. Artificial language is not used by anyone in any
communicative situation. Some primarese is artificial to the point
of being non-language, not even a divergent one.

THE CONSENSUS OF LANGUAGE AND THE UNIFORMITY OF PRINT

Two things are in the divergent child's favor. First, all speakers
have a range of comprehension that extends beyond the limits
of their own dialect. All of us can understand speech which differs from our own, particularly if we are in frequent contact
with such speech. As they grow older, urban children are in
increasing contact with a number of dialects other than their

own. Secondly, the English orthography has one great virtue in its uniformity across dialects. No matter how words are pronounced printers across the country usually spell them the same. Though we get some mavericks like 'guilty' and 'judgment' we spell 'pumpkin' the same whether we say 'pəŋkin' or 'pəmpkən' and 'something' the same whether we say 'səmpthin' or 'səmpm.' This standardization of print for a multidialectal speech suggests that part of the problem of learning to read for divergent speakers could be eliminated if teachers let children read in their own dialects and if teachers got rid of the misconception that spelling determines pronunciation. One child asked his teacher how to spell /ræt/. 'R-a-t' she said. 'No, ma'am' he responded. 'I don't mean rat mouse, I mean right now.'

POINTS OF DIVERGENCE AMONG DIALECTS

Now if we examine the areas in which dialects differ we can perhaps shed some light on the barriers divergent readers face. Let us start with sound.

Sound divergence

Intonation Dialects differ in intonation. Perhaps what makes an unfamiliar dialect most difficult to understand is its unexpected pitch, stress, and rhythm. Teachers often complain when they first begin to work with divergent speakers that they can't understand a word. But after a short time they seem to tune in on the right frequency. They catch on to the melody of the dialect. Since intonation is essential in understanding oral language, it is logical to assume that it must be supplied mentally by readers as they read in order for comprehension to take place. How much comprehension is interfered with if the teacher insists on intonation patterns in oral reading which are unnatural to the divergent reader can only be conjectured at this time. But there is no doubt that this is a source of difficulty to some extent.

Phonemes Phonemes are the significant units of speech sounds which are the symbols of oral language. All American dialects share more or less a common pool of phonemes. But not all dialects use these phonemes in all the same ways. They pattern differently in different dialects. Since phonemes are really bundles of related sounds rather than single sounds, it is likely that the range of sounds that compose a particular phoneme will vary among dialects. Vowel phonemes are particularly likely to vary. Even within dialects there are some variations. Good examples are words ending in -og, such as /dog/, /fog/, /frog/, /log/; or are they /dɔg/, /fɔg/, /frɔg/, /lɔg/? In my own idiolect I find I say /frɔg/, /fɔg/, /dɔg/, /lɔg/, but I also say

/cag/, /bag/, /smag/.

Obviously phonics programs that attempt to teach a relationship between letters and sounds cannot be universally applicable to all dialects. The basic premise of phonics instruction is that by teaching a child to associate the sounds which he hears in oral language with the letters in written language he will be able to sound out words. But a divergent speaker can't hear the sounds of standard speech in his non-standard dialect because he does not have them or because they occur in different places in his dialect than other dialects. The instruction may be not only inappropriate but confusing. When he reads the lesson he may then be forced to sound out words which are not words in his dialect. To illustrate: Take a child who normally says /də/ rather than /tə/ and /nəfin/ rather than /nəθin/. Teaching him that the digraph <th> represents the first sound in 'the' and the medial consonant in 'nothing' makes him pronounce words not in his dialect and throws a barrier across his progress in associating sound and print.

New reading materials and sound divergence among dialects
Recent attempts at producing beginning reading materials which have regular one-to-one correspondence between letters and phonemes will not solve this problem and may actually compound it since there will be a tendency for teachers to assume that the matched correspondence of sound and letter is to be uniform throughout the reading materials. For example, they might assume 'frog' and 'log' to have the same vowel sound and so teach the sounds to be the same when a student might well use /a/ as in 'father' in one and /ɔ/ as in 'caught' in the other. The matched phonemic-graphemic books assume that there is a uniform spoken set of sounds that can by ingenuity and counting of data be inscribed with a uniform written alphabet. This is not true, when the spoken language is viewed as a national-international phenomenon or when it is viewed as a local phenomenon in a heterogeneous cultural country such as one of our urban centers.

Transcription of the sound language in ITA faces the same problems. It has a wider alphabet and can therefore transcribe more literary and sensible English than the limited lexicon of the American linguistic readers. The British ITA materials, however, cannot be read literally except with the 'received pronunciation' of the BBC. When as an American I read about 'levers' in an ITA book I must say /liyverz/. The principle that spelling is the same across dialects is sacrificed and ITA spelling requires pronunciation narrowed to one special class dialect. Teachers using these materials need to make some adjustments for the dialects used by themselves and their students. There may be, no doubt is, a spoken language in common but it is not so uniform as is the common spelling system.

Another place where sound divergence among dialects affects

the handling of reading materials is the traditional sets of homophones. Homophones, words that sound alike, will vary from dialect to dialect. 'Been' and 'bin' are homophones in my speech. In another dialect 'been' would sound the same as 'bean' and in still another 'Ben' and 'been' would be sounded alike. Bidialectal students may bring up new sets of homophones. One teacher asked her class to use 'so' in a sentence. 'I don't mean sew a dress,' she said. 'I mean the other so.' 'I got a "so" on my leg,' responded one of her pupils.

Grammar divergence

The suffix Inflectional changes in words involve using suffixes or internal changes in words to change case or tense. In certain dialects of American English speakers say 'He see me' rather than 'He sees me.' They are not leaving off an 's'. There isn't any in their dialect. Similarly, plurals may not use an 's' form. 'I got three brother,' is common in Appalachian speech. One teacher reported to me that her pupils could differentiate between 'crayon' and 'crayons' as written words and respond to the difference by selecting plural and singular illustrations, but they read the words the same, one crayon, two /kraeyan/. The problem is not an inability to see or say the 's.' It doesn't seem to belong in the pronunciation of 'crayons.' The inflectional ending 's' to indicate plural is not in the grammar of this dialect.

Most Americans will add /əz/ to form plurals of words ending in /s/ /z/ /š/ /ž/ /č/ as in 'busses,' 'mazes,' 'washes,' 'colleges,' 'churches,' but in the Blue Ridge Mountains this ending also goes with words ending in /sp/, /st/, /sk/ as in /waspəz/ /pohstəz/ /taskəz/ (H.A. Gleason, 'An Introduction to Descriptive Linguistics,' New York: Holt, Rinehart and Winston, 1961, p. 62). This kind of difference will be reflected in the child's reading. The differences are systematic within the child's dialect. In terms of the school and teacher they may be divergent, or as we say, incorrect, but in terms of the reader and his speech community they are convergent, that is, correct.

Not only suffixes vary, but also verb forms and verb auxiliaries. When a child says, 'I here teacher,' as the teacher calls the roll he is not being incomplete. No linking verb is needed in this type of utterance in his dialect. There is a difference in the syntax of his dialect and other American English dialects. Fortunately such differences are minor in American English. One area of difference seems to be the use of verb forms and verb makers. 'We was going,' 'They done it,' 'We come home' all are examples of this phenomenon.

Vocabulary divergence An area of dialect divergence that people are most aware of is vocabulary. Most people are aware that 'gym shoes' in Detroit are 'sneakers' in New York, that in Chicago you may 'throw' but in Little Rock you 'chunk,' that a Minnesota 'lake' would be a 'pond' in New Hampshire. Perhaps there is less awareness of words which have similar but not identical meanings in different dialects. All words have a range of meaning rather than a single meaning. This range may shift from place to place. The meaning of 'carry' may be basically the same in two dialects but some uses will be correct in one dialect but not in the other.

Vocabulary differences among dialects may cause reading difficulty and must be compensated for by the teacher who uses texts printed for a national market.

I've dealt primarily here with the barriers to learning how to read that result when the readers have divergent languages. There are of course other important problems that grow out of the differences in experience, values, and general subculture of the divergent learners. Readers can't comprehend materials that are based on experience and concepts outside their background and beyond their present development.

THE READING PROGRAM FOR DIVERGENT SPEAKERS

Let's address ourselves to a final question. What is currently happening as the divergent speaker learns to read? I've found that divergent speakers have a surprising tendency to read in book dialect. In their oral reading they tend to use phonemes that are not the ones they use in oral language. Their reading often sounds even more wooden and unnatural than most beginners. There is some tendency to read their own dialect as they gain proficiency, but in general it appears that teachers are more successful in teaching preferred pronunciations than reading. What is lacking is the vital link between written and oral language that will make it possible for children to bring their power over the oral language to bear on comprehending written language.

There seem to be three basic alternatives that schools may take in literacy programs for divergent speakers. First is to write materials for them that are based on their own dialect, or rewrite standard materials in their dialect. A second alternative is to teach the children to speak the standard dialect before teaching them to read in the standard dialect. The third alternative is to let the children read the standard materials in their own dialect, that is to accept the language of the learners and make it their medium of learning. The first alternative seems to be impractical on several counts. Primarily the opposition of the parents and the leaders in the speech community must be reckoned with. They would reject the use of special materials which are based on a non-prestigious dialect. They usually share the view of the general culture that their speech is not the speech of cultivation and literature. They want their children to move into the general culture though they are not sure how this can be brought about.

The second alternative is impractical on pedagogical grounds in that the time required to teach children who are not academically oriented to another dialect of the language, which they feel no need to learn, would postpone the teaching of reading too long. Many would never be ready to learn to read if readiness depended on losing their speech divergence in the classroom. The problem is not simply one of teaching children a new dialect. Children, the divergent among them, certainly have facility in language learning. The problem involves the extinction of their existing dialect, one which receives continuous reinforcement in basic communications outside of the classroom. Labov's research in New York indicates that divergent speakers do not seem to make a conscious effort to use language forms which they recognize as socially preferred until adolescence. Younger children may hear differences but lack the insight to realize which forms are socially preferred. Of course, teenagers may deliberately avoid preferred forms, too, as they reject adult ways and adult values.

In essence the child who is made to accept another dialect for learning must accept the view that his own language is inferior. In a very real sense, since this is the language of his parents, his family, his community, he must reject his own culture and himself, as he is, in order to become something else. This is perhaps too much to ask of any child. Even those who succeed may carry permanent scars. The school may force many to make the choice between self respect and school acceptance. And all this must be accomplished on the faith of the learner that by changing his language he will do himself some good. As one teenager remarked to me, 'Ya man, alls I gotta do is walk right and talk right and they gonna make me president of the United States.'

The only practical alternative I feel is the third one. It depends on acceptance by the school and particularly by the teacher of the language which the learner brings to school. Here are some key aspects of this approach:

1 Literacy is built on the base of the child's existing language.
2 This base must be a solid one. Children must be helped to develop a pride in their language and confidence in their ability to use their language to communicate their ideas and express themselves.
3 In reading instruction the focus must be on learning to read. No attempt to change the child's language must be permitted to enter into this process or interfere with it.
4 No special materials need to be constructed but children must be permitted, actually encouraged, to read the way they speak. Experience stories must basically be in their language.
5 Any skill instruction must be based on a careful analysis of their language.

6 Reading materials and reading instruction should draw as much as possible on experiences and settings appropriate to the children. While special dialect based materials are impractical, we may nonetheless need to abandon our notion of universally usable reading texts and use a variety of materials selected for suitability for the particular group of learners.

7 The teacher will speak in her own natural manner and present by example the general language community, but the teacher must learn to understand and accept the children's language. He must study it carefully and become aware of the key elements of divergence that are likely to cause difficulty. Langston Hughes has suggested an apt motto for the teacher of divergent speakers: 'My motto as I live and learn, is dig, and be dug in return.'

My own conviction is that even after literacy has been achieved future language change cannot come about through the extinction of the native dialect and the substitution of another. I believe that language growth must be a growth outward from the native dialect, an expansion which eventually will encompass the socially preferred forms but retain its roots. The child can expand his language as he expands his outlook, not rejecting his own subculture but coming to see it in its broader setting. Eventually he can achieve the flexibility of language which makes it possible for him to communicate easily in many diverse settings and on many levels.

I'd like to close with a plea. You don't have to accept what I've said. I don't ask that you believe or that you agree with my point of view. My plea is that you listen to the language of the divergent. Listen carefully and objectively. Push your preconceptions and your own ethnocentrisms aside and listen. I think that you'll find beauty and form and a solid base for understanding and communication. And as you dig you'll find that you are indeed dug in return.

19 DIALECT BARRIERS TO READING COMPREHENSION: Revisited

with Catherine Buck

Much has been written in recent years on the possible influence of dialect differences on learning to read. A considerable amount of the momentum for this interest comes from the indisputable fact that speakers of low-status dialects of English have much higher rates of reading failure than high-status dialect speakers. Analyses of contrasts between high- and low-status dialects suggest that the problem in reading acquisition *could* be due to mismatches between the dialect of the learner and that of the writer.

In fact, this writer hypothesized some years ago that there would be a direct relationship between the degree of dialect divergence and success in learning to read (Goodman, 1965). Because this article has been widely reprinted and the hypothesis widely quoted, it is doubly important that I report that evidence from several years of miscue research has convinced me that the hypothesis, at least as it applies to the range of dialects spoken by white and black urban Americans, is untrue.

In the article cited above, I concluded that of several alternatives the approach most likely to solve the reading problems of speakers of low-status dialects is the acceptance by teachers of the use in oral reading of the dialect of the learners.

The same data that causes me to abandon my own hypothesis causes me to believe even more strongly that the solution to reading problems of divergent speakers lies in changing the attitudes of teachers and writers of instructional programs toward the language of the learners.

NEW HYPOTHESIS

I offer this new hypothesis:

The only special disadvantage that speakers of low-status dialects suffer in learning to read is one imposed by teachers and schools. Rejection of their dialects and educators' confusion of linguistic difference with linguistic deficiency interferes with the natural process by which reading is acquired and undermines the linguistic self-confidence of divergent speakers.

Simply speaking, the disadvantage of the divergent speaker, black or white, comes from linguistic discrimination. Instruction based on rejection of linguistic difference is the core of the problem.

THE EVIDENCE

For almost ten years my associates and I have been studying the reading process among urban kids in the Detroit area. The oral miscues of subjects reading a complete selection, which they haven't seen before and which is something difficult for them, are analyzed in order to get at the reading process. A miscue is any observed response (OR) which differs from the expected response (ER) to the text. Because of the location of the research project, somewhat more than half the subjects in our studies are black.

Early in our research we became aware that the expected response in oral reading is not an exact single response but a range of responses which depends on variability among the subjects in their oral language. Dialect differences must certainly be considered in judging whether a particular response (OR) is within the expected range. But even within dialects, considerable variation must be expected. In our area, for example, the words 'roof' and 'root' have two common pronunciations. Both are to be expected. At one point we discovered that 'with'm' was the most likely response to both printed phrases: 'with them' and 'with him' for all readers, all races, and all classes.

With our insights into the variability in ERs we became aware that all dialect difference that was purely phonological (a matter of pronunciation alone) was within the expected range for the readers being studied. What should one expect a reader to report orally in response to printed 'help them' if he would in his everyday speech normally say, 'he'p dem?' Clearly if he says in reading what he would say in speaking he is producing an expected response. In fact there might be more suspicion that a standardized pronunciation, unnatural to the speaker, might be a source of confusion. If he says 'help,' is he aware that it's an alternate for his 'he'p'?

We no longer even count as a miscue any OR that is simply a phonological variant in the reader's dialect of the printed word or phrase. What that means is that only miscues that involve inflection (mostly word endings), grammar or vocabulary will be found in our data.

Before leaving this matter of phonological dialect differences, I want to emphasize that teachers have tended to confuse attempts to change the speech of young learners with teaching them to read. This is, of course, not wholly the fault of teachers. The basal readers and other materials the teacher uses have frequently ignored all dialect differences. Exercises are provided in which 'pin' and 'pen,' for example, are treated as if they have contrasting vowel sounds. They do in some dialects, mine for one. But they don't in many others. Teaching pupils who do not use this difference in their dialects to hear and produce it (a more difficult task), can have no effect on their learning to read except to introduce discomfort, uncertainty, and lack of linguistic confidence.

Furthermore, spelling is standardized across dialects of English. 'Almond' is the spelling regardless of which of the five or more common pronunciations your dialect uses (with /1/ or without, with initial vowel /æ/ or /a/ or /ɔ/). Phonics programs based on single acceptable pronunciations are simply ethnocentric. The author of the program rejects everything which varies from his own speech.

Urban kids who speak low-status dialects have a linguistic advantage over speakers of higher status dialects which can work for them in learning to read if teachers are aware of it. They build an ability to understand the dialects of others in their community. This acquisition of receptive control over other people's dialects is a simple matter of survival. If you don't understand what teachers, policemen, store clerks, TV announcers, and other high-status people are saying, you can be in big trouble. This does not mean that divergent speakers learn to talk like the teacher; that involves productive control. But it does mean that what they find in print is not as hard to deal with for them as we once thought. Sims demonstrated this in her study of inner-city black English speakers (Sims, 1972).

Dialect-involved miscues represent a shift on the part of the reader to a surface representation which fits his own dialect rather than the writer's. Just as the sounds may shift, there may also be a shift involving a different rule for generating the surface structure from the deep structure - for example, the deletion of an '-ed' past tense morpheme because the reader's dialect doesn't require one. Or it may involve a dialect shift in choice of vocabulary, as when the reader prefers 'headlights' to the writer's 'headlamps.'

In a recently completed study of readers at low, average, and high proficiency levels in second, fourth, sixth, eighth, and tenth grades (Goodman and Burke, 1973) we found that no reader in our study is totally consistent in these dialect-based shifts. Readers who frequently eliminate - '-ed' endings in their readings will sometimes produce them. This is consistent with the findings of recent urban socio-economic dialect studies, including that of Shuy and his associates in the Detroit area (Wolfram, 1969).

These dialect studies show that dialect contrasts are not sharp and discrete among urban speakers, but show up more as a matter of preferences for certain alternatives.

In our research, dialect variations among the subjects are considerable between and within racial groups. Only a small number of subjects in the study, however, produce any notable percentage of miscues involving dialect. Furthermore, in every grade-proficiency group but four (10LA, 8L, 6L, 4A)[1] there are some subjects with no dialect miscues. Two groups (4H, 8H) have no subjects that produced dialect miscues. Only two subjects in the 2H, 10H, and 4A groups show dialect miscues.

All but one of the subjects with more than 10 per cent dialect miscues are black. But there are many black subjects with few dialect miscues and others with none. And there are white subjects with dialect-involved miscues.

Seven subjects among the total of ninety-four in this research showed more than 20 per cent dialect-involved miscues. All are black. These are found in groups as follows:

```
2HA:  1-31%    6L:   2-30%, 21%
 4A:  1-28%    8L:   1-25%
 6A:  1-23%   10L:   1-28%
```

These can be seen to be well-distributed, except that none are in any high groups. Black speakers in the high proficiency groups tend to do little dialect shifting in their miscues.

Those subjects with high dialect involvement tend to be more consistent in oral reading in using certain features of a black English dialect. No subject whose oral speech shows these features is entirely consistent in using them in oral reading, but these subjects come closest.

By far the most common kind of dialect shift involves changes in inflectional endings. Of seven relatively frequent types of dialect-involved miscues, the first four involve inflectional suffixes, one involves irregular verb forms, one involves 'be' forms, and the seventh involves confusion over base forms with 'ed' suffix.

The dialect features that occur most commonly are:

1 Use of null form of past tense morpheme: look/looked, call/called, wreck/wrecked, love/loved, pound/pounded, help/helped, use/used.
2 Use of null form of plural noun morpheme: thing/things, work/works, story/stories, prize/prizes.
3 Use of null form for third person singular verbs: look/ looks, work/works, hide/hides.
4 Use of null form for possessives: Freddie/Freddie's, Mr Vine/Mr Vine's, one/one's, it/its.
5 Regular present for past irregular forms: run/ran, have/had, keep/kept, do/did.
6 Be form substitution and deletion: was/were, is/are, we/we're, he be talking/he'd been talking.
7 Some readers tend to overcompensate for their tendency to delete 'ed' with a resulting confusion over past tense forms. This produced: likeded/liked, helpeded/helped, stoppeded/stopped.

The dialect miscues listed above are much more common than more complex transformations of grammar or substitutions of preferred terms. In fact, these other kinds of dialect miscues, though they occur, must be considered rare.

Here are some examples of less common miscues with dialect

involvement:

    OR It my little monkey here.
    ER Is my little monkey here?

    OR ...out loud.
    ER ...aloud.

    OR We got to tell.
    ER We've got to tell.

    OR A word what sounded good.
    ER A word that sounded good.

    OR His smiling muscle came
    ER His smiling muscle began to
        twitch again.

    OR He didn't have to worry
    ER He was not to worry

    OR hisself
    ER himself

    OR Classes left out.
    ER Classes let out.

Fortuitously, we chose one story for the study written by a British author which created dialect mismatch for all the subjects who read it and shed a light on the phenomenon of dialect shift from a different direction. 'Poison,' a story by the British author Roald Dahl, provided many uncommon uses of language for Americans. It was read by 8H, 10LA, 10HA and 10H groups.
    If the author himself had been the researcher listening to the retelling of his own story, he no doubt would have noted many examples to support the fact that the readers were speakers of a dialect other than his own. But Roald Dahl did not listen, American researchers did, and what they heard corresponded to their own system.

    1 OR   headlights
      ER I switched off the headlamps
          of the car.

    2 OR   minute
      ER Stop, Wait a moment, Timer.

    3 OR   around
      ER Look, could you come round
          at once?

These examples are produced not just by one reader, but by many and with dependability. Six of twenty-one readers substitute 'lights' for 'lamps.' Twelve say 'minute' instead of 'moment.' Fifteen prefer to say 'around' instead of 'round.' The phonological systems of the readers and the author, of course, differ far more radically than either their grammatical systems or their choices of lexical items for the same ideas.

The author tends to use certain adverbs without '-ly' that our American subjects add to fit the constraints of their dialects. His 'quick' is read as 'quickly' twelve times by our readers. (Do it quick.) 'Quiet' (lying very quiet) is less of a problem but it is changed to 'quietly' twice.

Old 'usage' problems pop up in this story including the grammar book '"lie-lay" bugaboo.' Five times 'lying' is changed to 'laying.' 'Laid' for 'lay' occurs twice.

British idiom leads to some other difficulties:

This sentence, 'It looked like a bad go of malaria,' produces eight miscues. Only one directly involves 'go' but four readers change the following word 'of.' It becomes 'from,' 'on,' and 'for' (twice). Two miscues involve 'it.' One miscue's on 'malaria.'

'He rang off,' a British alternate for hung up, produces four miscues. Two move to 'ran off.'

Clearly, written English is not a single dialect and the possibility of producing dialect-involved miscues depends on the writer as well as the reader.

Shifts in dialect in oral reading are less likely to occur than might be predicted from the speech of the readers.

To get a comparison, we listened to the electronically recorded retelling of the story by each reader who produced *no* dialect-involved miscues.

The retellings of those subjects who make no dialect miscues while reading reveal several facts of great interest. Of the thirty in this group, twelve use a dialect other than the author's in recounting their own versions of the stories. These readers include the full range of grade and level from the 2H reader who describes the main character of a story by saying, 'Freddie, he was thinking to be a scientist,' to the 10L reader who explained, 'Then Peggy was hungry because she didn't get no food.' And these readers are not all black youngsters. A white 4H reader, who reads with no dialect miscues, explains to the researcher that the baby brother Andrew is very unusual because: 'He said all them big words.'

Unfortunately, the baby is not 'A baby just like ordinaries baby...who cries and says words that doesn't, you know, that ain't true. Like da-da.'

And discovering this apparent deception, 'Mr Barnaberry asked him what was the idea.' The numerous subjects with no dialect-involved miscues, particularly among those children ranked 'high,' does not mean that we have a group of white speakers who use standard English only. Some of the most interesting examples of bidialectalism in retelling come from proficient black readers who show no dialect miscues in oral reading. They produce these examples of 'embedded questions':

1 They asked Harry did he really see it in the first place.
2 He called the doctor a few names and asked him was he calling him a liar.
alternate verbal constructions:
1 If I had wrote it, I'd have done it that way.
2 Andrew had bend over the crib.
3 He say it might be better to forget about birthdays.
And *double negatives*:
1 He said 'physiolical' and no baby never said that before.
2 He didn't do nothing right there.
From average readers come these examples:
1 Peggy was fighting with them and she surprise them and knock the coyote away from Chip and she start fighting with them.
2 So then that boy took out a dictionary and turned to the S's and start reading.
And from readers ranked 'low' we find these:
1 Then one of the men said 'Hold it! That wasn't no coyote.'
2 He hurt hisself or something.
3 He ain't - he hasn't ever ate a sheep before.

CONCLUSIONS

Shifts from the author's to the reader's dialect in oral reading occur among most of the readers in our study. They are never entirely consistent: the reader who tends not to produce '-ed' forms will produce some. Evidence of dialect in oral reading is less likely than in the subject's oral retelling; in fact, some readers with no dialect-involved miscues show frequent divergent dialect instances in retelling.

Less proficient readers show more dialect involvement, but we have no clear cause-effect evidence. Our study shows that black speakers of low-status dialects can be proficient readers. It does not show that dialect difference or dialect rejection is *not* a cause of difficulty in learning to read. But the most important thing to understand about dialect is that dialect-involved miscues do not interfere with the reading process or the construction of meaning, since they move to the reader's own language.

Low-status urban speakers learn to understand dialects other than their own in the larger community - that is, they acquire receptive control over these dialects, though they may never change the way they speak.

The readers in our study appear to have receptive control of the dialect of the author, judging by their own dialect, and to process forms foreign to their own dialects as they read.

What, however, would be the result of teacher rejection of the dialect-related miscues? We have one example in the tendency of readers to insert /ed/ endings on all past tense forms: 'smileded,' 'drownded,' 'askeded.' This is the result of teachers admonishing readers to 'be sure and sound out the ends of words.' The unnaturalness results from the reader attempting to produce forms inconsistent with his own dialect rules.

In fact, rejection or correction by the teacher of any dialect-based miscue moves the reader away from using his own linguistic competence to get to meaning toward a closer correspondence to the teacher's expected response to the text. Word for word accuracy, in a narrow sense, becomes the goal, rather than meaning.

We know that highly proficient readers produce few dialect-based miscues while reading with high comprehension. This has to be the result of increased receptive control over the high-status dialect.

But the appearance of greater accuracy is the result of proficient reading and not its cause. In encouraging divergent speakers to use their language competence, both receptive and productive, and accepting their dialect-based miscues we minimize the effect of dialect differences. In rejecting their dialects we maximize the effect.

Rejection, then, and not dialect differences, is the problem educators must overcome to remove the school imposed disadvantage.

NOTES

1 Groups of 5-6 subjects are designated by grade and level – for instance, 10LA means low average tenth-graders, 6L are low sixth-graders.

REFERENCES

Goodman, K.S. (1965), Dialect Barriers to Reading Comprehension, 'Elementary English,' vol. 42, no. 8 (December).

Goodman, K.S. and C.L. Burke (1973), 'Theoretically Based Studies of Patterns of Miscues in Oral Reading Performance,' USOE Project 9-0375 Technical Report.

Sims, R. (1972), A Psycholinguistic Description of Miscues Generated by Selected Young Readers During the Oral Reading of Text Material in Black Dialect and Standard English, unpublished doctoral dissertation, Wayne State University.

Wolfram, W.A. (1969), 'A Sociolinguistic Description of Detroit Negro Speech,' Washington, DC.: Center for Applied Linguistics.

We conclude this section with this in-depth treatment of ways of helping children who speak in a divergent dialect to become proficient readers. Some of the issues mentioned in earlier articles in this section are dealt with in a comprehensive discussion of dialects, the way they differ, and considerations and implications for the classroom.

20 URBAN DIALECTS AND READING INSTRUCTION

Perhaps the most easily observed and least understood characteristic of language is its immense variation. As one travels and
encounters speakers in other parts of the country, differences
in sound, vocabulary, and grammar are evident. Within a community differences in the language of social, economic, ethnic
and age groups are heard but frequently misclassified as careless, sloppy, degenerate speech or even non-language.

The key to this strange anomaly is the deep-seated misconception that language is either right or wrong and that all
deviations from right language are errors and deficiencies to
be stamped out.

In dealing with the implications of dialect variation for
reading instruction no insights are possible unless language
realities are understood. Over time or space speakers of the
same language develop differences which become systematic.
This is a universal characteristic of language. All languages,
English for example, are really families of related systematic
variants, called dialects. Any two dialects may have a common ancestral dialect or they may themselves be derived from
separate ancestral dialects.

Thus the major regional American English dialects are derived
from different regional dialects in England and not from a single British dialect.

Social, economic, or ethnic groups in a given community may
speak variations of a single regional dialect or they may speak
dialects with different antecedents. Working classes in northern
Midwest cities have been recruited from the South and Midlands
while rural and more privileged groups tended to move from
east to west. Each group brought their own regional speech.

Dialects in contact, like languages in contact, will influence
each other. The amount of influence will depend on the extent
of contact and the cultural, social, economic, and political
circumstances. So in London, for example, extremely different
dialects have exercised little influence on each other though
their speakers lived within a few blocks of each other.

The speech of blacks in the United States tends to vary from
that of whites in comparable social and economic strata within
the same region. This may be the result of a process of language
differentiation, due to patterns of segregation and migration.
But it also could be, as some have argued, that it results from
the influence of an ancestral plantation creole, spoken at one
period by slaves throughout the South, on the speech of

present-day black Americans. This creole had some roots in
the languages of West Africa.

The history is less important than the present reality.
Systematic language differences exist today. Because of the
dynamic nature of American cities and American society the
nature of urban language differences is particularly complex
and fluid. Evidence can be cited for convergence, further differentiation, and change. But nothing in historical or com-
parative linguistics could support the expectation that dialect
differences will ever cease to exist. In short, language difference is an expected, legitimate, universal phenomenon.

Each dialect is functionally the most useful for the speakers
who have developed it. Speakers of other dialects will be somewhat less effective in dealing with the common life experiences
of the group and somewhat less well understood than speakers
of the native dialect. No language, and no dialect of any language, is intrinsically superior to any other in coping with
any specific area of human knowledge or with learning in
general. Any advantage one language form might enjoy over
another is at the most temporary since each form can and does
adjust to the needs of its users.

The myth of language deprivation has a variant based on the
assumption that speakers of certain dialects are unable to learn
or deal with abstract concepts. This myth derives from treating
the speakers as poor speakers of someone else's dialect.

HOW DIALECTS DIFFER

Dialects differ in all aspects to some degree. Some aspects,
vowels for instance, are easily observed while others are more
subtle or get lost in misconception. Systematic difference often
is treated as isolated error.

Sound variation, systematic phonological difference, is often
what some people think constitutes the whole difference between
a Southern and a Northern 'accent.' The term 'accent' is not a
useful one as a synonym for dialect since linguists use it to
mean stress. It also results in confusing dialects of English
with English influenced by another language.

Vowel difference is notable in the way speakers of English
dialects would pronounce this list: been, bean, bin, Ben, being.
Any two or more of these will be homophones (sound alike).
Dialects of English vary in the number of vowels they use.
Furthermore, there is not a consistent correspondence from one
dialect to another. The vowel in the following group may be the
same or the group may split in two (though not consistently
for all dialects): *log, dog, fog, hog, cog, bog, frog*, smog,
flog, grog, jog. Those italicized rhyme for this writer (the
vowel is /ɔ/) while the others rhyme (the vowel is /a/).

/r/ and to a lesser extent /l/, particularly in final position,
vary considerably in English dialects; a speaker from Maine

and one from Michigan might hear each other's pronunciation of 'media' and 'meteor' as exactly opposite.

Consonants vary less notably than vowels but some variation does exist. Alternation of /ð/ and /d/ as in dis/this or /0/ and /f/ as in nuffin/nothing are examples.

Some consonants vary in certain sequences (Etna/Edna) or in clusters (Eas'side/Eastside) or final positions (col'/cold).

What complicates dealing with and accepting phonological difference is that there is an artificial phonology, sometimes based on spelling, that confuses many teachers on what is acceptable in any dialect. 'Just' is assumed to be always pronounced the same and /jist/ is rejected. Most people would say /jist/ when it is in a phrase such as 'just now,' and /just/ only when it is an adjective, 'a just man.' 'Can' is another word where artificial pronunciation is frequently advocated. I would say, 'I can/kin/ open the can/kən/.'

Grammar varies less among English dialects but the differences that result are most confusing to observers since there is the common assumption that a single set of grammatical rules applies to all English dialects.

Some differences are quite minor. Some Canadians might say 'he was taken to hospital' or 'he went to school.' Most Americans would say 'to *the* hospital' though they would agree on 'to school.'

In some American dialects one would say 'I asked him to go' or 'told him to go' but 'I had him go.' Others, notably Southern dialect speakers, would say 'I had him to go.'

Among speakers of some black American English dialects there is normally a deletion of the present tense of 'be' in many cases: 'He home,' 'I here,' 'She a good teacher.'

These same speakers may also not have an 's' form for third person singular verbs: I see, you see, he see.

'It' is used in some dialects where 'there' may be used in others: It's a chair in the other room for you.

Conditional statements can appear very different because of different dialect rules. 'If he does it' is equivalent to 'Do he do it.'

Such examples are offered here to indicate the range of ways dialects vary in grammar; even minor differences between pairs of dialects are too systematic and extensive to describe fully here.

Some grammatical differences, particularly when compounded with others and with phonological and vocabulary differences, can lead to major problems of communication.

Vocabulary is another major difference. Speakers may use different terms for the same concepts or referents. An 'elevator' in some dialects is a 'lift' in others.

Even more commonly, range of meaning may vary. In one dialect a 'frying pan' is identical to a 'skillet.' In another a 'skillet' is a special kind of 'frying pan,' one made of cast iron. To others the latter is a 'spider.' 'Carry' varies its range of meaning so that 'Carry Me Back to Old Virginny' doesn't mean the same thing to many people that it means in its original dialect.

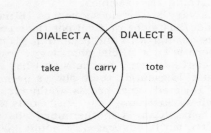

Figure 20.1

In Figure 20.1 notice that two dialects may have an overlap of meanings for 'carry,' but dialect A uses 'take' in some meanings where B uses 'carry' and dialect B uses 'tote' in some meanings where A uses 'carry.'

Vocabulary differences are often overlooked where terms mean almost but not quite the same thing.

Idioms in other people's dialects are easy to detect but those in one's own speech are frequently not thought of as idioms. Since idioms have unique meanings not suggested by the individual words they present rather special comprehension problems. 'Mind your head' may not mean much to an American who sees it as a sign in England, but 'watch out for your head' makes no more literal sense.

Dialects also differ in intonation. Pitch, stress, and pause patterns give a sense of poetry and music to other people's dialects. We are largely unaware on a conscious level of the same phenomena in our own speech. Yet without attending to intonational differences one could not understand the statement: All blackboards are not black boards. Unfamiliar intonation patterns make comprehension difficult since intonation keys phonological and syntactic patterns. Tuning in an unfamiliar dialect may in fact be mainly a question of picking up its melody.

The communication problems between speakers of different dialects are mutual; that is, a speaker of dialect A has about as much problem understanding a speaker of dialect B as the latter has in understanding him. Note that all speakers of different dialects have some communication problems; the problem is not confined to communication between blacks and whites.

An argument frequently used to support insisting on speakers of low-status dialects changing their speech is that they are hard to understand. To whom, though, are they hard to understand? Speakers of French are hard for English speakers to understand. But even little French children don't have much trouble understanding French.

Ethnocentrism permeates attitudes toward language. We think of our own speech as natural and that of others as funny-sounding. This gets entangled with feelings of superiority toward those in lesser social and economic hierarchies.

The speech of inferior people becomes inferior language. Good language is the possession of the superior social groups in society. In turn, strangers are classified socially according to the status of their speech.

Difference in language is not only, then, treated as linguistic deficiency, which it is not, but also as evidence of social inferiority, which it also is not. The twin doctrines of correctness and elitism are widespread in the general public. They are particularly found among educated people who believe themselves to be superior by virtue of their education and intelligence. Highly educated people frequently consider themselves the elite of society in all respects including language. Teachers are generally no exception. Elitist attitudes strongly influence their acceptance and rejection of their pupils' language. Many teachers are quite willing to accept simplistic characterization of low-status dialects as uncouth, sloppy, and incorrect. This is not to imply that they are undemocratic in their attitudes. They are frequently determined to help their unfortunate pupils become as good as they themselves are.

Attitudes toward the language of black people are quite similar to attitudes toward black people themselves. Racists have for a long time assumed observable language differences were the results of basic inferiorities among blacks and basic physical differences such as tongue, jaw, teeth, and mouth formations.

More enlightened people have explained what were assumed to be widespread language deficiencies among blacks as the result of cultural and environmental deprivation. Few liberally minded people are willing to accept the neo-racist conclusions recently advanced that blacks are genetically different in mental functioning from whites. They prefer to say that blacks are inferior because society has played nasty tricks on them. But the comparisons made are always to whites and it is the language of high-status whites that is treated as superior.

In such a view, the way to aid unfortunate blacks is to change them so that they are as much like whites as possible. A black pupil who speaks his own dialect of English effectively is to be treated like a deficient white.

All such attitudes are variations on a racist-elitist theme since all accept the language of a single status group and reject all others. The concept that poor people, black people, or people who are both could already possess language with any recognizable value is not even entertained.

Even many who have rejected as not possible the concept of cultural deprivation (human groups deprived of culture) have

not rejected linguistic deprivation which is equally not possible.
Today's urban complex in America is a dynamic kaleidoscope
of language. As population is recruited from south, midland,
and rural areas, in general, it pours into center city or industrial suburb bringing transplanted regional, racial, class dialects. These interact with pre-existing dialects as population
moves physically toward more affluent outer circles of the urban
complex and socially up the status ladder.

Until quite recently we have had no scientific studies of
language patterns in urban areas. Even dialectologists were
primarily concerned with the prestige forms in each geographic
area.

Now, though studies have only begun to probe urban language
patterns, we do have some basic insights.

Language differences do correspond to race and to social
class within races. Pure distinct dialects are not actually found,
however, in big cities. Forms dominant in the speech of one
group are found in the speech of other groups but to a lesser
degree. Swimming, sewing, running may tend to have /ŋ/ endings among one dialect group and /n/ among another but both
forms will be found in all speakers. The extent of influence is
apparently proportional to social distance. High-status whites
and blacks tend to be more alike in language than do speakers
at other status levels.

Within the life span of urban individuals their language flexibility increases. They become capable of understanding a wide
range of familiar dialects and are able to shift toward prestige
forms in situations that seem to call for them. This reflects
changing contacts more than it does direct teaching, though
causes are not easily separable.

The urban classroom, whether in inner core or affluent
suburb, will not be likely to present a homogeneous speech
group. This will be extenuated where there is a range of
backgrounds and socioeconomic levels. Areas of in-migration
will present special patterns particularly where enclaves of
speakers of transplanted dialects (Appalachian, for example)
result. Even more complex patterns are presented when there
are speakers whose native language is Spanish rather than
English, as with Puerto Ricans and Chicanos. The Spanish dialect of these speakers is, as might be expected, as low in
status as the English dialects they are most likely to learn.

IMPOSED DISADVANTAGES

Many of the problems for speakers of divergent dialects in
learning to read are avoidable and can be classified as imposed
disadvantages.

If a child comes to school and finds his teacher either rejecting his speech outright or smiling and saying 'We don't talk that
way in school, dear,' he becomes confused and ashamed about

his language. The language base on which his literacy can be
built is undermined or neutralized.

The confusion can be heightened if the teacher confuses
teaching reading with attempts at changing the speech of the
child. He reads. The teacher tells him he is wrong; but it
sounds right to him. So there must be some secret set of rules
to learning to read, some magic beyond his reach.

Teachers are not the only source of imposed disadvantage.
Materials for reading instruction are peppered with misconceptions of language differences. Phonics programs almost
invariably assume a single correct pronunciation for every
word. Auditory discrimination exercises are designed to teach
children to differentiate words which are the same to them -
'pin' and 'pen,' for example. To add to the learners' confusion,
remedial and compensatory programs are designed to eliminate
imaginary deficiencies. These hammer away at children's dialect
differences and frequently have the result of inhibiting reading development.

Even when teachers do not overtly reject children's language
they may create learning problems by not understanding the
learners. If children can't make themselves understood or find
they are continuously misunderstood with comic or tragic results
they give up trying.

Imposed language disadvantages are accompanied by imposed
cultural disadvantages. Materials and lessons often are built
around experiences not common in the urban culture of the
learners. Urban children, however poor, are not deprived of
experience. If anything, their crowded, noisy environment
bombards them with experience. But such experience, the
learner finds, is not like the experience that characters in his
book have. There is, in other words, a basic problem of reading programs being irrelevant to many urban learners.

Teachers, like others, often make the assumption that children
who speak low-status language do so because they are lacking
in aptitude for learning. That is, they assume certain pupils
are stupid simply because of their speech patterns. Furthermore, they confirm this belief by blaming the children for failure
to make themselves understood. The result is a low expectation
pigeon-holing of children before they even begin.

The vicious circle is reinforced by the use of tests of readiness and achievement which incorporate built-in bias against the
low-status language of the pigeon-holed children. Self-fulfilling
prophecy gives the teacher an excuse for not expecting achievement among the urban poor and the tests conceal much of the
actual progress the children do make.

REAL DISADVANTAGES OF SPEAKERS OF DIVERGENT DIALECTS

If the disadvantages that schools impose on speakers of dialects
that diverge from high-status ones can be separated from actual

problems in learning to read, then such problems will be much
more amenable to study. In fact, it is likely that the problems
will appear much less formidable obstacles to overcome.

READING AND PHONOLOGICAL DIFFERENCE

Though sound systems vary from dialect to dialect, spelling,
the written language patterning, is basically constant. 'Pumpkin' is the spelling whether it's 'punkin' or 'pumpkin' in speech.
'Picture' is the spelling whether the oral word sounds like
'pitcher' or has a /k/ in it. In fact, the standardization of
spelling across dialects is an advantage of English orthography.
ITA or other spelling reforms would sacrifice some of that
advantage since, in order to establish close correspondence
between oral and written language in one dialect, they must
move away in other dialects.

Words that sound alike, homophones, vary from dialect to
dialect. The picture/pitcher example is an illustration of this
variability. For/four also sound alike in some dialects and not
in others. No one group of speakers derives any particular
advantages or disadvantages from these similarities and dis-
similarities.

There is in fact no reason why phonological dialect differences
should be involved in reading problems. Phonics, defined as
the set of relationships between oral and written language,
will vary as much as the sound systems vary. The basic phonics
problem in reading instruction is that children are often taught
an irrelevant phonics, one based on someone else's sound
system. If it is understood that phonics is variable then the
problem will be largely eliminated.

Auditory discrimination tests are based on the two key misconceptions: (1) that there is a single right way to pronounce
every word, and (2) that children who can't discriminate
between sounds or oral words are demonstrating an auditory
problem. But there is no single correct pronunciation and
children who don't perform well on auditory discrimination tests
may simply be demonstrating their well-learned ability to ignore
differences in sounds which are not significant in their own
dialects.

READING AND VOCABULARY DIFFERENCE

There is not a single vocabulary shared by all literate users of
English. Those who share a common interest or educational background in a particular field will share a particular vocabulary
for that field but will differ in other fields. Doctors writing in
medical journals will choose terms that are likely to be understood by other medical people. Hot-rod enthusiasts will be able
to deal with the specialized vocabulary used in hot-rod

magazines.

But each writer will draw on his own dialect in writing and speakers of other dialects may in fact experience some comprehension problems that stem from vocabulary differences. Modern Americans have such difficulties reading Dickens and Shakespeare. Even Mark Twain used some terms differently than they are used in many current dialects of American English, particularly when he was trying to represent the dialect of the Mississippi River that Tom Sawyer and Huck Finn spoke. British and American people have some difficulty understanding the terms used in each others' newspapers.

Problems of divergent vocabularies are therefore not unique to speakers of low-status dialects. Personalized reading programs in which the language of the learners is used as a base and in which children are free to pursue their own interests in choosing reading materials can largely overcome this problem area. Two principles are important in expanding the vocabulary of learners: (1) Language can not be learned in a vacuum apart from experience. Teaching isolated words in lists or having children do dictionary work on unfamiliar words is unlikely to have much pay-off. Vocabulary grows as it is needed to cope with new ideas and situations. (2) Bridges must be built between the existing vocabulary of the learners and terms used by others. If a child normally says bucket, the desirable goal is to help him know that some people call it a pail; the goal is not to insist on his abandoning his own term in favor of the other.

Sensitive teachers who listen carefully to children can anticipate vocabulary problems and build the necessary bridges. In a version of the 'Three Billy Goats Gruff,' an old folk tale which retains, as do many such stories, the dialect form of an earlier era, the troll is tossed into the 'bern.' Even teachers may need to find some term in their own vocabulary with which to match that. Reference is also made to curling stones. Canadian youngsters would be more likely to understand that term since curling is a popular sport in Canada.

What parent or teacher has not had to interpret the word porridge in 'The Three Bears' for their children?

READING AND SYNTACTIC DIFFERENCE

Though syntactic differences between American English dialects are relatively minor, they are sufficient to cause some difficulties in communication. Phonological difference need not be a problem at all in reading; vocabulary difference is a problem to a greater extent but an easily recognized one; but syntactic difference is a more subtle and pervasive form of difficulty, particularly so since the role of grammar in comprehending language and particularly in reading is not well understood by teachers and text writers. Confusion over unfamiliar grammatical patterns is likely to be misunderstood as phonics problems or inability to deal with concepts.

Urban children, especially those who speak low-status dialects, have some advantage over rural children who live in more isolated linguistic communities. Such rural children may seldom encounter, face to face, speakers of dialects other than their own. The mass media may be their only awareness of speakers of other dialects. But the urban child comes into increasing contact with the varied forms of language spoken in his community as he grows older. Ironically, the inner-city child is more likely to acquire the ability to cope with the dialect differences within the urban complex than is a more privileged suburban child. He has both the need and the opportunity to do so since he frequently must comprehend speakers of higher status dialects. He will not necessarily learn to speak in alternate ways. As he begins to develop pride in his own culture and heritage he may even disdain to do so, but he will come to comprehend these alternate language forms. Certainly by adolescence he will be able to handle the grammatical patterns of familiar dialects not his own whether he meets them in oral or written language.

The six-year-old reading beginner is not yet so facile, however. He may, in fact, be seriously hampered in learning to read materials which utilize grammatical patterns outside of his syntactic system. A key factor in learning to read is the child's ability to recognize written language as an alternate parallel form to oral language. The young reader must trust his linguistic judgment as he reads if he is to derive meaning. Beginners who encounter language forms that do not in fact sound like language to them are likely to have difficulty achieving this key understanding. Unnatural patterns in traditional pre-primers create something of the same problem for all readers. They are like no child's oral language.

OVERCOMING READING PROBLEMS FOR SPEAKERS OF DIVERGENT DIALECTS

Several alternative solutions to the problem of language difference have been suggested. One is to teach all children so-called standard English before reading instruction. An opposite approach is to literally teach the child in his own dialect by writing materials in that dialect.

There is, however, a more attractive solution. It involves accepting the dialect of learners and building on it while eliminating imposed disadvantages. Here are the elements of such an approach.

1 Early reading instruction would utilize language experience materials. They would be composed by the children, in their own language, about their own experiences. Language differences

within classrooms would be treated positively and alternate forms of experience stories would be developed if children desire them.

2 Relevant materials would be utilized at all stages of instruction.

3 As children move into reading published materials they would be encouraged to read in their own dialects. Teachers would be careful to avoid confusing the child by rejecting his shifts toward his own dialect as he reads.

4 The movement of urban children toward the comprehension of the range of dialects in their community would be encouraged and their ability to cope with a range of unfamiliar dialects in print would also be encouraged.

5 Throughout such a program teachers would try to anticipate possible sources of difficulty stemming from differences in vocabulary and grammar.

6 Most important, teachers would guard themselves against introducing elitist, racist views of language into their classrooms.

In such a program it should be possible to work with children, not at cross purposes to them; to build on language, not reject it, and to find strength in children where previously only weakness was seen.

SPELLING

This is a thought-provoking report of a study conducted by the Goodmans focussing on the spelling ability of their then six-year-old daughter. It provides considerable insight into the strategies and abilities of this young learner. The article concludes with possible implications for the classroom teacher. This study precedes by ten years or more the current research on the natural spelling development of young children such as that of Reed, Henderson, Graves, and Yetta Goodman herself.

21 SPELLING ABILITY OF A SELF-TAUGHT READER

with Yetta M. Goodman

Some children learn to read before they go to school. This is a fact that teachers and educators have been aware of for some time, for considerable attention has been given to early reading.[1] Less attention has been given to other literacy skills - spelling, for example - that children may develop before they begin formal instruction.

We have undertaken a study of the language and literacy skills of one self-taught reader. We are reporting here our findings on the spelling techniques she used and the generalizations she developed.

At the time of the study, Kay was six years and five months of age. She is an intent child who loves to learn. Her keen ambition and her love of learning may account in part for her ability to read and comprehend materials at a fifth-grade level, as measured by Gray's Standardized Oral Reading Paragraphs.

Kay's environment is rich in language experiences. She has always been read to, listened to, and talked to. Singing, poetry, nursery rhymes, and oral family language games are daily fare in her home. She has puzzles and picture lotto games, but her favorite recreation at home is to pretend that she is a teacher or a librarian; she sets up three or more dolls in front of her and reads to them.

With no instruction Kay was reading independently by the age of five years and six months. At the time she was studied, she had had four months of formal reading instruction in school. Her teacher uses a sight-word approach and pays some attention to beginning consonant sounds. Kay had received no formal instruction in spelling.

For those who feel that such knowledge is pertinent, at the age of six years Kay had an intelligence quotient of 117, as measured by the Kuhlmann-Anderson Intelligence Tests.

Kay was given sixty-five words to spell. The words were taken from 'Billy Whitemoon' by Ruth M. Tabrah, a story in a third-grade book-two reader.[2] To prepare the test, all the words in the story were divided into five groups: nouns, verbs, adjectives, adverbs, and function words.

Function words have little lexical meaning but play vital roles in signaling the structural meaning of utterances. Some linguists call these structure words.[3]

To assure an adequate sampling of the five types of words in the story, the first thirteen words in each group were selected for the spelling list. They were the first thirteen words in the order of appearance.

Table 21.1　Words spelled incorrectly on each of three tests

Test words	First test	Incorrect Spelling Second test*	Third test*
there	thar		
carefully	carfullle	carfully	
quickly	cucklie	cuckly	
or	ouer		
when	whne		
just	jist		
own	oen	oen	
much	mah	mush	
leaves	leves	leves	
beauty	butey	butey	
weather	wather	wather	
highway	hiheway	higeway	
broke	brook	brrok	
carry	cary		
color	coler	coler	
heavy	havey	havey	havey
dead	did	daid	
young	yong	yong	
every	eavry	avery	
travelers	travlars	travalers	travalers
hunters	hanters	hanters	hanters
shoulder	sholder	sholder	
prove	proove	proove	
rustle	rasal	rasel	
shoot	shot	shoet	
little	littial	littil	
cotton	coten	coten	coten
straight	srat	strat	strat
spring	spreng		
bright	bragt	brigt	
should	shood	shod	
Indian	Indien	Indin	
swamp†		swap	
Winnebago†		Winnie ba-go	Winnie bago
Total	23　　32	28	6

* Space indicates that words were circled or spelled correctly at that testing.
† Given in second and third tests only.

Kay was given the first spelling test before she saw or read the story. To minimize the effect of fatigue she was given about ten words at a sitting over a period of several days. Each word was pronounced and used in a sentence.

After the spelling test, Kay was asked to read the story aloud. She was then retested on the words she had originally misspelled (see Table 21.1). As a third and final test, she was given a list of all the words. In this test each word was presented three times across the page. One spelling was correct; two spellings were incorrect. Whenever possible Kay's misspellings were used.

Kay was told: 'Look across the row at all three words. I will say the word and then use it in a sentence. You decide which one word is correct and put a circle around it. Only one word in each row is correct.'

On the first test Kay spelled these words correctly: 'boxes,' 'summer,' 'things,' 'dance,' 'closer,' 'alike,' 'happy,' 'poor,' 'long,' 'most,' 'soon,' 'off,' 'with,' 'too,' 'this,' 'over,' 'ices,' 'same,' 'push,' 'sit,' 'home,' 'who,' 'any,' 'his,' 'hear,' 'very,' 'back,' 'out,' 'fish,' 'win,' 'leap,' 'hunt,' 'pick.'

On the second test she spelled six additional words correctly: 'there,' 'or,' 'when,' 'just,' 'carry,' 'spring.'

On the first test, Kay spelled thirty-three of the sixty-five words correctly. During the post-reading test, she correctly spelled an additional six of the thirty-four words she was given. In her oral reading, Kay mispronounced two words: 'swamps' and 'Winnebago.' The two words were added to the spelling list on the second test. When she was presented with the list of sixty-seven words in the third test, she was able to recognize the correct spelling of sixty-one of the sixty-seven words presented. 'Winnebago' and 'swamps' remained on this list.

Therefore, although Kay could write correctly 58 per cent of the words, she could recognize 91 per cent of the correct spellings and was able to handle adequately in her reading close to 100 per cent.

To see whether the words Kay spelled correctly had any relationship to their appearance in basal texts, these words were compared with a composite list from five widely used reading series.[4]

Table 21.2 shows that the words that Kay consistently misspelled were all from second- and third-grade textbooks and were perhaps less readily available for frequent observation in her reading to date.

Kay uses at least three patterns in her spelling. The first is remembered configuration. When she uses this technique, she spells the words correctly or almost correctly by remembering how they look. During the test, she often closed her eyes tight, as if she were trying to see the word. Silent consonants were a problem for Kay. 'Straight' she spelled 'srat' in the first test and 'strat' in the second; in the third test, she circled 'strat.' But 'bright' she spelled 'bragt' in the first test, 'brigt' in the second test, and she circled the correct spelling in the final test.

Table 21.2 First occurrence of test words in five basal readers

Composite word list*	Numbers of words spelled correctly on:		Numbers of words spelled incorrectly on:	
Textbooks by Grade level	First test	Second test	Second test	Third test
1–0 (pre-primer) . . .	4	0	0	0
1–1 (primer)	5	2	1	0
1–2	6	2	2	0
2–1	10	1	3	0
2–2	4	1	5	2
3–1	1	0	2	0
3–2	3	0	15	4
Total	33	6	28	6

* Whenever a word did not appear, it was considered a 3–2 word.

Kay also uses sound-symbol generalizations that she has developed. For example, she spelled 'prove' as 'proove' in both the first and the second tests. In the final test she was able to choose the correct spelling. Between the first and the second tests she apparently acquired a generalization of the 'ly' morpheme. In the first test she spelled 'carefully' as 'carfullle' and 'quickly' as 'cucklie,' using different digraph possibilities. In the second test, however, she used the correct digraph in both: 'cuckly' and 'carfully.' In the final test she chose the correct spelling for each word.

It is important to note that she never let her sound-symbol generalizations interfere with spellings she was sure of. She spelled 'some' and 'summer' correctly even though she had generalizations to the contrary. This finding seems to imply that she also learned some of the limits of the applicability of her generalizations. In the few instances where Kay said she could not spell a word and required urging, she used sound-symbol generalizations.

The third technique Kay uses in spelling is to look for recurrent spelling patterns. When she was asked to spell 'own,' Kay say, 'How come "only" is spelled o-n-e-l-y, but we say the word "one."' She was not correct, but she was looking for recurrent patterns in the spelling of words.

In the first spelling test, Kay showed that she had mastered all problems with so-called sounded consonants. She had difficulty with silent consonants although she remembered some of the configurations so that 'highway' was spelled 'hiheway' in the first test and changed to 'higeway' in the second.

Kay's greatest problem in spelling is vowel phonemes. Her sound-symbol generalizations are least useful here. In this difficulty she confirms what Fries wrote: 'The heart of the practical spelling problem for English lies primarily in the representations of the vowel phonemes'.[5] She used the wrong graphic representations of vowel phonemes in twenty-two of thirty-two errors on the first test and twenty-two of twenty-eight errors on the second test.

One problem was the type of word in which a single vowel phoneme is represented by a digraph or trigraph (for example, 'there,' 'own,' 'beauty,' 'leaves,' 'weather,' 'heavy,' 'straight'). Sixteen errors on the first test were of this nature. Of the six additional words spelled correctly on Test 2, only one contains a digraph that represents a vowel phoneme.

Table 21.3 Relative difficulty of types of words

Word Type*	Correct Test 1	Additional Correct Test 2*	Additional Correct Test 3†	Incorrect	Total
Nouns	5	0	7	3	15
Verbs	7	1	5	0	13
Adjectives	4	1	5	3	13
Adverbs	10	1	2	0	13
Function Words	7	3	3	0	13
Total	33	6	22	6	67

* Words spelled correctly on Test 1 were not given on Test 2.

† No words that were spelled correctly on Test 1 were misspelled on Test 3.

Kay's spelling performance was analyzed by word types to see whether certain types were especially easy or especially difficult for her (see Table 21.3). She found verbs and function words somewhat easier than other types. She had little difficulty with adverbs. It is probable that the controlled-vocabulary story she read has greater variations in nouns and adjectives than in other categories.

Kay's ability to handle function words is interesting. These words have little or no meaning out of context and are thus difficult to learn in spelling lists, even though they may be short and very common in language. Kay may have less difficulty with these function words than other children do because she learned them in context.

Kay can read and understand a large number of words that she is unable to spell. She can also recognize the correct spelling of many words that she is unable to write correctly.

She uses several approaches to spelling that she developed as she learned to read without formal training. She seems to rely chiefly on remembering the whole word, though when she is attempting to spell a word that she does not remember, she uses sound-symbol generalizations and common spelling patterns. She appears to be aware of the limitations of applicability of spelling generalizations. Vowel phonemes, particularly those represented by two or more letters, appear to cause her the greatest difficulty.

This study has shown that spelling can be learned naturally without instruction. At least one child has learned to spell without studying lists of words in isolation and without learning rules or generalizations.

The child who has achieved some language competence before coming to school highlights the importance of individual differences. The question is not what to do with this child but what to do about differential rates of learning and readiness development of all children.

Can teachers justify teaching spelling generalizations to all children at the same time, even if they are grouped, when it is obvious that some are not ready for the generalizations and some have long since developed the generalizations for themselves? Even more difficult to justify is the teaching of lists of spelling words to children who already know the words or are in no position to learn them.

The teaching of subsidiary skills in language arts in reading, spelling, composition, grammar, handwriting or literature must be approached diagnostically, and appropriate remedial measures should be taken at the proper time with the proper child.

We hear the advice: 'What's good for one is good for all.' The slogan is not appropriate in helping children become literate.

NOTES

1 Dolores Durkin, Children Who Read before Grade One, 'Reading Teacher,' vol. XIV (January 1961), pp. 163-6.
2 Emmett A. Betts and Carolyn M. Welch, 'Along Friendly Road,' New York: American Book Company, 1963.
3 Kenneth S. Goodman, A Communicative Theory of the Reading Curriculum, 'Elementary English,' vol. XL (March 1963), pp. 290-8.
4 David R. Stone and Vilda Bartschi, A Basic Word List from Basal Readers, 'Elementary English,' vol. XL (April 1963), pp. 420-7.
5 Charles C. Fries, 'Linguistics and Reading,' New York: Holt, Rinehart & Winston, 1963, p. 195.

IN CONCLUSION

We have created this section to conclude Part One of this volume because we believe that together these three articles present a comprehensive, up-to-date coverage of many of the concerns for children and their development that have motivated the Goodman work.

'I want to proclaim a revolutionary doctrine' says Goodman in this article. 'Revolutionary in two full senses. One is a total change of vantage point from the traditional...but it is revolutionary also in the sense that it gets at the basic roots of things....We live in interesting times, in revolutionary times... the schools are a battleground.'

This article deserves to be read if only because it permits tremendous insight into the motivations and concerns that have prompted much of the Goodman writing. It contains keen insights into the situation existing in schools, as Goodman sees it, and puts language and the child in their rightful place. A critique of Goodman's research once complained that Goodman was not 'dispassionate.' Here he reveals some of his passion.

22 MANIFESTO FOR A READING REVOLUTION*

To paraphrase another manifesto, I think there is also a spectre haunting education today, and particularly does it haunt those of us who are involved with language and reading. I have perhaps seen it first in southern and northern California, but I have seen it in Seattle and in the midwest and southeast, in Canada and in the other English-speaking countries, and in countries where kids learn to read in other languages - in French or German, for example.

This is a revolution in two full senses. One is a total change of vantage point from the traditional one that we have used involving the way we have looked at the problems we have been dealing with for a long time - things which haven't really changed, except that sometimes when the vantage point is changed things are seen in totally different relationships. What was important before looks less important, and some of the things that weren't even thought about suddenly emerge as being very important.

But it is revolutionary also in the sense that it gets at the basic roots of things. Radical, in the original use of that term, it is really getting to the sources.

I read in newspapers and I see in publishers' advertisements that there is supposed to be a movement back to the basics going on in the United States. I would like to suggest that basics in reading means getting back to the essential relationship between language and its use by people to convey meaning, not back to some good old way in some good old day where everybody learned to read, a day that never existed.

The revolution I am referring to involves much more than reading, although I am going to focus on that part. But it seems to involve reading particularly because reading is always somehow in the white-hot light of every controversy and every battle in education. It is the thing that gets parents most upset and that groups can manipulate for their own purposes. It gets publicity in newspapers. It would surprise me if any group made a big splash about the way art is taught in school, but making a splash about the way reading is taught is a proven way to get a lot of attention in the community. In fact, in California a candidate ran for the senate on a phonics platform not very long ago.

*The third Peter Lincoln Spencer Lecture, honoring the founder of the Claremont Reading Conference.

I want to proclaim a revolutionary doctrine, then. The revolutionary doctrine is that literacy has to be the natural extension of language-learning, not something new, not something different, but something that in fact grows out of and builds on the natural human tendency to communicate. Language is an individual and social invention, something that is integrally related to that drive that we have to make sense out of our world and to interact with other people as we come in contact with that sense. We are born dependent. We are born social animals, and if we cannot communicate with people around us we cannot survive. That communication goes far beyond the initial preoccupation with food and warmth and security.

One important issue has been misunderstood and has tended to make people separate reading somehow from considerations that deal with the function of language in general: why is it that everybody who is human learns easily, and without any professional assistance from schools, to listen and to communicate with oral language in whatever is the language of the community or the sub-community? Why is it that everybody doesn't learn to read and write in a literate society as easily with as little instruction? The answer to that has to be seen in a couple of things. The very fact that we have tried so hard to teach kids to read and write is partly responsible for why some of them don't learn. Or to put it another way, maybe it is a tribute to the marvelous language-learning ability of kids that they learn to read anyway in spite of some of the dumb things that we do in the name of helping them.

One of the things we have to understand is that since language is a social invention and all human societies develop oral language, there is an integral relationship between that oral language and the immediate face-to-face situation that is common to all human societies everywhere. That kind of language is very strongly situationally bound. In the history of any individual, written language develops at a point where there is a need for communication beyond the here and now, the face-to-face; that is, communication over time and over space. We need to be able to communicate with people who are not present, even with people who are not alive.

When the society reaches the point where it has a culture that needs to be preserved; where it has reached the point of complexity where there are people who need to communicate with each other who do not see each other or perhaps even know each other, that is when written language comes about. If you understand that, you can understand why every child learns oral language with the possible exception of those who cannot hear it. But not all children acquire literacy.

It is important to understand that reading is language. It isn't like language or a process that uses language, it *is* language. And for any literate person in a literate society there are four language processes: speaking and listening, and their counterparts writing and reading. Two are productive and two receptive. The processes are alike but the uses for them are different. And we have to understand in school that if we make children aware of language processes and enhance their awareness of the function of written language they are going to learn easily and painlessly. They won't grow up to be kids who can read but hate to read or people who can't read yet are desperately trying to find ways to function in a literate society without being able to.

These are revolutionary times I am suggesting. The Chinese have a curse that I'm sure you have heard: May you live in interesting times. Interesting times aren't placid or peaceful. In interesting times, in revolutionary times, it is sometimes hard to tell which way the winds are blowing. There seem to be so many counter-pressures and trends; there are revolutionary ideas and there are counter-revolutionary ideas and sometimes it is hard to tell which is which, particularly when the language and the metaphor are borrowed for both purposes. There are, in our society, people who are trying to lock in permanently the status quo. One place that they are trying particularly hard to do this is in the schools. The schools are a battleground. I don't have to tell you that, those of you who are desperately trying to teach what you believe in and at the same time have to check off the skills and behaviors that are specified by a law or an administrative decision. There isn't any safe ground for anybody; even if you'd like to get out of the battle scene, you can't. There is no safe place to retreat to because you still have to deal with the kids and the pressures, and the administrators and the tests and all of the things that are involved.

There are two sources of pressure that I feel are causing us to be at a particularly critical point in this revolution. Maybe I should make a personal confession first. Long before I began to do research on language and particularly on reading, I had made a commitment as far as education was concerned. I had arrived at a basic belief which I think has been fundamental to everything I have done whether as a teacher, researcher, or writer. Maybe the most important thing that I took away from my undergraduate teacher education is the admonition that in education our business is accepting people for what they are, taking the kids where they are, and helping them to grow in whatever direction they are growing, to the extent that we can, accepting them and building on what they are. I believe in kids. I have to tell you I am very happy to report that my research supports my original prejudice. In fact, the more I understand about reading and language and the more I understand what other people have learned from their research, the more convinced I become that that is as much if not more true in language and reading as it is in any other field. The kids have tremendous linguistic strength, both as language users and as language learners. They share a remarkable human ability to learn language and they have achieved a remarkable competence in language long before they come to us to help them

acquire literacy. That's scientific fact. Linguists, psycholinguists, child development students who have looked at language development across cultures and across human societies
have discovered that this is universal. All human beings learn
language. They learn it easily; they learn it well and fortunately for them, they learn the language most important to them,
the language most necessary for survival and effective growth
within the cultures in which they live. That is true whether
they live in Watts or in the inner city of Detroit or the Australian bush or an affluent suburb in an American city. It is not
a possession of privileged people or people who grow up in
highly developed affluent cultures or industrial societies. It is
a universal of human development, a universal of human society.

You may have read of studies that have been done by behavioral psychologists that have attempted to demonstrate that
human language achievement is not unique. Some of them have
been done with porpoises; one of those that was most widely
publicized recently was done with chimpanzees. Somebody has
finally succeeded in teaching one young female chimpanzee to
communicate a set of utterances in such a way that the chimp
has even used a few sentences that were not specifically taught,
apparently using the rule that was deliberately taught and
then applying that rule. They set up, at enormous expense in
terms of money and manpower and talents, a kind of computer
controlled environment and the chimp was taught to push buttons on the computer that had visual forms, something like
color forms. The chimp can even push a 'please' button and
another, a 'period' button, at the end. These are necessary
because the 'please' button turns the computer on and the
period signals that the message is over. You have to remember
that computers are no smarter than we teach them to be.

The demonstration was supposed to have proved that language
is not unique to human beings; in fact, it proves the opposite.
Look at the enormous expense and the years of failure that
preceded this moderate success and then compare that with
what any human infant accomplishes with no such expense and
no fancy elaborate equipment and no team of highly trained
behavioral psychologists constantly there revising the curriculum as the experiment proceeds.

What it *has* demonstrated is the remarkable human ability that
exists.

We know so much now about language and children's acquisition of language and how language works that even if nobody
were worried about anybody learning to read and write we
would still have to cope with that knowledge; we would still
have to apply it; we would still have to modify our curricula,
what we do and how we do it, to take into account that new
knowledge. Of course, considering that we have been less than
fully successful and particularly less than fully successful with
the minority populations in our country, then I think we have
to look at it even more seriously. There are answers here that

can lead us to better understandings and better solutions of the literacy problems.

I am convinced that we know enough about language to eliminate totally illiteracy in any functional sense. I don't mean that everybody is going to be able to read equally well. Obviously there are many things besides the basic acquisition of literacy involved in whether you understand something that you have read, just as there are things involved in whether you understand something that you have heard. But I mean that we ought to be able to eliminate the apparent disadvantages that keep some people from learning to read.

That means that I don't believe in learning disabilities. I don't believe that you can explain away even a fraction of 1 per cent of the population having any difficulty in reading on the basis of something being wrong with them. For too long we have looked for things in the kids, explaining why they are not learning, and we have to face the fact that the main thing that we should have realized is that kids were learning to read in proportion to how far they have to come to accommodate to a narrow view of what schools accepted. It is very interesting that if you walk into any remedial reading classroom, at least in the United States, you can predict that the large majority of the kids in the remedial reading program are going to be males compared to females. Unless somebody can demonstrate, and I don't believe they can, that there is some kind of sex-linked gene that keeps people from learning to read, I think we have to accept that simply as another evidence that boys, for cultural reasons, are often less willing to conform than girls are to the kinds of demands we make on them, and the limits we set on what we accept and what we won't.

The other source of this revolutionary push is almost a negative one. We have had forced on us in ways that we cannot ignore, because some of them are written into law, the kind of dehumanizing, systems oriented, highly structured, view of learning that so narrows us that we are left with no room for treating kids as individuals, or treating them as human beings, or for any kind of constructive professional insight that the teacher can carry on. In some programs, the teacher is literally tied to a script and told not to vary from that script in wording. The only thing you can vary is the pace. That means that individualization is over and over again taking kids over the things that they are resisting until they finally acquiesce and give us the responses that the script calls for. That is called individualizing learning. There is across the country a strong reaction among teachers to this dehumanization and to the deprofessionalizing of the act of teaching in the classroom.

A key tenet of this revolution is that reading is a language process that can be studied and understood the way other language processes can. It is not something new that a kid is learning for which he has no basis. That leads to my next tenet that a reader is a user of language. And if you under-

stand that language is always used in relationship to meaning
and communication and ideas, then you can understand that
people learn to read to the extent that it is a functional kind
of process.

I said before that written language and oral language differ
in their uses. One of the things that we have to understand
is that when you grow up in a literate society there is a great
deal of intrinsic motivation to learn to read. But it isn't in
learning to respond to language with sounds, to bark at print.
It isn't in learning to deal with the workbooks and the basal
reader, or to do programed or highly structured tasks. It
has basically to do with needing to understand written language
and that is nowhere better illustrated than in a little boy learning to find the right toilet. It is more important for boys than
girls because if you don't know which door says 'men' and which
door says 'women' you have to go with your mother into the
other place. That's functional reading. That's highly motivated.
The same thing motivates the kid to go to the supermarket and
find which box of all those boxes says 'Count Chocula' on it
because he or she has become highly convinced that 'Count
Chocula' is essential to the good life. That's motivation. It
doesn't have anything to do with green stamps or candies or
pats on the back or even smiles from the teacher. Please don't
think that I'm against teachers smiling at kids. What motivates
children to learn language is that they need to understand it or
they need to use it to express ideas that they have. In a literate
society that is all around us. All we have to do is mesh in with
it, pick up on it, build upon it.

The third key tenet is that language is a means to an end and
not an end itself. Nobody ever learned to talk simply for the
sake of learning to talk. You learn to talk because you have
something to say. Maybe you have heard the story about the
little boy who was four years old and had not said anything
intelligible. He had been to all kinds of experts and nobody
could find an explanation. One day at breakfast he said, 'Hey,
the toast is burnt!' When the hubbub had died down and everybody stopped hugging him his mother said, 'Why didn't you
ever speak before?' He said, 'I never had anything to complain
about.' As a matter of fact, about the only way you can keep
normal children from learning language is to anticipate their
needs constantly so that they really don't have much need for
communication. Even then they will learn to communicate with
people other than their parents.

There are some focal points in this revolution that I have been
talking about. The first one is a new respect for children and
particularly for them as language learners and language users.

I have a flag in mind for our revolutionary army. It is a half-
full water glass on a plain white field. You remember the Peace
Corps ads from several years ago in which there was a water
glass and a voice that said, 'If that glass looks half empty, don't
bother to apply to the Peace Corps. But if it looks half full,

come and see us.' I think that is symbolic because it says we
have been too preoccupied for too long with what children cannot do, what they are not ready to do, what they don't care
to do. We have lost the significance of what they already have
going for them that we can build on.

Children are language users. They have learned without our
help the remarkable ability to use language. They have acquired
through that drive for meaning control over the system of language, and they have learned in the process something that no
porpoise or chimpanzee has ever learned or is ever going to
learn. They have learned to say things in response to new
experiences and new situations that they have never heard.

The thing about human language that people so often miss is
that it changes, that it has to change and all of us have the
ability to invent it. All of us do invent it and its invention is
so continuous that it not only changes all the time, but it also
is then possible for us to deal with the new experiences that
every individual has and that every generation has.

If you think back to those first communications from outer
space when people were dealing with experiences that humanity
had not encountered before, there was language being made
before our very ears and eyes. I still remember the astronaut
who cut himself off in the middle of a sentence and said, 'Oh
my gosh, I hope my English teacher isn't listening now!' Somewhere he got the idea that it was bad to create language, that
if you are using language that you realize is original that's
something bad. Well, it isn't bad at all. It's an essential of
human language.

If we understand these things, then we have the base for
making literacy the extension of natural language learning of
all humans. But it means then that we have to respect the
language of all language learners, and that means inner-city
black kids and Chicano kids who speak two languages, neither
of which is a high-status form of a particular language.

A new respect for language is also necessary. Let me tell
you what I mean by that. Through the attempts at advancing
the understanding both of language and language learning
and the curricula that go with it, there have been two oppos-
ing positions that have both gotten in the way. One is a
tendency to say language is so self-evident that it doesn't need
to be studied; everybody learns it, so why do we need scientific
study of language? With that view, we stayed with the commonsense *misconceptions* that make it difficult for us to appreciate
everything that is going on so that we can begin to understand
a process like learning to read.

The opposite is equally unfortunate: the tendency for people
to say language is a great mystery: it is so complicated, nobody
will ever understand it. Therefore, forget about understanding
it and instead just do a stimulus-response kind of thing. Nothing
bothers me more at professional conferences than somebody
prefacing an hour-long speech or a two-hour workshop by

saying, 'Nobody knows how language works, therefore...'
And then the therefore is anything goes as long as it works. It
took the medical profession a long time to get to the point where
they could say 'We won't permit people to practice quack remedies. They have to demonstrate validity and soundness of a
remedy before we will even let them experiment. And then we
will only permit it to be used in highly controlled experimental
ways.' We simply don't permit somebody to say, 'I've got a
cure for cancer,' and then see whether it works or not by trying it on a dying cancer patient. But we have been doing that
in school for a long time. Almost any quack remedy can be tried
in school, particularly if people make loud enough and outlandish
enough claims for it.

   If you understand and respect language, if you understand
that language is rule governed, that the most remarkable thing
about human beings is that they learn a finite set of rules that
nobody can teach, making it possible for them to say an infinite
number of things, then it is also necessary to understand that
you cannot chop language up into little bits and pieces and
think that you can spoon feed it as you would feed pellets to a
pigeon or a rat. As a matter of fact, I think the image of the
rat is in the minds of many of the people who make hierarchies
of skills and check lists of what children have to learn in first
grade, second grade and third grade. It is as if reading can
be chopped up and you can say 'This is the first grade slice
and this is the second grade or this is the first month of the
first grade and this is the second month.' Language doesn't work
that way. One of the lessons that we have to learn is that the
learner has to have the whole right from the beginning. What
would happen if we undertook to teach kids to talk and we did
it by standing over their cribs, or even better locking them
into a dark room where a recording played sounds at them until
they repeated the sounds? And then we moved to the blending
stage and we taught them to blend the sounds. And then we
moved to the one syllable word stage and we taught them to
say words until they could master a 10 000 word vocabulary.
And then we were ready to have them learn to produce sentences with simple combinations. And finally after that we said,
'OK, now you are ready for a conversation.' We would have
remedial talking classes - with big conferences all over the
country and an International Talking Association.

   We have learned a lot of things. One of those things is that
language is learned from whole to part: that language is treated
by learners as if it were part of the concrete world as long as
it's involved in the meanings that people are coping with and
trying to understand. It is when you take the language away
from its use, when you chop it up and break it into pieces, that
it becomes abstract and hard to learn. In these two basic focal
points, respect for the learner and respect for the language,
one of the things I must underline again is that I am not talking
about select youngsters, I'm not talking just about children who

are the good learners, and the ones who are willing to put up with all the nonsense we subject them to. I mean all children; when somebody says that special education kids or minority kids or bilingual kids or anybody else needs a more structured program because 'they can't learn that way,' that statement is saying there are some sub-human human beings, that there are ways that people learn and there are ways that *those* kinds of people learn.

As a matter of fact, turning it around the other way, the children who for various reasons are less tuned to school or less able to deal with abstraction, are the ones who most particularly need relevant language experiences in school. Where language makes sense and children can see that sense, the payoff is in understanding. *Those* kids particularly who are school and achievement oriented because of their cultural and family background, will put up with more nonsense and somehow overcome and learn anyway.

Rat psychology is very big now. Let me make a simple statement in relation to what I said before. It is easy to demonstrate that kids can learn like rats. That doesn't mean that they should be taught that way. We should understand that rats can't learn like kids and that particularly when we are talking about language learning or human learning and the role of language in it, we have to understand that there are some uniquely human phenomena. The lessons learned from conditioning rats and pigeons and other living species do not answer the questions about how you go about teaching kids to read. I am particularly talking about rats not only because of the influence of behavioral psychology on teaching and methodology but because it has also been the basis for most of the testing and evaluation programs developed recently. The easiest way to organize an assessment program is to determine the sequence of skills and test them and check them off in a neat order. If language worked that way, there might be some arguments in favor of that. But it doesn't. Furthermore, since nobody has ever demonstrated that there is a hierarchy of skills, or if there is one, what it is, any hierarchy of skills built into a testing system is in fact arbitrary. Unfortunately, what happens is that the teacher, the curriculum writer, the material writer, the curriculum director, is confronted by the tester who says 'You want me to test what you're doing, you've got to tell me what you're teaching.' When you start telling him, he says 'you have to fit my evaluation model.' Soon he is saying, 'If I can't test it, you can't teach it.' There is something very peculiar about that logic.

There is a crisis in education, an accountability crisis now, one the assessment people have gotten themselves into because when they come back and say, 'We don't know how to test what you are teaching,' it demonstrates that they don't know their business. When they then say to us, 'Tell us how to test it,' our answer should be, 'that's your business; mine is teaching or developing curriculum, I can tell you the sound basis for what we are doing. I know how to tell when the kids are making progress, but I can't fit it into something that we can measure in a standardized test applied once a month so that we provide that so-called hard data.' Examples of evidence why I think the testers are in a crisis, why I think we have to hold them accountable for their ability to do what they said that they could do, are readily available. One example is the Jensonian conclusion, drawn from a set of studies on intelligence tests, that asserts that some people, notably black, learn differently than other people, that they have genetically determined minds which work differently. I think that demonstrates an absurd conclusion from some faulty kinds of evaluation, evaluation that isn't relevant or usable with some groups of people and probably not even with the people for whom it works well. Second example: recently the Right to Read program funded, at great expense, a study by the American Institute for Research to determine which programs were highly effective programs in teaching reading. They did a broad screening; they received several thousand nominations; they identified 222 programs as effective; and then they chose from those twenty-five which were later narrowed to twelve. These have been widely publicized as 'exemplary reading programs.' If you read carefully, the only criteria used in deciding whether those were effective, exemplary programs were pre-test and post data from a standardized reading test. They didn't even bother with criterion referenced tests. In the end, when you look at the list of so-called exemplary programs, either everything works or nothing works because there are no common characteristics among all the programs. They cover the range of possibilities.

Perhaps again it is the teacher who makes the difference. But if that is so, we have to learn what it is that the teacher is doing that is different. What has really been demonstrated is the total poverty of using the available tests to learn anything useful about programs, or success of curricula, or methodology, or teachers or kids. I can tell you that our own research has shown repeatedly that, particularly among minority or immigrant children, tests grossly underestimate actual reading competence. For a long list of reasons they don't seem to do well on the tests. One reason is that the tests don't measure reading competence.

Testing has created a Procrustean bed that all of us are having great discomfort lying upon. In the Greek myth, Procrustus had a bed he let his guests use, but if they were too short for it he stretched them and if they were too tall he cut off their legs so they would fit. That is what has been happening with tests. By trying to fit everything into a narrow assessment framework, we have created a national calamity that is destroying our curriculum and our children. The situation is so bad in terms of abuse of tests that we ought to declare a five-year moratorium on the use of *all* standardized tests, until the test makers can get some sense into the tests and the uses they permit to be made of them.

I could criticize many more things but I would rather conclude with some positive things we have learned from scientific investigations of language and reading that provide a strong base upon which to build a new revolutionary position:

Language is learned from whole to part.
Meaning is the intrinsic motivation for language learning
    including reading
Language is far more than a bag of words.
You understand what something means before you know what
    the words are.
There isn't any sequence of skills in learning to read, it has
    to be all together from the very beginning. It also has to be
    relevant and meaningful from the beginning.
Kids reveal their strengths in the very mistakes that they
    make.
We have to encourage risk-taking. We have to make children
    willing to take chances and keep the focus on meaning even
    if they do not know all the words.
We have to learn to work with kids, to build on the strengths
    that they have rather than to be at cross-purposes to them.

I have left out one important point in this revolution. I asked for a new respect for learners, a new respect for language. I have to add a request for a new respect for teachers. Teachers can make the crucial difference but not as fountains of wisdom, not as sources of knowledge, not as actors with a script. Teachers must be informed professionals who understand language and language learning, who know how to monitor the process so that they can help it happen, and who don't need tests to tell them whether children are learning how to read or not.

Let me say something about accountability. I can say it really simply. The only people we are ultimately accountable to as teachers are the kids we teach. That accountability has to transcend everything else if this revolution is to be successful. On behalf of the kids, I'd like to welcome you to the revolution, comrades.

In this article Goodman criticizes the view that sees learning to read as the 'acquisition of a series of skills.' 'Many children,' he says, 'will have lost all confidence in their own ability to get sense from print. They will be the victims of overskill....'

'Learning literacy is like learning a second language in that functional need and continual exposure are more important than the quality of instruction.'

Goodman believes that it is time we moved from the primitive practices of skill technologies, that we 'relegate them to the museum of folklore and superstition in which they belong.'

23 ACQUIRING LITERACY IS NATURAL: Who Skilled Cock Robin?

An old English folk song asks the question 'Who Killed Cock Robin?'. I've parodied that question in the title of this paper because I believe that many of the problems in literacy instruction in the world today are misunderstood because learning to read has been treated as a matter of acquiring a series of skills.

In the literate nations - particularly America - we've built a technology of reading skills. On a world basis, literacy can be easily seen to be proportionate to the need for literacy within any society or subgroup of the particular society. Even within literate societies, different ethnic, cultural and economic groups show notably different patterns of acceptance of literacy and literacy instruction.

But as we've built a technology of instruction in literate societies, we've created pathologies of failure that are independent of the need for language, the nature of language or the natural learning of language. The technology we've built treats reading as something difficult to be systematically taught skill upon skill. Though this technology has no foundation either in theory or research, it has acquired, over time, a credibility partly due to pedagogical tradition - we continue to do what others have done before us - and partly due to its arbitrary specificity. Skills are arranged sequentially and hierarchically and drills and exercises are multiplied and duplicated to teach the skills. Research fills the professional literature reporting experiments on the most effective ways of teaching the skills, creating the illusion that the skills themselves have a base in scientific research.

Achievement tests based on the skill hierarchies become the means for determining the extent of acquisition of literacy. Performance on these tests becomes synonymous with reading itself. Low scores on tests are offered as proof of failure and a new technology is created to find the pathological causes within the non-learner's failure to acquire the skills. And more drills and exercises are multiplied and duplicated to remediate the deficiencies and teach the skills.

Networks of professionally trained diagnosticians, clinicians and remediators are created to test, diagnose and treat the disabled learners.

The acquisition of literacy has been so obscured by equating it with the acquisition of skills that strength is mistaken for weakness and instruction is often at cross-purposes to natural language learning. The sources of problems in learning to read and even the extent of such problems are also obscured.

Furthermore, skill technologies are transferred into literacy programs in developing societies where they work even less well than in the established educational systems of highly literate societies where opportunities for natural acquisition of literacy are more abundant.

How well schemes for teaching literacy work is always a complicated issue to judge since learners are often able to overcome artificial structures to resist having literacy fractionated and to learn written language much as they learned the oral. The key seems always to be that the learner experiences functional need for written language. Language serves the communicative needs of individuals and societies and development of language including literacy can not be understood outside of the social-cultural context of learners.

In changing societies where massive literacy campaigns are conducted among people of all ages who had no prior opportunities to learn to read and write, the success of such programs is far less a result of the methods or even the quality of instruction than it is of the reality and extent of social change. If a people feel a real need to be literate because of changed roles, values, opportunities, or experiences and if written language becomes truly accessible and functional then many of them will become literate easily and well.

I'm not suggesting that instruction is either unimportant or unnecessary. I am arguing that instruction must be related to the realities of language and language learning in cultural, social contexts.

Oral language develops in all human societies. It is both a personal and social invention. It makes it possible for human societies to achieve a level of interaction unique among living species. We can truly share our problems, needs, thoughts and experiences. Oral language serves the face-to-face, here-and-now communicative needs common to all human societies.

For all but the deaf, oral language is the most accessible and useful form for such immediate communication. It is the form individuals develop first. Quickly, their thrust to communicate causes their personal language to move toward the forms, norms and structures of the language of the family and the community. The need to communicate becomes intertwined with the need to fully participate in society. Language is the necessary means to both. But neither the individual nor society ever lose their ability to create language to meet new need. Language remains always open, always adaptable, ever changing to represent new experiences, concepts, values or environments.

Oral language is suitable for all functions except those that require that language be preservable over time or transmittable over distance. When human societies reach a point of complexity where their ideas, concepts and experiences become too complex for preservation through the oral tradition and when society itself becomes so complex that individuals must be in regular communication with others outside the immediate community, then the societies invent the means for such communication and written language comes into being.

Sometimes the need is limited and only a small corps of literate people is needed to serve as the historians or the scribes of the society. Mass literacy represents a stage in social development in which every individual needs written language for full first-class participation in the culture.

Gutenberg's invention of the printing press has been credited with making mass literacy possible. But it is probably more accurate to say that the need for widespread literacy caused the invention of the printing press. Recent developments of quick, easy, inexpensive, high-quality reproduction devices facilitate written communication but they didn't create the need they serve. They are responses to that need.

Written language is as natural as oral in human society. In fact, it is a natural extension of the human ability to create language to deal with each communicative function as it develops.

Language is universally human. The form it takes depends on the function it must perform. Deaf people cut off from sound develop a visual language, manual sign, as an alternative for face-to-face communication. Blind people, cut off from sight, use their sense of touch to read Braille.

If there are human communities that have not developed literacy they are not proof that literacy is less natural than oral language but rather that language develops as the functions for it develop.

Differences between oral and written language which will affect how they are learned, result from the differences in their use. Because of its special function, written language is more likely to be used out of the situation context in which oral language is commonly embedded. It tends to be used to express ideas that are more complex and abstract than oral language. Both language forms have some common functions too, of course. A sign that says 'keep off the grass' is just as concrete and situationally embedded as the equivalent oral command. Oral discussions may become quite abstract.

Still, it is the differences and similarities in the functions of written and oral language that hold the key to understanding how acquisition of literacy is like or unlike the acquisition of oral language. We have made the critical mistake in the past of ignoring function and teaching reading and writing as the mastery of abstract form. In doing so, we have ignored the intrinsic motivation to learn to read and write that development of functional need brings about. We have ignored the lessons learned from studies of language acquisition about language development as growth in the competence to understand and be understood through language.

We made literacy something separate and apart from language and its use. We made it a set of abstract skills to be mastered

sequentially as a prerequisite to use. We skilled and over-
skilled readers and then sought to help those who couldn't find
their way to meaning with a dose of remedial skill instruction.

All language is used and learned in the context of expressing
and comprehending meaning. Human infants sort out, from the
sensory bombardment they receive through all their senses that
which is significant and that which is not. They categorize,
organize, relate as they continually seek to comprehend. They
sort language out of their noisy environments and begin relating it to its functions. In the process they develop not only
control over a set of symbols and a vocabulary but also a set
of rules for generating and comprehending language not previously experienced.

For most people in all human societies the movement toward
virtually full control of at least one form of at least one oral
language is swift and easy. By age four they are highly competent.

In literate societies, children begin acquisition of literacy in
much the same way. They sort out from the environment the
print and its relationship to everything else within that environment. They will be most aware of the print that has functions
which overlap those of oral language such as that which names
and identifies - logos and brand names on cars, cereal boxes,
peanut butter jars, or their own names - that which controls -
signs for stop, exit, no parking. If they have a lot of experience with books and newspapers, they may become aware of
the more abstract functions of providing information or entertainment through literature.

If the acquisition of literacy lags behind that of oral language
at the age of school beginning, it is a demonstration of the
slower development of the functions of written language and
not proof that literacy is either harder or less natural to learn.

Just as in acquiring oral language, children are finding order
in written language, developing control over its system as they
seek to comprehend and express. They become aware of the
form as they experience the function, they learn the parts from
the wholes, generalize and expand their functional competence.

For most children becoming literate, they have the advantage
of being already quite advanced in oral language competence.
They control the rules and basic language structures as well as
the terms and idioms. They can express and comprehend,
through oral language, their understandings, feelings, concepts. The two most important resources that any learners bring
to learning to read and write are their competence in the oral
language and their undiminished ability to learn language as it
is needed for new functions.

The role of literacy instruction in school is to facilitate the use
by learners of these resources. To be most successful, instruction accepts and expands on the base of literacy already begun.
The school's focus is on expanding awareness in the learners
of the personal-social functions written language has for them.

This often means enhancing and enriching the classroom making it a highly literate environment – one in which the learners are immersed in functional written language. Children must be continually in meaningful interaction with each other, with teachers, with unseen authors, with others *through print*. This is also true for those acquiring literacy at any age.

The optimally effective teacher in such a school is not the technician sequentially teaching and testing the skills assumed to be components of reading. Rather, a teacher must be knowledgeable about linguistic and cognitive development, insightful in monitoring the progress of learners in acquiring the ability to get and express meaning through written language, able to plan experiences to help children to learn.

Much is now known about how language works. We understand that in producing language speakers or writers start with meaning, create an underlying or deep language structure to represent it, and then produce a surface representation either in speech or in print which must be full enough to be comprehensible to the listener or reader.

We understand that the listener or reader samples from the speech or print, predicts and assigns underlying structure and seeks meaning as efficiently as possible.

Effective language teachers need not be linguists or psycholinguists. But they must be knowledgeable about language functions and processes.

There is a comfort and orderliness that appeals to teachers in sequential skill hierarchies. They particularly lend themselves to very formal and structured classrooms. But the emptiness of such hierarchies and irrelevance to actual development in reading is observable in any skill oriented classroom. In such classrooms, there always are two kinds of learners; one kind do well on the skill drills because they have enough control of the reading process to deal with the parts within the wholes. They don't need the skill instruction. The second kind have great difficulty with the sequenced skills because they are dealing with them as abstractions outside of the meaningful language process. Such learners can't profit from skill instruction unless they can transcend it and find their way to meaning on their own. Unfortunately, the difficulty they experience is often cause for more intensive instruction in skills even more removed from real functional written language. While their peers move on to more natural language with decreasing proportions of time spent on skills these learners are subjected to remedial skill instruction.

By the time they have satisfied their instructors that they can produce grunts for letters, blend sounds, sound out words, syllabicate, match words that have beginning, middle or final sounds or letters and attack, perceive, identify, recognize, analyze and synthesize words, many of them will have lost all confidence in their own ability to get sense from print. They will be the victims of overskill. Poor cock-robin!

Even if they should later overcome the fragmentation, they will have been so phonicated, so syllabified, so verbalized that they will always regard reading as dull, tedious and onerous. They will read only what they must and never of their own choice for pleasure or relaxation.

In countries with extensive literacy instruction, there are far more people who can read to some extent but don't than there are people who can't read at all. There are even people who read well enough to become highly educated who seldom read anything for their own pleasure. For them, there is no pleasure in reading.

Illiteracy in developing countries must be seen as the result of two factors: lack of functional need for literacy and lack of opportunity to acquire literacy.

Earlier, I argued that literacy campaigns in developing nations can only succeed when the conditions in the society make literacy both necessary and available.

There must be reasons for people to need to use written language - there must be signs, forms, books, newspapers, magazines, street signs and addresses to be read. Only then will substantial numbers of learners respond to instruction. If the cultural conditions are right, even nonprofessional teachers using common sense methodology will appear to be successful. Highly professional teachers can make a major difference but when the need is real many learners will transcend weaknesses in instruction.

Learning literacy is like learning a second language in that functional need and continual exposure are more important than the quality of instruction.

In many cultures some social, ethnic, occupational or economic groups may need and/or value literacy more than others. Indeed it may be possible in some countries that some people will not need to be literate to become respected members of their immediate communities while others in the same countries do need to be literate. Even within communities, it is possible that some individuals, families or social groups will attach greater value and importance to literacy than others. Response to literacy instruction will certainly be proportionate to the value and need. That doesn't mean that some groups will learn and some won't. It means that there will be significant differences in the relative degree to which literacy instruction is accepted.

I've been using the term 'acceptance of literacy instruction' because I am arguing that literacy learning is not a passive response to instruction. Instruction can help to motivate and facilitate, even guide learning but it can not produce learning in a passive, disinterested or hostile learner. Even behavior modification forces active involvement of the learner through rewards or punishments.

I believe that schools can help to rebuild a sense of the functions of written language in pupils who have not yet developed such function. But there are limits on what schools and teachers can accomplish alone in this respect. The community itself must examine the uses it makes of written language and the real value that literacy has in the culture of the community. Schools can participate in changing the conditions and values of society but only as part of a much broader concentrated effort.

Illiteracy in developed nations presents a different picture. There may be subcultures which are very much like the developing nations within them - for example, some Native American groups in the United States. But the bulk of illiterates in countries with universal education are people who have had instruction but can't or who believe they can't get meaning from print.

These illiterates tend to have certain common characteristics. Very often, they can produce phonic approximations for virtually every word. They have the skills they've been taught but can't make them work. So they think that successful readers know some magic tricks that turn the disjointed cacophony into meaning. They tend to accept the opinion of past teachers that they can't read because they lack skills. They believe readers always know every word. So each word they meet that they don't know is one more proof of defeat. Above all, they are convinced they will never read successfully even when they are already partially successful. That's because they don't regard what they are doing as reading unless they have conscientiously used their skills to attack the words.

Deskilling reading instruction and placing greater emphasis at the beginning on building the personal-social functions of reading will help to prevent such cripples from developing. Keeping the focus of both the learner and the teacher on meaning will provide both the necessary context for learning and basic means of evaluation and self-evaluation. Readers who understand that success in reading can be easily judged by whether what is read makes sense will tend to drop non-productive strategies even if teachers advocate them.

I can't offer a neat simple sequence of testable steps in the deskilled alternative to beginning reading instruction, I'm advocating. My approach starts where the learners are; it extends and establishes functional uses for written language; it employs *only* whole, real, relevant, meaningful language; it encourages risk-taking, meaning-seeking, hypothesis-testing. In other words, it treats learning to read as language learning. It treats teaching reading as helping people learn to get meaning from print. And, if you want to get back to basics, getting meaning is where it's at.

Too often in the past we tried to build technologies without a base in scientific concepts and understanding. We had alchemy before chemistry, astrology before astronomy, witch-doctors before modern medicine. Let's move on now from our reading skill technologies and relegate them to the museum of folklore and superstition in which they belong.

We conclude with this comprehensive article by the Goodmans, the fruit of many years of observing young learners and inter- acting with authorities in a number of fields relevant to reading. It is the most complete statement they have made on beginning reading.

It is the obvious choice for concluding Part One of this volume, because it offers a unique, unified, in-depth perspective of learning to read that integrates important information from relevant research from a number of countries that could be described as being on 'the cutting edge of understanding.' A very important article for teachers and teacher educators.

24 LEARNING TO READ IS NATURAL

with Yetta M. Goodman

When a human society experiences the need for communication over time and space then written language is developed. Until that time language is used in a face-to-face, here-and-now context and oral/aural language suffices. But when a society is literate, written language is functional for the society and the members in that society must learn the written form. We believe they learn it in a similar fashion as oral/aural language. Written language includes two of the four language processes. Reading is the receptive and writing is the productive form.

Children are born into a family, a community, a society in which language is used. Children are born dependent. Furthermore humans are social animals. They need to interact linguistically and communicate in order to survive and to participate.

Almost all children acquire language easily and naturally. They do so within the 'noisy' situations in which they are interacting with parents, siblings, and others. Strongly motivated by the need to understand and be understood they sort out and relate language to non-language, acquire control of symbol and rule systems, use language appropriately for appropriate purposes, build an impressive, even precocious, repertoire of utterances and become able both to understand and produce language they have never heard before.

Their language moves rapidly toward the familiolect and dialect that surrounds them, so rapidly that some scholars have come to view language as innate while others have seen it as an example of conditioning through stimulus and response. Our own view is that language is both personal and social invention. Both the individual and the society never lose the ability to create language. It is communicative purpose that motivates language development and which moves children toward the language around them. We believe as does M. Halliday (Halliday, 1975) that function precedes form in language acquisition. The ability to create language makes it possible for individuals to express original thought in original, yet understandable, language and for society to cope with new situations, new circumstances, new insights.

Children growing up in a literate society begin to encounter written language before they personally experience the need to communicate beyond face-to-face situations. All of them become aware of and able to use written language to some extent.

They become aware of books, signs, captions, printed containers, logos, handwriting in the day-to-day experiences they

have. They recognize stop signs, read cereal boxes, scribble
letters, write their names, follow familiar stories and join in
the reading.

For some children their awareness of written language and its
uses leads so naturally to participation that they are reading
and writing, even inventing their own spelling rules, before
they or their parents are even aware that they are becoming
literate. The process of acquisition of written language parallels
for such children that of acquisition of oral language.

Our contention is that acquisition of literacy is an extension
of natural language learning for *all* children. Instruction that
is consistent with this understanding facilitates learning.
Instruction that does not build on the process of natural language learning will, in some respects, be at cross purposes
with learners' natural tendencies, will neutralize or blunt the
force of their language learning strengths, and may become
counterproductive. Learners may then have to overcome barriers placed in their way in order to become literate.

ESSENTIALS OF INSTRUCTION FOR NATURAL LEARNING

We believe that children learn to read and write in the same way
and for the same reason that they learn to speak and listen.
The way is to encounter language in use as a vehicle of communicating meaning. The reason is need. Language learning
whether oral or written is motivated by the need to communicate,
to understand and be understood.

The essential process of beginning reading instruction involves these key understandings:

1 Understanding how language functions in conveying meaning.
2 Understanding how communication of meaning functions as
the context in which language is used and learned.
3 Understanding the subtle differences and similarities in
use of oral and written language.
4 Understanding the personal social motivations that lead
children to learn or not learn language.
5 Understanding the cultural factors that make the acquisition of literacy of more or less personal importance to children
of differing backgrounds.
6 Understanding the natural process of acquisition of literacy
some children achieve.
7 Understanding all children's self-initiation of literacy in
literate societies.
8 Understanding how to create programs and environments
that enhance the natural motivations, awareness, experiences,
and cultural variables so that reading is acquired naturally
by all children.
9 Understanding the roles teachers must play as guides,

monitors, environmental arrangers, and stimulators to help the process happen.

NATURAL, NOT INNATE

This view of development of literacy as natural is not the same as the view held by those who regard language as not learned but innate. Many of those who espouse such a position have tended, reasoning back from the apparent lack of universality in acquisition of literacy, to treat oral language as innate and written language as acquired.

Mattingly (1972, pp. 133-47) summarizes such a view:

> The possible forms of natural language are very restricted; its acquisition and function are biologically determined... special neural machinery is intricately linked to the vocal tract and the ear, the output and input devices used by all 'normal' (quotation marks ours) human beings for linguistic communications....My view is that...speaking and listening are primary linguistic activities; reading is a secondary and rather special sort of activity that relies critically upon the reader's awareness of these primary activities.

That leaves Mattingly by his own admission rather surprised 'that a substantial number of human beings can also perform linguistic functions by means of the hand and eye. If we had never observed actual reading or writing we would probably not believe these activities possible.'

Mattingly's use of 'awareness' in describing reading is a focal point. Oral language is a 'syntactic, creative process' which is not 'in great part deliberately and consciously learned behavior like playing a piano....Synthesis of an utterance is one thing; the awareness of the process of synthesis quite another.' Mattingly is led then to conclude that reading unlike speech requires very deliberate awareness of linguistic process.

This view makes the learning of oral and written language very different. Learning to read is seen as not 'natural' like listening, but a deliberate conscious, academic achievement dependent on awareness of certain aspects of oral language.

Since we view language as personal-social invention we see both oral and written language as learned in the same way. In neither case is the learner 'required' by the nature of the task to have a high level of conscious awareness of the units and system. In both cases control over language comes through the preoccupation with communicative use. Awareness of the uses of language is need. But in neither case is it possible or profitable for the competent language user to be linguistically aware in Mattingly's sense. In reading, as in listening, pre-occupation with language itself detracts from meaning and produces inefficient and ineffective language use.

NOT A GARDEN OF PRINT EITHER

Our position is also not Rousseauian. When we use the term
natural learning we do not regard the process as one of unfold-
ing in an environment free of obstructive intrusions. Teaching
children to read is *not* putting them into a garden of print and
leaving them unmolested.

Language learners are active participants in communication
with unseen writers.

They are seekers of meaning, motivated by the need to comprehend, aware of the functions of print and adaptive to the
characteristics of print. The environment must certainly be
rich in print, a literate one. But reading instruction, particularly beginning instruction, has a vital role to play in creating and enhancing the conditions that will bring the reader's
natural language learning competence into play. Children must
be among people who talk in order to learn to speak and listen.
But that's not enough. Their need to communicate must also be
present for learning to take place. This is also the case in
acquiring literacy.

Instruction does not teach children to read. Children are in
no more need of being taught to read than they are of being
taught to listen. What reading instruction does is help children
learn.

This distinction between learning and teaching is a vital one.
Helping children learn to read is as Frank Smith has put it,
'Finding out what children do and helping them do it' (Smith,
1973, pp. 183-96). That's possible given children's language
competence, language learning competence, and the social function of written language. Teaching children to read has often
meant simplifying and fractionating reading into sequenced
component skills to be learned and used.

With the focus on learning, the teacher must understand and
deal with language and language learning. The learners keep
their minds on meaning. With the focus on teaching both
teachers and learners are dealing with language, often in
abstract bits and pieces. The need of the learners for making
sense may help them to use their language learning competence
to circumvent such instruction. But that demonstrates how we
have tended again as Frank Smith has said to find easy ways
to make learning to read hard.

Halliday has stated a position we can agree with:

> There is no doubt that many of our problems in literacy
> education are of our own making; not just ourselves as
> individuals, or even educators as a profession, but our-
> selves as a whole society, if you like. In part the problems
> stem from our cultural attitudes to language. We take lan-
> guage all too solemnly - and yet not seriously enough. If
> we (and this includes teachers) can learn to be a lot more
> serious about language, and at the same time a great deal

less solemn about it (on both sides of the Atlantic, in our different ways), then we might be more ready to recognize linguistic success for what it is when we see it, and so do more to bring it about where it would otherwise fail to appear. (Halliday, 1971, p. viii)

THE DIFFERENCE BETWEEN ORAL AND WRITTEN LANGUAGE

'What is common to every use of language,' says Halliday, 'is that it is meaningful, contextualized, and in the broadest sense social' (Halliday, 1969, pp. 26-37).

Modern linguistics correctly shifted the main focus of linguistic concern from written to oral language several decades ago. It's unfortunate that many linguists began to equate speech with language to such an extent that written language came to be treated as something other than language. Such a view is unscientific since it is largely unexamined and illogical: if written language can perform the functions of language it must be language. Mattingly, rather than being surprised that people can perform linguistic functions by means of hand and eye, must be prepared to modify a view of language that would make such linguistic reality surprising. Written language in use is also meaningful, contextualized and social.

For literate users of language, linguistic effectiveness is expanded and extended. They have alternate language forms, oral and written, that overlap in functions but which have characteristics that suit each for some functions better than the other. Let's consider the basic characteristics of the alternate language forms so that we may see which uses they are better suited for (Table 24.1). Speech lends itself easily to here-and-now, face-to-face uses. Writing is best suited for use over time and space. Certainly the need for extending communication between people separated by time and distance was the social cultural reason for development of literacy historically. In some early societies this social need required literacy from only a few people who functioned either as a kind of signal corps or as the archivists of the communities. The Persians used a small corps of literate Hebrew slaves to handle communication across their empire.

In other societies the need for and uses of written language become more pervasive. Religious communities that hold the belief that each individual must share in a body of knowledge stored in print documents will develop widespread literacy.

Oral language is of course the first language form for most individuals even in literate societies. This primacy means that for a period of their lives children will use oral language as the first means of dealing with all the language functions. Evidence exists, however, that very young children have some awareness and make some use of both the form and function of written language long before their control of oral language has become fully functional.

Table 24.1

Input-output medium	Oral	Written
	Ear/voice	Eye/hand
Symbolic units	Sounds and sound patterns	Print and print patterns
Display	Over time	Over space
Permanence	Instantly perishable unless electronically recorded	As permanent as desired
Distance limits	Distance between encoder and decoder limited unless amplified or electronically transmitted	Distance between encoder and decoder unlimited
Structure	Phonological surface representation of deep structure and meaning	Orthographic surface representation of deep structure and meaning

Our contention is that we can explain both acquisition and lack of acquisition of literacy in terms of the internalization of the functions of written language by children. Let's start with a simple example: Children in a developing nation go off to a village or boarding school where they are taught basic literacy, among other things. The functions of written language they encounter in school may have no parallels in their homes. Instruction may deal with the mechanics of reading and writing and not even attempt to establish need or linguistic function. Instruction, literacy, and materials may even be in an unknown language. Success in initial acquisition of literacy will certainly be limited in any sense. If any mechanical skill is achieved it is unlikely to become functional. Furthermore, when the pupils leave school there will be little or no use to be made of written language. The village culture is one with little use for print. Since there are strong patterns in many countries of early school drop-out before the third or fourth grade, progress in developing literacy is unlikely.

Halliday has presented a view of children's models of language that we wish to apply to written language. Halliday states that 'the child knows what language is because he knows what language does.' Children in literate societies use written language

to various degrees and for various social, personal purposes.
Halliday considers that these functions appear in approximate
order and he believes that they develop before the child learns
the adult language. In building initial literacy it is important to
understand that function precedes form in language development and that children have acquired all functions before they
come to school (Halliday, 1975, p. 244).

Halliday's Functions of Language are:

Instrumental: I want
Regulatory: Do as I tell you
Interactional: Me and you
Personal: Here I come
Heuristic: Tell me why
Imaginative: Let's pretend
Informative: I've got something to tell you

The extent to which children become aware of how each function is dealt with in written language will be influenced by which
ones are most commonly served by print and which continue to
be best served by speech in their cultures and communities.

Children in literate societies are aware early of the regulatory
function. The function of 'STOP' signs is quickly learned. One
six-year-old was asked why she thought it was important to
read. 'You might be out driving. And you might want to park.
And there might be a sign that says "No Parking." And a man
might come out and say "Can't you read?"'

The people who write the copy for the Saturday morning TV
cartoon shows work hard at establishing the 'I want' function so
that millions of preschoolers will be able to spot the 'Count
Chocula' box and say 'I want Count Chocula.'

Letter and note writing represent the interactional function
of language. Many children become aware of letters, enjoy
receiving them, dictate letters to be sent to grandparents, and
begin to play at or actually produce letters. Parents often leave
notes for children. But the 'me and you' function begins to
illustrate the important differences between the two forms of
language in use. Conversation is oral interaction. Usually it is
strongly situationally supported. Speaker and listener are
together, response is quick, topics usually relate to the situational context itself. Pointing, facial expression, body movements, all support successful communication. Interacting through
print is not situationally supported (the context is more abstract),
response is delayed and the respondent unseen; language must
express aspects of messages that are indicated in other ways in
oral conversation.

Two differences are involved in written interaction as compared
to oral. One is the absence of supportive situational context.
Writing shares this condition with telephone use. It's interesting
that the extension of oral interaction to telephone conversation
causes children to refine and extend the function. But telephones

provide immediate response, written letters result in delayed responses.

The second attribute of written language that distinguishes oral and written interaction is that the writer, the partner in communication with the reader, is most often unseen and un-known; the young reader may in some sense be aware of the message but not its source. This difference also shows in other written language. Signs tell you to 'keep off the grass.' Who wrote and put them there may not be something children have considered.

Children may be no more concerned with who puts stories in books than they are with who puts milk in bottles. In fact the message appears to be coming from the language itself, or its context in the case of signs.

Some children become aware of the personal function of writ-ten language perhaps earlier than others. They may be in a very egocentric stage at the time when they are aware that they have written names. This written representation of self becomes a way of identifying what is 'mine.'

One of our graduate students recently reported an experi-ence of a ten-year-old fifth-grader who was considered learn-ing disabled. Reading is so far from having a personal function for him that he encountered the name Miguel four times in a story before he recognized it as his own name. Then he was amazed to find it in print.

On the other hand, a three-year-old, asked to write his own name, scrawled an A. That's Ali, he said. Then he drew a picture with an A discernible in its center. That's Ali on his bike. His graphic name was his image.

If Halliday is right about a sequence in development of lan-guage functions, then it is interesting that the last three, heuristic, imaginative, and informative, are the functions for which written language is most heavily used in literate societies.

As language functions are extended beyond the immediate concerns, needs, and interactions of children to exploration of the real world, the world of ideas, and the world of what might be, language expands, takes on new textures and begins to transcend the immediate contexts in which it occurs.

The language of children expands to serve their needs as they become fully interactive with their communities.

Halliday (1969) suggests that the informative model of language which is the abstract use of language to talk about ideas may be the only model of language that adults articulate but it is a 'very inadequate model from the point of view of the child.'

He indicates that if our concept of language is to be helpful to children it must be exhaustive. It must take into account all the things language can do for children. In reading that means using street signs, buying favorite toys and foods, finding favorite TV programs, writing and reading notes from parents left under magnetic markers on the refrigerator, reading stories that expand the creative and fanciful world of play, using books to discover how to make a sock puppet or read a recipe from the box to find out how to make marshmallow Rice Krispies crunch.

Readers in our society who are the readers who *do* read, as opposed to the readers who *can* read, use reading for all its varied purposes. We must focus more and more attention on how written language is used in society because it is through the relevant use of language that children will learn it. They will learn it because it will have meaning and purpose to them. Written language, too, can then fit into Halliday's statement that what is common to every use of language is that it is meaningful, contextualized and social.

WHEN AND HOW DOES READING BEGIN? THE RESEARCH BASE

Reading begins when children respond to meaningful printed symbols in a situational context with which they are familiar.

The onset of this process probably goes as unnoticed as the point in time when listening begins.

Yet there is lots of evidence in the literature that suggests that some kind of print awareness starts in children at a very early age without formal instruction.

Frank Smith (1976, pp. 297-9) makes several points relating to the onset of reading:

> The first is that children probably begin to read from the moment they become aware of print in any meaningful way, and the second is that the roots of reading are discernible whenever children strive to make sense of print before they are able to recognize many of the actual words.
>
> Third, not only are the formal mechanics of reading unnecessary in these initial stages, they may well be a hindrance. It is the ability of children to make sense...that will enable them to make use of the mechanics....Fourth, words do not need to be in sentences to be meaningful, they just have to be in a meaningful context...

The awareness of print seems to develop as children learn to categorize the large amount of print information that surrounds them in a literate society. As they drive down a highway, walk down a street or through a shopping center, or watch television, they are bombarded with print media. Children learn to organize their world and make sense of it. When printed language is part of that world, children will use that aspect of the environment if it is functional and significant to their life and culture. Gibson (1970, p. 137) reports on children who at four could not only 'separate pictures from writing and scribbles... they could separate scribbles from writing.'

After being aware of print as different from other graphic information, the child begins to assign meaning to the print in the environment.

Ingrid Ylisto (1968) studied preschoolers who had no formal instruction responding to signs in situational context and concluded 'In reading as the child interacts in a print culture his awareness and recognition of printed word symbols become more and more autonomous. He abstracts the printed word symbol from the contextual setting, classifies and orders it and systematizes or assimilates it in a language system he knows.'

Our recent pilot research substantiates this movement from children learning to read printed symbols in familiar situational contexts toward more reliance on language contexts.

Children from age three on have been asked to respond to common signs in their environment. Certain signs are recognized in the situational context only. Circle K Market may be recognized when the family drives by the store but the logo may not be recognized on a match book cover. However, certain logos like McDonald's and Coca Cola are recognized as long as the print retains its distinctive form even when away from the golden arches or the sexy bottle.

Children's responses to signs suggest that they are concerned with the meaning of the graphic unit more than the representation of the name itself. Some children seeing Chicken and Stars in white block letters similar to how it is printed on the can will say 'That's Campbell Soup' and they respond to the logo 'Campbells' as Campbell Soup as well. One three-year-old called signs of Burger Chef, Burger King and McDonald's all McDonald's but when shown the sign of a local hamburger place which was more distinctly a sit-down as opposed to take-out place, the child said 'That's a restaurant.' Children are categorizing using associations other than significant graphic features to read. One 2½-year-old calls Myna and Mother (when she sees them written) as Mother. Myna is her mother's name. Her father's name is Mark. When Myna, Mark, Daddy and Mother are all presented to her, she interchanges Daddy and Mark, but never confuses Mark with Mother or Myna. In the beginning of reading children may relate concept of meaning to a graphic unit and not be concerned with an exact oral representation. So it is not surprising when a kindergartner responds to each graphic alternative of his name as 'That says Jimmy' whether the name is written Jim, Jimmy, James, or James Jones Junior.

Just as oral language meanings are developed and used in ongoing everyday experiences so written language is learned through functional use.

Marie Clay (1972b, p. 28) has studied five-year-old entrants to New Zealand's schools. She suggests that children are print aware when they ask 'What's that say?' in response to a TV advertisement or when telling a story from a picture story book they might sigh and say 'I can't read all the words but I know what they say.' She describes children who are reading a book obviously not following the print but using a book like a pattern such as 'Once upon a time...' or 'Mother said, Do you want a piece of cake?' Instead of the familiar 'Reading is Talk Written Down' these children indicate that 'Books Talk in a Special Way.'

As children respond to written language in its contextual setting, they begin to respond to significant features and may even use some metalinguistic terminology to suggest their developing rule structures.

One child suggested 'Revco has the same face as my name' (Roberta).

But for the most part children *use* language. They become interested in signs that help them control their lives. Men - boys - Senors are all important signs to learn to read. 'Exit' signs are important and many preschoolers respond to them appropriately although one doctor's son at age four responded to it by saying 'I know that's not X-ray.'

Charles Read (1975) and others have made us aware of the children who seem to be developing rules of written language through their invented spellings.

> Certain pre-school children print messages, employing an orthography that is partly of their own invention. They represent English words with the standard alphabet and are thus compelled to classify distinct phones in some way. They do so according to articulatory features, making judgements of similarity that are quite different from those that most parents or teachers might make. (Read, 1975, p. 329)

Marie Clay suggests her own model of beginning reading and how children begin to develop rules about written language. She sees:

> Beginning reading as a communication system in a formative stage. At first the child is producing a message from his oral language experience and a context of past associations. He verifies it as probable or improbable in terms of these past experiences and changes the response if the check produces uncertainty.
>
> At some time during the first year at school visual perception begins to provide cues but for a long period these are piecemeal, unreliable and unstable. This is largely because the child must learn where and how to attend to print. (Clay, 1972b, p. 153)

Clay (1976) suggests that how children view the significance and function of written language in their own particular culture may provide the basis for success in reading. She studied Pakeha, Maori and Samoan children in New Zealand. Statistics indicated that 'the English language skills did not relate closely to progress in reading. While every Samoan group had the poorest average scores on each language test at every age, the Maoris had the poorest reading averages' (Clay, 1976, p. 337).

She suggests these reasons: The Maoris had little contact with printed material prior to entry to school and had few opportunities to learn concepts about print. The Samoan children do not have homes filled with reading books but their culture provides oral Bible reading in the home. A Sunday school teacher also reported '...four-year-old Samoan children who come to Sunday school all want to write. They take the pencils and paper and write.' This teacher described relatives back home involved in selling various crafts at the market-place to tourists on Boat Day. While working they are 'reading their mail from New Zealand and frantically writing their answers so that the boat which only stays a few hours can take the letters back to New Zealand....Children would see high value placed on written messages.'

'The Samoan child who speaks two languages, who is introduced to a book and to written messages in his home, who is urged to participate fully in schooling and is generally supported by a proud ethnic group with firm child-rearing practices, manages to progress well in the early years of his school without handicap from his low scores on oral English tests' (Clay, 1976, p. 341).

Readers know how to use written language long before they can talk about it. Downing, Clay and Read have all reported that children can't respond appropriately with terms like 'word,' 'letter,' 'number,' in the fifth and sixth year. However, it is important to consider that the labels may follow the concepts (Clay, 1975; Downing and Oliver, 1974, pp. 568-82).

HOW BEGINNERS DIFFER FROM PROFICIENT READERS

In our research on the reading process in readers with widely different levels of proficiency we reached certain key conclusions:

1 There is only one reading process. Readers may differ in the control of this process but not in the process they use.
2 Non-proficient readers show problems in getting it all together. They tend to get bogged down in preoccupation with letters and words and lose meaning.
3 The major difference in readers of varying proficiency is their ability to comprehend what they read.
4 Older non-proficient readers seem to have acquired nonfunctional skill. They can produce phonic matches or nearmisses for words. They can handle short phrases. But they don't get much sense from what they read and seem not to expect sense (Goodman and Burke, 1973).

In fact it appears that a gap has developed for some children between the skills of reading and any useful function of language. So much focus has been placed on form and those functions explored through reading have been so removed from the functional needs of the learner that reading becomes a school subject and not a useful language process.

Even when some degree of functional reading competence is achieved through instruction it often leaves people with so strong a distaste for reading that they only read what they must, particularly avoiding literature and educational materials, the most common school-related written language.

Beginners may follow four basic paths in moving into literacy: they may move forward from the natural beginning they've made gaining flexibility and control of the process as they expand the functions of written language they control; they may be distracted from function by instruction, coming to regard reading as an essentially non-functional, non-linguistic school activity; they may themselves bring their natural growth and school instruction together, choosing from instruction that which facilitates instruction; they may develop functional literacy outside school while developing a school behavior which is non-functional but satisfies school and teacher demands.

The key to these different results lies in the readers' perception of the functions for reading; the extent to which reading is functional in their culture; the extent to which instruction is facilitative, building on natural development; and the extent to which school experiences are relevant to the functional needs of the learners.

That people can achieve literacy under less than optimal conditions, even in very unlikely circumstances, is more a tribute to the universal human ability to acquire and use language than it is proof that educators can afford to be unconcerned about building programs that create optimal conditions.

Beginners have a sense of function that we have demonstrated has already led to some beginning of literacy before instruction. Shifting their focus to the forms of written language does not make them like proficient readers since the latter never sacrifice function to form even when they encounter misprints.

HOW DOES PROFICIENT READING WORK

Our research on reading miscues has been primarily concerned with developing and testing against reality a theory and model of proficient reading (Goodman, 1974).

We've come to view proficient reading as a process in which readers process integrated graphophonic, syntactic and semantic information as they strive to construct meaning. Reading consists of optical, perceptual, syntactic and semantic cycles, each melting into the next as readers try to get to meaning as efficiently as possible using minimal time and energy. That involves sampling from available cues, predicting syntactic structures and subsequent graphic cues, confirming or disconfirming predictions, correcting when necessary, and accommodating the developing sense as new information is decoded.

Efficiency, using minimal cues, and effectiveness, constructing meaning, depend on the readers being able to maintain focus on meaning. For that to be true, the material being read must be meaningful, comprehensible and functional to the reader. Unlike Mattingly we are not surprised at the facility readers develop nor at the fact that reading actually becomes more efficient than listening; again this difference turns out to be not a basic distinction in the two receptive processes but one that results from the conditions of use. Listening need only happen as rapidly as speech is produced; reading has no such constraint so it happens more rapidly with no loss of comprehension. We could listen as efficiently as we read; we just don't need to.

Proficient reading and listening processes are parallel except for the form of the input, their speed and, as we repeatedly said, the special uses we make of each. Proficient readers do not recode print as speech before decoding it. Why should they depend on a less efficient process and how could they be given the greater efficiency of reading?

It is not their ability to listen but their underlying ability to process language to get to meaning that beginning readers rely on to develop reading competence. The strategies we have described the proficient readers using are already used effectively and efficiently by children beginning to read their native language. Within meaningful, functional use of written language, they naturally, quickly and easily learn to use these same strategies with the new graphic inputs in the new contexts.

THE NATURAL SEQUENCE: A THEORY AND SOME PREMISES

We believe, as we've said, that motivation is inseparable from learning. Recognition of function, the need for language, precedes and is a prerequisite for acquisition.

The crucial relationships of language with meaning and with the context that makes language meaningful is also vital. Learners build from whole to part and build a sense of form and structure within their functional, meaningful experiences with language.

Written language development draws on competence in oral language since both share underlying structures and since for most learners oral language competence reaches a high level earlier. As children become literate the two systems become interactive and they use each to support the other when they need to.

As children expand their views of the world and become more concerned with things beyond the immediate they find more need for the informational and literary uses of written language.

We believe that it helps educators in understanding the reading process to study what proficient readers do when they read.

But it's a serious mistake to create curricula based on artificial skill sequences and hierarchies derived from such studies. To build facilitative instruction, we must understand not only how language processes work but how and why they are learned.

Our research has convinced us that the skills displayed by the proficient reader derive from the meaningful use of written language and that sequential instruction in those skills is as pointless and fruitless as instruction in the skills of a proficient listener would be to teach infants to comprehend speech.

METHODOLOGY AND MOTIVATION

We take as our principal premise in designing initial reading instruction that our goal is to create conditions that help all students to learn as naturally as some do.

Here we will focus on instruction for children growing up in a highly literate society. But in passing we must reiterate our premise that literacy will not be acquired if the community and society do not use literacy to any significant degree for any significant purpose.

Our initial instructional concerns are twofold: (1) to determine and expand on the literacy learners have already achieved (2) to establish and expand awareness of the function of literacy.

An old but essential educational premise is that education takes the learners where they are and helps them grow in whatever directions are legitimate for them.

That turns out to be essential in building initial literacy. In the balance of this paper we'll explore some in-school activities that school and teachers can include in initial reading instruction. What we're proposing are elements in a program; it is not yet a full program.

FINDING OUT WHAT THEY CAN READ

If teachers take children for a walk around the school, the neighborhood, or a supermarket they can get quick insights into the literacy kids have already attained. With a Polaroid camera a pictorial record can be brought back to the classroom. 'Show me anything you can read and I'll take a picture of it' is all the teacher needs to say. This sense of what they're reading is important for the teacher but it's also important for the kids who will discover reading isn't new, it's already part of their experience.

Marie Clay's sand test gets at kids' concepts about print (Clay, 1972a). The tests relate to her concept that careful observation of children is a basic requisite to facilitative instruction. Noting how children handle books, how they respond to print, how they relate print to meaning are things that teachers

can do with or without the test. The teachers must be an
informed monitor, able to see where the kids are and helping
them to find function and build competence.

Creating a literate environment. The classroom and school
must become an environment rich in functional use of written
language. That means there must be lots of written language
pupils will need and want to read. It does not mean that every
chair, table or window should be labeled. The uses of written
language must be both natural and functional. Furthermore,
it will be helpful if the kids are involved in creating the literate environment. That will give some sense of where written
language comes from. Dictating a set of 'Rules for Taking Care
of Our Hamster' is an example of their participation.

Work, play and living. Play is the child's equivalent of the
work world of the adult. In language development it forms a
valuable adjunct to the real-life experiences of children. They
can read real letters but they can also create a classroom post
office which delivers letters and notes between class members.
We need to bring back into kindergartens and primary classrooms the stores, kitchens, gas stations, play houses and other
centers for dramatic play.

Reading something. Language, reading included, is always a
means and never an end. Reading is best learned when the
learners are using it to get something else: a message, a story,
needed information. Literacy development, therefore, must be
integrated with the science, social studies, math, arts, and
other concerns of the classroom. In isolation it becomes non-
language and non-functional.

Reading and writing. Reading needs to be kept in constant
relationship to writing. Wherever possible composition in written
language should be related to reading activities.

Utilizing all functions. Halliday's seven functions make a good
guide for generating learning experiences for initial and con-
tinuing reading instruction.

Since most forms of writing are almost completely outside a
situational context, it's important to begin in school with those
situationally supported functions that children have already
begun using: the instrumental, regulatory, and personal (Table
24.2).

TEACHERS

In all that we've said we see the teacher as making the crucial
difference between whether some or all will learn to read. The
teacher's role, in our view, is a complex one.

Table 24.2

Function	*Experiences and activities*
Instrumental: (I want)	Sign-ups for activities or interest centers Picture collages with captions: things I want Play stores, gas stations, etc. Reading cans, boxes, posters and ads, coins and paper money Orders for supplies: things I need
Regulatory: (Do as I tell you)	Signs Directions Rules for care of class pets, plants, materials
Interactional: (Me and you)	Notes from the teacher for children on a message board e.g.: Tom, did you bring your absence excuse? Margaret, remember your music lesson at 10 a.m. Class Post Office: Encouraging note writing between pupils Games involving reading
Personal: (Here I come)	Books about self and family, pictures with captions Individual language-experience stories with character to identify with
Heuristic: (Tell me why)	Question box Single concept books Science experiments Instructions to make things Recipes
Imaginative: (Let's pretend)	Story-telling Hearing picture-story books read and joining in Acting out storied read, creative dramatics which teacher writes down Read-along books and records, comic strips
Informational: (Something to tell you)	Message boards Bulletin boards Notes to pupils paralleling school messages to parents Resource books Class newspaper Weather board Community newspaper, TV guide Content textbooks

Kid watching. To build on what kids have learned and to facilitate natural acquisition of reading the teachers must be insightful kid watchers. They must know what to look for, how to look, what it means. As children progress they must be able to monitor the progress, building on strengths and helping over hang-ups.

Environment arranger. Teachers must be able to create the literate environment which will facilitate learning. They must constantly be bringing kids in contact with relevant, functional print.

Interactor. The teachers will be the literate adult using print in functional ways to interact with the learners.

Motivator, stimulator and encourager. Teachers have major roles to play in helping children to recognize functional need, stimulating children's interests and encouraging and responding to their efforts.

REFERENCES

Clay, Marie M. (1972a), 'Sand - The Concepts About Print Test,' Auckland: Heinemann Educational Books.
Clay, Marie M. (1972b), 'Reading: The Patterning of Complex Behavior,' Auckland: Heinemann Educational Books.
Clay, Marie M. (1975), 'What Did I Write?' Auckland: Heinemann Educational Books.
Clay, Marie M. (1976), Early Childhood and Cultural Diversity in New Zealand, 'Reading Teacher,' January.
Downing, John, and Peter Oliver (1974), The Child's Conception of a Word, 'Reading Research Quarterly,' vol. IX, no. 4.
Gibson, Eleanor J. (1970), The Ontogeny of Reading, 'American Psychologist,' vol. 25.
Goodman, Kenneth S. (1974), The Reading Process, 'Proceedings of the Western Learning Symposium.'
Goodman, Kenneth S., and Carolyn L. Burke (1973), 'Theoretically Based Studies of Patterns of Miscues in Oral Reading Performance,' US Office of Education Project no. 9-0375, April.
Halliday, M.A.K. (1969), Relevant Models of Language, 'The State of Language Educational Review,' 22.1, University of Birmingham Press, November.
Halliday, M.A.K. (1971), Foreword to 'Breakthrough to Literacy,' Los Angeles: Bowmar.
Halliday, M.A.K. (1975), Learning How to Mean in Eric H. Lenneberg (ed.), 'Foundations of Language Development,' New York: Academic Press.
Mattingly, Ignatius (1972), Reading, the Linguistic Process, and Linguistic Awareness, in Kavanagh and Mattingly (eds), 'Language by Ear and by Eye,' Cambridge, Mass.: MIT Press.
Read, Charles (1975), Lessons to Be Learned from the Pre-School Orthographers, in Lenneberg and Lenneberg (eds), 'Foundations of Language Development: A Multidisciplinary

Approach,' vol. 2, New York: Academic Press.

Smith, Frank (1973), Twelve Easy Ways to Make Learning to Read Difficult, in F. Smith (ed.), 'Psycholinguistics and Reading,' New York: Holt, Rinehart & Winston.

Smith, Frank (1976), Learning to Read by Reading, 'Language Arts,' March.

Ylisto, Ingrid P. (1968), An Empirical Investigation of Early Reading Responses of Young Children, unpublished dissertation, University of Michigan.

Part Two
ISSUES IN EDUCATION

TESTING

In education today in many countries, but particularly in the USA, our preoccupation with testing and with statistics is incredible. Management, from whom we first borrowed testing many years ago, has long since dropped its use in favor of more flexible and efficient means of evaluation. Unfortunately, education appears to be well and truly hooked on testing.

Testers try to test something that people begin to call intelligence, and testers try to test something people call reading. But then the very people who make the test become infatuated with their own creations. They forget they are only tests and begin to say the thing measured is intelligence; or it is reading. In research journals the writers are extremely careful to use terms in precise rigorous ways that other researchers demand, terms like 'significant,' 'correlation' and 'validity.' But researchers will quickly move away from talking about correlations between scores on tests and begin to talk about correlations between reading and intelligence. We create a test and just by enduring, the test comes to be regarded as having God-given validity. We begin to forget where it came from and what it was we started to do.

In the following three articles, Goodman expresses his strong concerns about the construction and use of tests in education, views that he has expressed for some time, views that appear to be gaining some momentum at least in the USA, where the need for change is probably greatest.

'Do you have to be smart to learn to read?...You don't have to be smart to learn language,' says Goodman in this article, 'And we have to stop treating written language as if it is not quite language.'

This is a scathing attack on the design and use of tests, and a clear account of the need to apply what we now know about language learning to the teaching and testing of reading.

25 DO YOU HAVE TO BE SMART TO READ? DO YOU HAVE TO READ TO BE SMART?

In attempts to relate intelligence and reading, we create artifacts to measure reality, and then, somehow, begin thinking of them as if they, themselves, were reality. Testers try to test something that people begin to call intelligence, and testers try to test something people call reading. But then the very people who make the test become infatuated with their own creations. They forget they are only tests and begin to say the thing measured is intelligence; or it is reading. In research journals the writers are extremely careful to use terms in precise rigorous ways that other researchers demand, terms like 'significant,' 'correlation' and 'validity.' But researchers will quickly move away from talking about correlations between scores on tests and begin to talk about correlations between reading and intelligence. We create a test and just by enduring, the test comes to be regarded as having God-given validity. We begin to forget where it came from and what it was we started to do.

Buros's 'Mental Measurements Yearbook' started as a way of improving the quality of testing. The idea was that if you subjected tests to critical review, bad tests would fall away and good tests would replace them. What's remarkable in the field of reading is that the majority of all the tests ever published are still commercially available. Reading tests have become accumulations of subskill tests having no supportive theory or research, and based simply on things people thought kids should be able to do in learning to read.

We assume that performance on intelligence tests is intelligence, the competence to learn. We assume that performance on reading tests is reading, the competence to get meaning from written language. In getting correlation between the tests, we are licensed to play the 'why' game, in which we reason that intelligence and reading are highly correlated, therefore...

One 'therefore' is that you have to be smart to learn to read. Moreover, if there is a high correlation, then not only do you have to be smart to learn to read but the degree to which you are smart determines the degree to which you learn to read. Yet, some smart kids don't learn to read easily; so, we decide there must be something wrong with those smart kids. (If there weren't something wrong with them, they ought to be able to read; *therefore*, let's blame it on something being wrong with them.)

They're smart, so they must have perceptual problems, or

learning disabilities, or dyslexia (dyslexia is the affliction of not being able to learn how to read), or poor motivation, or some kind of a learning disability.

Another insidious 'therefore' is something called reading expectancy, which you find discussed in some very respectable textbooks. Assuming intelligence and reading are correlated, a child who has an IQ of 80 should not read as well as his peer group. Likewise, we should be dissatisfied with a child with an IQ of 120 who is not reading better than his peer group. It seems the statistical conclusion turns into a prediction to be applied to individual children.

But what about the unintelligent children who don't have any trouble learning to read? For them a remarkable explanation is invented: over-achieving. How that is possible in the correlational theory I haven't been able to figure out, yet. Perhaps somebody will say that it isn't 1 to 1 correlation, it's more like 6. Or perhaps some will simply say, 'We really are doing a good job with those dumb kids, aren't we?

But there are other explanations for the correlation between performance on intelligence tests and performance on reading tests. One possiblity is that both kinds of tests result from common factors: cultural bias, linguistic bias, a focus on abstraction in both tests, an academic bias focusing on the kind of things that are school-oriented. Another is motivation - the degree to which the child cares about the test. Still another similar kind of thing is test-wiseness, just the general ability to take tests. Dick Venezky (1971) discovered, in relationship to a study he was doing of performance on auditory discrimination tests, that if you gave kids the same test three days in a row, by the third day you could eliminate between-group differences.

Intelligence tests and reading tests may really be the same tests. The contents of the test are so overlapping that they aren't different tests, and they aren't measuring different things at all; the tasks are really the same or equivalent tasks so the results are similar. With the pressure of accountability in test performance, the production of tests becomes a self-fulfilling kind of thing. One dimension of this: everything one measures is supposed to have a bell-shaped curve when you're done. If I want to publish a test and after a group sample don't get a bell-shaped curve, what should I do? I tinker with the test until I do get a bell-shaped curve, even if it doesn't give me the right distribution.

Let's play the reading-intelligence relationship against some linguistic realities, now trying to differentiate reality from performance on intelligence tests and performance on reading tests. One statement can be made on the basis of decades of language research. You don't have to be smart to learn language. People at the widest possible range of intelligence learn to talk. They may not all be talking in equally wise ways, but they're all talking.

We have to be careful not to confuse reluctant performance with incompetence. Labov (1972) has demonstrated very well that kids labeled 'linguistically deficient' or the favorite phrase, 'nonverbal' may well be nonverbal only in situations where teachers are trying to get them to talk about school things, but their linguistic competence shows in other nonthreatening situations when they are communicating with each other. People talk about performances on the Illinois Test of Psycholinguistic Abilities. All the ITPA measures is performance on the Illinois Test of Psycholinguistic Abilities. It doesn't get at the language competence that the child has that he can make use of when he chooses to do so, or when he feels comfortable about using it.

Some things we thought we knew about language development have to do more with cognitive development. When a child begins to think conditionally he begins to speak conditionally and there isn't much conditional speech until he reaches a certain conceptual level. That may sound a little like a relationship between intelligence and language, but only in the sense that you don't start talking about some things until you understand them. But there is a great deal of the world that small children do think about and do begin to understand in their own ways and do begin to talk about in their own ways. What it amounts to is that almost no child is below the cognitive development level which is necessary for language to develop.

LEARNING THE LANGUAGE

'Language By Ear and By Eye' (Kavanagh and Mattingly, 1972) includes articles by people who think that what humans have a capacity to learn is speech and speech is language. Speech is the form of language most available to them and therefore the one they learn first. But the work that Ursula Bellugi (1970) has been doing with deaf children of deaf parents, who have a visual language available to them as a first language, has demonstrated that those kids can learn sign language as easily and effectively as any hearing child can learn to talk. She studied a deaf child who had an almost parallel language development pattern to hearing children.

It's *language* that children have the ability to learn. When we talk about oral and written language we have to understand that for most people, oral language comes first, but for literate people, written language is not a secondary representation of speech, it's an alternate language form. If one accepts the premise that humans take the most direct route to the information they're seeking, it's illogical that they would take the route of going from written language, to speech, to meaning when they can go from written language to meaning directly. The preoccupation with phoneme-grapheme correspondence or phonics in any form in reading instruction is at best a peripheral concern.

What we're trying to teach when we teach reading is how to get meaning from print. The fact that the child is already a competent language processor and knows how to get information through language is a help. He simply has not yet developed an alternate parallel mode of doing it. What he knows about language, however, is exactly the same. We have to stop treating written language as if it is not quite language.

In a literate society there are four language processes. Two are productive; two are receptive. Reading is no less a receptive language process than listening is, and as long as we continue to use terms like 'decoding' to mean, not going from language to meaning, but from one language representation to another, we're missing this basic point. That's not decoding; that's a kind of recoding. There are lots of kinds of recoding that you can do, but they don't get you to meaning. This misuse of decoding began from two sources: (1) the work of early linguists who believed oral language to be the most universal language experience, and (2) an old preoccupation with the idea that when you read you have to somehow say everything to yourself before you can process it, a very inefficient process and one that no reader really does, though some of them try because that's what they've been taught to do.

Language is always a means and never an end in itself. Nobody ever learned to talk because he wanted to; nobody ever learned to talk because it's fun to talk. Language is learned because you have ideas to communicate and because other people have ideas to communicate to you and also because it's a very convenient, useful medium for manipulating experience and developing concepts and representing them to yourself and to other people. When language is divorced from its use in communication, it becomes a set of abstractions; it becomes something that's much harder to learn. Verbal-learning researchers have reported that nonsense that looks like English is easier to handle than jumbles of letters that don't look like English. That's because the closer language is to its use, the closer it is to its basic relationship to meaning, the easier it is to handle, and the easier it is to learn.

Most reading tests fracture language, chop it into pieces, pull things out of their use, turn them into abstractions and then test the performance that kids employ to handle the much more difficult task. On the basis of their performance, the testers assume that they've learned something about the reading competence of the children involved. Teachers very often have important information to feed back to theoreticians and researchers about the puzzling kid in the third grade who has no trouble reading, but can't pass the unit test with the phonic and word attack skills. He can't do any of those things that he's supposed to need to do to get meaning from written language but he has no comprehension problems, and the teacher is so confused about it that she even says, 'But when he gets to the fifth grade he might have trouble.'

LEARN AS A WHOLE OR PART?

Language is indivisible: it ain't no salami that you can slice as thin as you want and still have all the pieces look like the whole salami. When you break it up, each piece not only changes its relationship to the whole but changes its physical characteristics.

Language is also learned from whole to part, from general to specific. Testers have followed an incorrect model partly because of the atomistic focus of many learning theorists that starts with parts and builds up to the whole. Rather, learners go from the general, move toward the precise from the whole, to a clear kind of information processing that makes it possible to handle very fine kinds of differences.

My conclusion is that you don't have to be smart to read. I think we have to ask ourselves seriously why if children learn to talk without our help, they don't learn to read with our help? One of the obvious answers is that we've been working against them instead of with them. Instead of facilitating the use of language as an information-processing system, we concentrate on language-like abstractions. In some systems, the child never encounters anything that makes sense until long after he's started something that's been called reading instruction. And then, if he has trouble dealing with the abstractions, we take him into remedial programs that are more abstract. The funny thing about this, which teachers again frequently report, is that the child who got it the first time didn't need the practice, and the child who didn't get it seems never to profit from the practice.

We teach and test word names as if that was what is important rather than how to get to meaning from written language. The word becomes an end in itself. Teachers say to me 'Yes, he read the story and he understood it, but I'm going to take him back through it because he didn't know all the words.' It would be a strange world if nobody attempted to read anything unless he knew all the words.

Why is it that, if I were to walk into a remedial reading class any place in this country, I could predict that well over 75 per cent of the children in that class would be boys? Do boys intrinsically have more of those things that get in the way of learning to read? Are they less intelligent than girls? Or does the way we teach reading put more of a strain on boys than on girls? I suggest that one of the problems is that we force kids to adjust to the way school does things, instead of adjusting the school to the way children do things. Our success of teaching reading depends not on the basis of their intelligence, but on the basis of how relevant school is and how willing or able they are to learn our way.

In another way, our teaching children to read may be a measure of their ability to overcome inadequate instruction. Nobody has devised a method of teaching reading that has succeeded in keeping even half the children from learning to read. I think a measure of tremendous language learning capability is that a six-year-old can surmount all the hurdles that we put in his way and still learn to read (but, that really fouls up reading research and clouds testing issues).

The need for reading is not as immediate or universal for all children as the need for speaking and talking. We have to help them see the immediate value of reading and writing as an alternative system to speaking and listening. We don't have to give children Green Stamps or candies to get them to learn to read unless what we're trying to get them to read is so irrelevant and has so little connection with any kind of reality that it has to be extrinsically rewarded. Language doesn't need extrinsic rewards. Communication is enough, understanding is enough. If you don't understand, you try it another way. Information seeking is a universal human acitivity that should be fostered in reading instruction.

We cut children off very often from their own language in the process of teaching them to read by confusing language difference with language deficiency. In some programs, when a child says something which he has known previously to be right, the teacher will say, 'No, dear, that's wrong.' The teacher holds up a pencil and says 'Is this a cup?' The child is supposed to say 'No, that is not a cup, that is a pencil.' If the child says, 'That ain't no cup,' that's a wrong answer; it's rejected. If language is rejected, then we frustrate and confuse the child at the point of his greatest strength. How can you build reading competence on language competence if we destroy the faith in the fact that he has it in the first place? If what sounds right to him is continually portrayed as being wrong (with a smile on the face or otherwise), there can only be confusion, and the nonverbal child is the child who's smart enough to know that if you shut up you are less likely to be criticized. The same thing happens in writing; after the third rewriting, when the composition is about half its original length, one concludes the less you say the fewer mistakes you make, if mistakes are to be punished.

WHY CAN HE READ?

Following the wrong learning theory in much reading teaching and testing leads to things I call pigeon-pecking programs. Skinner could easily teach a pigeon to peck when he sees 'peck' and not to peck when he sees 'don't peck.' But that's not reading, that's not language in the sense that humans have the ability to learn it.

After teaching children reading skills, you give them a reading skill test that is just like the instruction. If the children look good on the test, then 'the program works.' The problem is that nobody ever carries that to its logical extension bit by bit,

every little pigeon-pecking piece, until the millennium is
reached and the kid is a reader. Somehow in between, he
becomes a nonreader or he becomes a reader. How he becomes
a reader on that basis is never very clear, since the approach
never carries him far enough that it could complete its logical
development. It's a kind of behavioral stairway to nowhere
that's built - if the reader learns he must complete his own
stairway.

Without knowing much about language processes or how
experience and language are related, teachers who have empathy
for children and who are good observers realize that if you
start with children's experiences in their own language it is
easier to begin to talk about things that are relevant and meaningful and easier to begin reading instruction. Unfortunately,
these teachers have been vulnerable to people who say, 'Yes,
but how are you going to make sure they learn the skills?'
Teachers take a good idea and then try somehow to satisfy the
accountability people. They get so busy with the checklist
that they lose the good idea. Teachers shouldn't worry about
skill development as long as the process is whole and meaning
is kept in focus. Lewis Carroll said in 'Through the Looking
Glass,' 'Take care of the sense and the sounds will take care
of themselves.'

We've thought of reading in extremely naive ways. We
thought reading was a matter of seeing a word and naming it,
or when you came to a period you took all that stuff that you
stored, reviewed it, and said 'What does that say?' We failed
to see reading as a process that is continually trying to get to
the meaning: trying to make sense out of the experience one is
having with written language.

Do you have to read to be smart? Growing up in a literate
society does put some demands on people. Doors have 'exit'
over them. One of the things little boys are very eager to learn
is which door says 'men' and which door says 'women' because
until they do, they have to go with their mothers. That becomes
a measure of independence in a literate society. Maybe a better
place to begin reading instruction is by analyzing the things
that are most necessary and most universally require the ability
to read.

There isn't any doubt that written language isn't quite as
important as it once was. We have electronic ways of communicating over time and distance, making it possible to send messages,
the original purpose of written language. Through electronic
media, millions of six-year-old children have had experiences
that adults never had until they were much older.

You don't have to read to be smart, but it's pretty hard to be
fully functioning in this society without being able to read. And
that's one of the things children discover who have trouble with
learning to read in school. You can preserve your self-image
and be a good guy anyway and even live a fairly good life without being a terrific reader.

A problem regarding the role of reading in learning is that we let ourselves romanticize and overrate the literature function of written language. The basic function of written language is not literature; that's a kind of secondary benefit that you get from it. Certainly, if you get a child interested in a good book that he wants to finish, it's going to help him in developing his reading ability. A more basic question is being able to use reading to learn. There's a general practice that's almost as old as the printing press that I call the 'here-read-and-learn' method. It's my second unfavorite next to the 'listen-to-me-talk-and-learn' approach, the lecture system. The view somehow is that all learning can take place through reading, once one has mastered the reading process. This view is reflected in the fact that high school teachers say those junior high teachers didn't do a good job, and the junior high teachers say if those elementary teachers had taught the child to read they wouldn't have any trouble.

I would like to suggest that everybody is functionally illiterate to some extent. Ability to read and understand anything depends very much on what the reader brings to that particular reading situation. I get graduate students who come up to me saying they tried to read Chomsky in the original with no success. My answer to them is 'You have a reading problem,' which startles them a little. But it is, in fact, a reading problem. If you can't understand what you're reading, you have a reading problem. Of course, this has to do with appropriateness, and the kind of background the teacher provided before he says 'Read chapter four in your social studies book.' It has to do with thinking through what kinds of concepts are being dealt with in the reading material, and then asking what a person would have to know to be able to get knowledge from that.

I'm not supporting the elimination of instruction through reading; rather, I'm supporting the idea that one can learn a limited amount through reading – the limit being the background the learner brings to that particular reading situation. Getting smart isn't simply being able to read. We have to be very careful that we understand the function of written language in learning in order to even begin to get at this question.

When the teacher says that if the child hasn't learned to read by the time he's in the fourth grade, he's going to be a failure in school, what he's really saying is that by the time a child is in fourth grade, if he can't read and learn on his own, he's in trouble. It's the child who can overcome that handicap we label a success. The view is unfair and a rather naive one in terms of what a general reading ability would mean to anybody's ability to learn anything. There are special strategies that have to be developed to help people to use special kinds of language. It's very interesting to see adults reading maps, for instance; it's not a universal reading ability.

I've been very negative throughout much of this, so I'd like to propose a more positive alternative. Test misuse has reached a level that would justify a five-year moratorium on such tests. Test makers won't drop the bad tests and really begin to develop tests that have some sound basis until we stop buying the bad tests. It's a very simple economic question. They are profit-making corporations and they are not about to stop publishing something that is still selling.

Another thing is focusing on the child's immediate need for literacy – not only to help children become better readers, but also help them to become smarter since language and learning are in the proper intertwined relationship. We should follow the axiom: no language without experience and no experience without language. If we keep the focus, not on some future need, but on immediate payoff in reading now, then we have self-motivation.

We also have to use real language as naturally as possible so children can deal with it the way they have already learned to process language. The differences between written and oral language are based more on their use than on any intrinsic differences between the processes. We have to keep language together and not fragment it, not break it into pieces. From the very beginning, the child needs to be reading whole, relevant, interesting language that makes sense.

We have to start with vital kinds of things, mundane kinds of things, like what the sign says on the ladies' room and the men's room, and move toward the wide range of uses that written language makes possible. We have to keep reading in the context of the information the child is seeking – that is meaning. He's processing language, but he's thinking meaning and that's the significant thing about keeping it in a meaning context. The more children learn how to read, the more they're going to learn through reading.

I want to finish with a very profound question in terms of the teachers who are out on the firing line of trying to teach children how to read. How do you know the child is making progress in learning to read? It's a question I get asked from teachers who are trying to shift away from traditional to more soundly based kinds of reading approaches. I answer the question with a question. How do you know a child is learning to talk? The answer is that if he makes himself understood, he's learning to talk. If he understands what somebody says to him, he's learning to listen with understanding. We expect children to express a wider and wider range of ideas successfully and to understand a wider and wider range of language. So, you also know a child is making progress in reading if he understands a wider and wider range of written language.

REFERENCES

Bellugi, Ursula (1970), Reported at Michigan, Applied Linguistics Conference, Ann Arbor, Michigan.

Kavanagh, James F., and Ignatius G. Mattingly (eds), (1972), 'Language By Ear and By Eye,' Cambridge, Mass.: MIT Press.
Labov, William (1972), Academic Ignorance and Black Intelligence, 'Atlantic Monthly' (June), pp. 59-67.
Venezky, Richard, Robin Chapman, and Aichen Ting (1971), 'The Effect of Mode of Elicitation in Articulation Testing,' Wisconsin Research and Development Center, Technical Report 154.

'Never in the history of education have reading tests enjoyed as much status as they do today.'

'No test, however cleverly it's constructed, can substitute for the insights which professional teachers can get from working closely with children.'

This article provides a comprehensive treatment of the problems, limitations, and abuses of reading tests. It provides much food for thought and raises many important questions and issues dealing with test design and use, both now and in the future.

26 TESTING IN READING: A General Critique

Never in the history of education have reading tests enjoyed as much status as they do today. They provide a data base used increasingly as a means (often the sole means) of evaluating pupil progress, teacher effectiveness, and program success. They are used in research studies to compare methods and materials. They are linked by law in several states with special or basic state support for the schools. Schools and school systems are publicly compared on the basis of rankings of pupil populations on reading tests. Election campaigns often center on pupil performance on reading tests. Publishers and private contractors are sometimes paid on the basis of student performance on reading tests.

It is always desirable to re-evaluate the evaluators we use from time to time. With so many crucial educational decisions being based on reading tests, this re-evaluation becomes urgent.

USES OF READING TESTS

Above, reference has been made to some of the current uses of reading tests. Only two basic uses of reading tests are legitimate. They are as follows:

1 To measure the effectiveness with which any person uses reading to comprehend written language. Within this, the two main concerns are (a) flexibility in comprehending a wide range of materials and (b) degree of proficiency as compared to other readers or as compared to some absolute scale of proficiency in comprehending written language.
2 To diagnose the strengths and weaknesses of readers as an aid to planning instruction which will help to make them more effective.

Testing for each purpose will vary depending on the theory of the reading process, and of reading acquisition which the tester uses. In some cases, readiness tests will be used if the tester believes that there are nonreading tasks that must be mastered as prerequisites to successful acquisition of reading.

A major weakness of current reading tests is a failure to articulate views of the reading process and of learning to read as a basis for building the tests, subtests, and test items.

Tests are often built on eclectic traditions of what is important in reading and learning to read. These are sometimes
derived directly from popular instructional reading programs;
but just as often the instructional programs derive their ration-
ale from the tests on the theory that if something is commonly
tested it must be important. This misuse of tests results in a
self-justifying cycle that institutionalizes tradition.

That cycle tends to block progress in improvement of reading instruction through the application of new insights from
research, theory, and practice. The tester says we must test
what is being taught; and the teacher says we must teach what
is being tested. Innovation programs are judged on the basis of
performance by pupils on traditional tests which incorporate
the same faults that the new programs seek to overcome in old
programs.

Since tests grow from tradition rather than articulated theory,
they develop subtests with large areas of overlap, while leaving gaping holes that are not tapped at all.

The successful reader is treated as a possessor of bundles
of skills rather than as a user of written language. Traditional
semilogical, sequencing criteria and hierarchical arrangements
are imposed on these skills which are isolated, for ease in
testing, out of any context of language use which they may
have.

In the absence of a strong base in reading theory, current
reading tests substitute sophisticated test theory. Surrounded
by norms, percentiles, measures of significance and other
statistical armor, the tests give an impression of scientific
validity which conceals their hollow cores.

Tests, any tests, will produce statistical results with populations that take them. These results can be mathematically
manipulated. By adjusting the test items on the basis of the
statistics they produce, one may achieve neater statistical
patterns. But in fact one may never draw conclusions whose
significance goes beyond the validity of the assumptions on which
the test is based.

Criterion-referenced tests, those which measure achievement
of stated goals rather than comparing to a statistical norm, are
even more in need of being rooted in a strong theory. In reality,
they tend to be selected skills arbitrarily sequenced.

Statistical fallacies in reading testing
There are a number of key statistical fallacies that are widely
incorporated into justifications for misuses of reading tests.
A few will be explored here.

Norming over diverse populations. Sophisticated test theory
dictates that norms or percentiles should be developed by
administering the test to a structured sample of the general
school population. Care is taken to include the right proportion
of urban, suburban and rural pupils, white, black and other;

east, west, north and south, and so on. These national norms
on percentiles are then published. The implication is that the
text is valid for use nationally. Though test-makers often suggest that schools may wish to use regional or local norms, there
is a clear implication that individual pupils, classes, schools and
districts may be usefully compared to the national norms.

But now let us introduce just one condition. Suppose that the
tasks and questions on the tests are selected so that they favor
one group (white, suburban, middle-class eastern pupils) over
all others. This could be the result of choosing to deal with
experiences and concerns more common among the favored
group. Differences between groups then would be at least partly
the result of the relative relevance of the test and not any
actual difference in reading effectiveness. Furthermore, simply
using local norms would not remedy this problem, since pupils'
scores would reflect the degree to which they matched the
favored group in background. Now add to this problem regional
and social dialect differences, and the justification for national
use of the test through a structured sample is even more highly
suspect. Only if the test-maker argues that in fact all pupils
should be judged by the degree to which they compare to a
high-status group is such norming justifiable, and such a
judgment involves value questions that cannot be answered
statistically.

The importance of small variations in test performance.   The
statistical treatment of raw scores on reading tests makes it
possible to equate them to grade placement – the grade of the
average pupil who achieved the score in the norming trials.

Since the test must use a limited number of items because
of time considerations, the differences, particularly at the
upper and lower ends of the scale between the average score
in two adjacent grades, may be only a few items. One more
question right can add several months to the grade equivalence
of a pupil. Consider this in relation to the relevancy questions
raised above and it is clear that a slight bias against a group
can explain statistically significant differences in group means.

Sky-hooks, split-halves, etc.   To cope with questions of
whether tests are testing what they should and doing it consistently, a number of statistical devices have been employed.
One used particularly for new tests is to correlate them with
other older tests. If a high correlation is achieved, then validity
is assumed. However, if the new test is in fact measuring what
the old test did, then why is a new test needed? And if the new
test employs new insights, why expect it to correlate with the
old? This sky-hook method of anchoring tests to each other
clearly says nothing about the extent to which reading is really
being tested. A current federally funded project seeks to
establish a new test to which all current tests could be correlated. Such a test, appropriately called an anchor test, would

surely anchor reading permanently to the past. Similarly, using split-half techniques to prove that a test is consistent within itself proves only a symmetry on whatever biases are built into the test and does not offer evidence about the value of the test.

Hard is hard but why is it hard?
Test theory requires that some items should be missed by most pupils, and some items by a few, with the rest of the items ranging in-between. Further, the high scorers should be the ones getting the hard items right, and the low scorers should be the ones getting the easy items wrong. Close examination of reading-test items reveals that the items are often difficult for irrelevant reasons: ambiguity, equally correct wrong alternatives, and so forth. The fact that few people get them right may indicate that they are hard, but it may also indicate that they are irrelevant or poorly written. The fact that the right pupils get them right may demonstrate more that high scorers are good at thinking like test writers than that they are better readers. Again, what is important is that statistical evidence cannot substitute for intrinsic criteria in judging the relevance or difficulty of items.

Related to this statistical fallacy is an artifact that results from weighting certain items by virtual repetition (a series of very similar items). A pupil tends to get all like items right or wrong if in reality his performance reflects knowledge or lack of knowledge. A minor lack becomes magnified into a major weakness. An example of this is the syllabication sections of certain tests.

Averaging ends and means
A statistical fallacy occurs in many reading achievement tests when an overall score is calculated which combines scores on 'skill' subtests with those on comprehension. Since skills are ostensibly the means by which comprehension (the end product of reading) is achieved, such a score is meaningless.

Counting in diagnosis
Statistics that produce summary scores are much easier to manipulate than those that relate to complex phenomena in detail. The effective use of diagnostic testing is often defeated by being more concerned with quantity of errors or a grade level equivalence, than with the specific phenomena revealed by performance on the reading tasks involved. Number of reading errors or items wrong gives little diagnostic information.

DESIGN PROBLEMS IN CONSTRUCTING READING TESTS

Aside from the statistical fallacies confusing test use and misuse, there are a number of design problems that test-makers have not yet solved adequately.

Convergence.   One of the most difficult design problems in writing tests is that there must always be a right answer. This leads to focus on convergent responses – on those that match the preconceptions of the test-maker. Two groups are hampered by such tests: culturally divergent groups whose experience does not match the testers, and creative thinkers who are able to see 'different' relationships. If you march to the beat of a different drummer, the test penalizes you.

Pupils who know too much.   Multiple choice responses are designed to mislead pupils with common misconceptions. Since a misconception is better than no concept at all, pupils are penalized for knowing a little and will be wrong more than chance would predict. Even worse off is the pupil who knows more than the test-maker. He will often reject the 'right' answer because he recognizes it as a misconception or over-simplification.

What they learn vs What they know.   In testing comprehension, it is easy to end up testing general knowledge. The pupil may be able to answer the questions without reading the test selec-tion. To overcome this problem requires a measure of prior knowledge or tests on material all pupils lack background for, The latter is a virtually impossible task.

How test-wise are the subjects?   Pupils vary greatly in their control of devices for scoring higher on tests. Only some pupils have learned simple devices like skipping troublesome items, quick identification of tasks, eliminating obvious wrong choices to narrow the range of possible options, going to questions without reading test paragraphs or answers without reading questions, and so forth. There appears to be no way to neutralize fully this effect, which is also linked with the pupil's basic desire to do well (or his indifference).

Honesty.   Related to the latter problem is one of honesty. This is a complex problem because many pupils avoid using techni-ques that would produce higher scores. They think that is like cheating. In fact, those who give reading tests often behave hypocritically. Test-makers discourage guessing, tell pupils to read each item before looking at the answers, refer to the tests with smaller children as 'a game we're going to play.' They tell pupils that the test is only to help them and that the score they make is unimportant.
    But in fact the score is the only part of the test in which the test-makers are interested, and decisions are made on the basis of the test scores, which may well affect the learner adversely – placement in a low track, for example. The pupil who is honest and trusting becomes a statistical victim.

How they do vs What they do. Since test-making involves counting right answers, there is a tendency in trying out test items to ignore the basis on which pupils respond to questions. In many cases, pupils are producing both wrong and right answers for the wrong reasons. Subtests turn out to be testing something quite different from what they claim to test. Auditory discrimination tests, for example, turn out to be testing largely the ability to deal with abstractions. Some pupils on such tests will resort to matching spelling patterns, producing a fair number of right answers without being able to abstract sounds from sound sequences.

Making the test clear. Pupils frequently do not understand what the task is that a particular subtest requires of them. It is quite likely that this accounts for a considerable amount of the variation of performance, particularly among younger children.

Distortion of tasks. Finding a format for test items that is suitable for inclusion in a group-administered reading test frequently results in a distortion of actual reading tasks. Some examples follows:

  1 *Items too short.* Research on reading miscues has demonstrated that short items are harder to read than longer ones because reading involves building up expectations on the basis of redundancies.[1] A sentence is proportionately harder to read than a paragraph, a paragraph harder than a page, and an isolated word hardest of all. Since short items predominate in tests (words, phrases, sentences), reading test items will be harder than reading stories or other natural materials.
  2 *Words in isolation* are particularly hard to 'read' because there are no grammatical cues from the sentence structure or meaning cues from the context to help identify the word meaning, yet many subtests deal with isolated words.
  3 *Comprehension questions that can be treated like nonsense.* Many questions are stated in such a way that readers may answer them by transforming the question to a statement and searching the text for a match without necessarily understanding. They manipulate the sentence patterns as if they were nonsense like the jabberwock. Q. What did the momeraths do? A. The momeraths outgrabe.

ABUSES OF TESTS

There are uses of tests that clearly violate the publisher's advice on limitations in their use.

One common, recent abuse is giving tests at too frequent intervals. Many requirements for reporting progress in reading

as often as once a month are built into contracts for research
or demonstration projects. In the name of accountability, tests
are being used to measure small increments of progress which
they are simply not designed to handle. Factors such as regression toward the mean (a tendency for high and low scores to
move toward the mean on repeated testing) become very important. Immediate, often temporary, results become more highly
valued than long-term, permanently held gains.

If jobs, funding, and professional status and pay are made
contingent on pupil performance on reading tests, then the tendency to teach to the test and to build curricula around the
test will become a major trend. Instead of the curricular goals
being centered around effective reading, the goals become
performance on specific tests. Instead of tests functioning as
a measure of achievement, they are turned into ends in themselves. Even if they had a sound theoretical base, that would
be unfortunate. In their current state, it could be tragic. It
could lead to a new kind of widespread functional illiteracy.

Another abuse of tests that we have touched on earlier is
the use of test scores without close examination of each pupil's
test performance. It is not enough to say Mary Lopez is reading on the 2.2 level. Her responses to subtests and items must
be examined closely so that her strengths and weaknesses
are revealed. Standardized reading tests are given wholesale
to masses of students. But their results must be interpreted
for each learner if they are to be useful in improving that
child's reading. Every child has a right to be treated as an
individual and not as a test statistic.

A related problem is the use of tests as exclusive means of
evaluating pupils' reading effectiveness, ignoring more
extensive evidence of competence because it is less easily
quantifiable. Teachers will frequently treat a low scorer on
a standardized test as a poor reader, even though they observe
him functioning as an adequate reader every day in class. The
quantifiable performance on tests is so intimidating to the
teacher that he will not trust his own professional judgment.

Often the pupils perform poorly on the test because it is
irrelevant to them and penalizes them for linguistic, experiential, and cultural differences (not deficiencies). Instead of
rejecting the test as irrelevant, wholly or partly, teachers and
administrators accept the test and misjudge the achievement,
strengths and weaknesses of the pupils. Programs are then
planned to remediate deficiencies that never really existed.

Other abuses of reading tests occur in evaluating new methods
and instructional materials. Frequently, little consideration is
given to the basic soundness of the method or the materials
or the principles on which the tests are based. Rather they are
judged largely by how well pupils do on pre- and post-tests.
While effective instruction must ultimately be judged by the
learning it produces, progress in improving instruction cannot
come by using a trial-and-error technique for evaluation. Not

all programs are worth trying, nor can the test results be usefully interpreted if the instructional program is not thoroughly
analyzed.

If instructional methods and materials are built around tests,
it is likely that pupils will improve their performance on the
tests. The most extreme version of this is to use the test items
as the instructional program, asking the pupils to respond
over and over until they produce right answers all or almost
all the time. This ability to do well on the test is then assumed
to prove learning has taken place because the learner now can
produce a test score characteristic of a proficient reader. Performance is assumed to reflect the reader's competence exactly,
no matter how it is produced.

What is not understood is that all behavior is the end product
of a process and that competence is not behavior, but control
over the process. Behavior, in the form of test performance,
can be used to infer what competence exists in reading, but
this requires an interpretation of the behavior based on understanding how reading works.

Deciding, on the basis of unexamined reading-test scores,
such vital aspects of the child's future as the class, group,
or track to which he will be assigned is a terrible abuse of
reading tests. It jeopardizes the pupil's future and does not
even offer a basis for improving his reading proficiency, since
pupils who are very different in reading may achieve similar
scores.

READING THEORY: KEY QUESTIONS TEST-MAKERS MUST ASK

The earlier parts of this paper have portrayed reading tests as
rather primitive, eclectic, and atheoretical in all aspects except
for their use of sophisticated test theory.

The questions reading test-makers must deal with to produce
better and more useful tests are clear; however, there is no
agreement yet on the answers.

Major questions that must be answered in building better tests
are (1) what is reading; (2) what are the essential skills and
strategies that a successful reader must possess; and (3) what
are the purposes and uses of reading? These will be considered
in order.

What is reading?
Elsewhere the author has stated that 'Reading is a complex process by which a reader reconstructs, to some degree, a message
encoded by a writer in graphic language.'[2]

Whether one accepts this definition, which carries with it the
concept that reading must result in meaning to be considered
reading, or some other definition, one must still base test construction on some coherent definition.

The following group of related questions must also be

answered:

1 Can reading skill (for example, matching letters to
sounds) be separated from the quest for meaning in teaching or testing?
2 At what point can reading as a process be separated from
its uses?
3 Does the reading process necessarily involve oral language at all, or is it entirely a matter of deriving meaning
from written language?
4 Is the reading process different at various stages of
development, or is it the same, varying mainly on the
effectiveness of the reader?
5 Is reading a general ability, or is it one that varies with
content, interest, or task within each reader depending on
his own background?
6 Is the reading process the same or different across people, languages, cultures, or orthographies?

Though there are implicit answers to these questions in many
current reading tests, it appears that the test-makers have
made assumptions often without considering the issues involved.

What are the essential skills and strategies that effective
readers possess?
Reading tests have generally employed subtests to get at what
are assumed to be essential reading skills and to monitor their
development. To justify such practice, the following questions
must be answered:

1 Can essential skills or strategies be isolated for testing
without changing their relative values, their basic uses,
or the reading tasks in which they occur?
2 Are such strategies or skills universal across people,
contexts, purposes, languages, and orthographies?
3 Is there an essential sequence in learning to read, i.e.
must some skills or strategies be learned before others?
4 How are reading skills or strategies to be understood in
terms of how language works and is used?

What are the purposes of reading?
Language, including reading, is always a means and never an
end in itself. This is true whether one is talking about the
proficient user or one just learning. Meaning, either its expression or comprehension, is always the end for which language
is the means.
Ultimately, then, any reading test must measure the success
of the reader in comprehending written language. It is meaningless to consider performance on skills tests a measure of
reading achievement. What counts at all stages of development
is what the reader understands as a result of reading.

Test-makers must be concerned with the following questions:

1 What is comprehension; how does it work, how is it achieved, how varied is it?
2 What different problems face the reader who is reading to acquire knowledge, as compared to one who is reading for a message already within his conceptual grasp?
3 What role does the reader's background and interest play in successful reading?
4 How does critical reading differ from other reading?

FUTURE READING TESTS

Diagnostic reading tests in the future will need to focus on reading as it really occurs in natural language. This suggests the type of task now found in informal reading inventories. But the diagnostic test of the future will be designed so that the strengths as well as the weaknesses of learners will be made clear. A shift will need to be made away from counting errors to analysis of performance, to get at the underlying competence.

Achievement tests will need to deal with comprehension in a range of reading situations. They will need to avoid irrelevance. And they will need to get at the reader's ability to use written language effectively. Group tests may well disappear. They sacrifice too much for the sake of economy of time.

Still, however, the main improvement needed in the area of testing is in use. No test, however cleverly it is constructed, can substitute for the insights professional teachers get from working closely with children.

NOTES

1 D. Menosky, A Psycholinguistic Description of Oral Reading Miscues Generated during the Reading of Varying Portions of Text by Selected Readers from Grades Two, Four, Six and Eight, doctoral dissertation, Wayne State University, 1971.
2 Kenneth S. Goodman and Olive S. Niles, 'Reading Process and Program,' Urbana, Ill.: National Council of Teachers of English, 1970, p. 5.

This is a modern parable that 'illustrates the poverty of logic behind the attempt to solve fundamental educational problems through legislatively mandated minimal competencies.' It concludes with some positive suggestions for professional educators.

27 MINIMUM COMPETENCIES:
A Moral View

'I've got a problem' said the student. 'I don't read very well.
I think my writing is awful. I'm not too good at arithmetic
either. I'm going to graduate from high school soon. Can anyone help me?'

'I know you've got a problem' said the teacher. 'I've got one,
too. I've done the best I could to teach you. But you just
haven't achieved very much. And you're not the only one. I
wish someone would help me.'

'I wish I could help you with your problem,' said the administrator. 'I've got one, too. The low achievement in your class
is reflecting badly on me. I've provided you with materials,
remedial specialists, inservice education but it hasn't helped.
I wish someone could help me solve this problem.'

'We'll help,' said the state legislature.

'Great,' said the student.

'Marvelous,' said the teacher.

'I'm saved,' said the administrator.

'We'll solve the problem,' said the legislature. 'We'll make sure
that no student ever graduates from high school without minimum competencies in the basics. There'll be no illiterates graduating from our schools.'

'Terrific!' said the student. 'How will you make sure I get
those minimum competencies?'

'We'll make the administrator accountable,' said the legislature.

'Accountable!' said the administrator.

'From now on you must test all graduating seniors. If they
can't pass the basics at tenth grade level we won't let you give
them high school diplomas. And you may not promote anyone
from the ninth grade who scores below sixth grade in the
basics,' said the legislature.

'Did you hear that?' said the administrator to the teacher.
'I'm holding you accountable for getting those students ready
for the test.'

'But how will I do that?' said the teacher to the administrator.
'I've picked up some new ideas from my in-service class. Shall
we try them?'

'Nothing of the sort' said the administrator to the teacher.
'Too much is at stake here. This is no time to try new ideas.
Forget the frills, too. We've got work to do.'

'Frills?' said the teacher. 'What do you mean by frills?'

'Anything that's not on the test,' said the administrator.

'Back to basics,' he said, 'and that's an order.'

'Now, then,' said the teacher to the student, 'let's get at
your problem. Put your book away, we've got some exercises
to do.'

'I think I've got two problems now,' said the student.

This modern parable illustrates the poverty of logic behind
the attempt to solve fundamental educational problems through
legislative mandated minimum competencies. In such attempts
competency is equated with test performance, the curriculum
is narrowed and totally dominated by the tests, latitude for
professional judgment by administrators and teachers is min-
imized, innovation and application of new insights and methodology are made impossible, and the student is doubly punished
for the failure of the whole educational system. And in all
this there is no seeking of causes, no concern for analyzing
problems, no applications of research or theory, no new solutions.

This is not to say that the effort is not a sincere one. Surely
the advocates of mandated minimum competencies have the best
interests of students as their goals. But such mandates are
nonetheless unfortunate. They aggravate the problem, placing
unbearable pressure on teaching and learning while offering
no positive help.

The effectiveness of minimum competency testing depends on
the truth of some or all of five propositions:

1 Failure to achieve is due to a lack of school standards.
2 Student failure is largely the result of lack of teacher
concern for student success, or teacher mediocrity or both.
3 Solutions for teaching-learning problems are built into
current, traditional materials and methods.
4 Test performance is the same as competence; furthermore,
existing tests can be used for accurate individual assessment and prediction.
5 If students are required to succeed they will.

None of these propositions, however, is true. The whole
attempt to help learners through mandated minimum competencies turns into an attempt to blame someone for the failure of
the system.

It's time for professional educators to reject such attempts
as destructive and unsuccessful and to put the focus back
where it belongs - on seeking real substantive solutions to
real problems.

We must study the students who are not succeeding, not just
test them. We must examine curricula, methodology, theory
and classroom practice, not just students. We must build
objectives relevant to learners and consistent with scholarship,
not simply mandate standards.

In the field of reading this all means seeing the problems of
literacy in the context of what we know about the uses and

learning of language. It means finding linguistic strength even in the system's losers. It means helping reading teachers to be more competent, not treating them as untrustworthy incompetents. And it means taking the lid off the pressure cooker of mandated minimum competencies before it blows off.

GENERAL EDUCATIONAL ISSUES

This is a satirical look at the fascinating exercise in logic involved in the attempt to solve school problems with performance contracts. The author predicted with accuracy that performance contracting would lose popularity quickly because it offered no new inputs into solutions of educational problems and because there is no substantial profit to be made in performance contracting.

28 PROMISES, PROMISES

'It's not so much the input that counts as the output'; so said the San Diego Schools' leading authority on performance contracts in a conversation with this writer recently.

This is a rather remarkable but succinct distillation of the arguments in favor of performance contracts as a solution to school problems. Implicit in it are a number of assumptions: (1) *The ends justify the means.* Means are in fact not to be considered except in terms of evidence that they do indeed work. Validity, soundness of basic premises, theoretical assumptions, consistency with research, all are to be left to the contractor. (2) *Any unplanned, incidental effects on learners are not of importance.* As long as the ends are spelled out as behavioral goals and the contractor promises to achieve those goals; never mind the bed-wetting, self-esteem, anti-social acts, or effects on other areas of learning. Such concerns are 'fuzzy-minded.' (3) *Besides it's easier to stipulate end products than a program to achieve them.* (4) *Educators have no input worth considering* (other than choosing whose promises to believe) and teachers in particular, by virtue of past failures, have forfeited the right to make educational decisions. They are to become efficient technicians, trained just enough to carry through the contractor's program but not enough to interfere with it. In fact a pep rally might be better than in-service training since the main thing is that teachers have faith in and enthusiasm for the program.

Performance contracts in reading represent a fascinating exercise in logic. (1) We do not know how to teach black children to read, likewise chicanos. (2) Furthermore, nothing we have ever tried has been effective in substantially improving the reading achievement of black and chicano pupil populations. (3) Therefore, we will seek bidders to accomplish this hitherto unaccomplished task. (4) We will accept those bidders who make the most definite promises, stated most unequivocally. (5) However, promises can be broken. Hence, we will require them to agree that, if they cannot keep their promises, they are to forfeit part of their profit. (6) A promise made, backed by a willingness to risk loss of payment, is a promise kept. Note: if, however, the contractor will not agree to take the risk, we will accept his promises anyway. (7) The unsolved problems of teaching black and chicano children to read will be resolved.

Since no new input is necessary, implicit in this logic are the assumptions that: (1) Reading programs have been unsuccessful before because the publishers did not make promises (or at least sincere ones) (2) Threats of loss of profit were absent in past relationships between publishers and educators and/or (3) Speculators have been quietly sitting with the key to reading instruction waiting for the advent of performance contracting at which point they will surface, make promises, fulfill them and live profitably ever after and/or (4) The solutions to problems in reading instruction are self-evident and all that is necessary is for a business organization to systematize the instruction. (5) Non-profit agencies have not been able to provide funds sufficient to provide successful reading programs, but profit making agencies will do so, and make a profit besides, using the same revenue sources.

The possible applications of the performance contract to other human problems using this logic are limitless. For example: (1) *Crime*. Government agencies sign performance contracts with private companies to eliminate, or alleviate to a specified level, the criminal behavior in a given community. The ends-means or input-output assumption may require that certain prior practices such as assumption of innocence, right to privacy, constitutional liberties be permanently or temporarily set aside. But after all, past efforts have certainly not reduced crime and no one would argue with the goals. (2) *Health*. The applications of the performance contract to human health problems boggle the mind. A community could enter into contracts for cures to diseases such as cancer. One can also foresee a governmental agency or citizens group entering into a performance contract with a patent medicine supplier to halt an epidemic. If the contractor fails to meet the objectives he forfeits his profits. Even an individual might agree with his physician to a performance contract. For example if he is suffering from a heart condition the doctor might contract to keep him alive for X years. A sliding scale could be developed whereby the physician receives only part payment if the patient dies in less than X years. Quacks should not be excluded from bidding since output, not input, is what matters. What could be more reassuring to a patient, as he goes into an operating room than that his doctor will receive no compensation if the operation is unsuccessful. That would surely be a prime example of accountability. (3) *Space*. How much more secure those astronauts would have been at the time of the explosion in their space vehicle if that vehicle had been built under a performance contract. Furthermore, the expense of the huge NASA staff could be greatly reduced if input were no longer a concern and only output mattered. We could leave it to the contractor to deal with all input trivia secure in the knowledge that faced with a loss of his profits he would not promise what he could, in fact, not achieve. (4) *War*. The Pentagon, the State Department and three administrations have not been able to achieve the goal of ending the Vietnam War. Performance contracts could be let that would end the war by a specific date with no more than X

American casualties, no less than Y enemy casualties and no
more than W new areas of military involvement. (Again out-
moded considerations such as bans on the use of chemical and
bacteriological warfare might be ignored as long as the end was
achieved.) In fact we might contract out all American involvement in international problems. To be fair we could give one
company the Middle East, another the Soviet Union; still another
could guarantee to cope with Red China. After that why not
divorce, drugs, child raising, the Generation Gap. And then,
why not - why do we need elected officials? Why not a performance contract to run the country? Too complex? OK, we will
break it up. Separate performance contract to run each cabinet
level department. Think of the savings on Congress alone which
has demonstrated by its past performance its inability to handle
the job.

The author prefers to bid on the Treasury and promise a
balanced budget, lower taxes, and a reduced national debt. He
will get 2 per cent if he succeeds and 1 per cent if he does not.

This paper is an informative fantasy of a 'military-industrial conspiracy to capture control of education in America.' It was written following Goodman's participation in a USOE evaluation of federally funded Educational Laboratories and Research and Development Centers.

29 MILITARY-INDUSTRIAL THINKING FINALLY CAPTURES THE SCHOOLS!

I'm known among my close friends as a reasonably sane guy. But lately I've been having this wild paranoia. I fancy that there is a military-industrial conspiracy to capture control of education in the USA. Now don't laugh.

I imagine state legislatures imposing an industrial cost accounting system on the schools of their states. I hear initials like PPBS and it seems to me that someone is trying to cost out education on cents per unit of information added per learner.

Thoughts of military sounding 'systems approaches' overwhelm my reason. I think that government agencies are pressuring school administrators to regiment teachers and pupils so that time, space, movement, deployment of staff, allocation of materials, decision-making procedures, and authority all take on a precision characteristic of a military manual or a Ford production schedule.

In this dementia I seem to read technological treatises that offer feasibility studies for the replacement of human teachers with computers and technology.

When I sleep I dream of schools turned over to private industry at so much per head. I see long lines of curriculum directors happily waiting to be next to contract out their responsibilities to Xerox, General Learning, or Westinghouse. I see deans of colleges of education marching under the AACTE banner gleefully dismantling their curricula while they build modules and mini-modules. Student teachers turn before my eyes into look-alike, sound-alike teachers who are doing the same thing at the same time in look-alike classrooms peopled with look-alike, sound-alike children.

I thought I had myself convinced that this was all the result of my own anxieties, produced by an undigested late evening off-campus workshop. But then I had a weird hallucination. It was so vivid, I cannot yet make myself believe that it didn't really happen.

In my 'trip' it began with an invitation from NCERD (National Center for Educational Research and Development), a subsidiary of USOE (United States Office of Education), to join a panel of outside 'experts' to evaluate the educational labs and R&D centers. We were to recommend whether their efforts were of value and whether they should receive the funds they were seeking for the following year. My panel's area of responsibility was 'curriculum.'

You will understand how absurd it is for me to believe in the reality of this fantasy when I tell you that NCERD, after organizing a 'systems approach' to the whole evaluation process, self-destructed. We were, however, subsequently contacted by a new group, the Task Force on Labs and Centers, National Institute of Education. Mysteriously their address is 'Code 600.'

The curriculum programs we dealt with ranged from aesthetics to computer programing. Several dealt with math. A number focused on reading and other aspects of language arts. One proposed to spend one million dollars in the next five years on children's folklore. (Now that surely couldn't be, since the world hasn't spent that much on studying children's folklore in all time.)

Three of these PPBS's were entire lab or center programs. One stands out even against this surrealistic background: The Southwest Regional Laboratory (SWRL is its acronym. How could that be real?).

SWRL HAS A SYSTEM

SWRL had just moved into its four million dollar building. SWRL has a system. It is producing a text that describes the documented experience of construction of their building. It applies the 'principles of "construction management" and "fast tracking" to the planning and construction of a facility dedicated exclusively to the conduct of educational research and development' (SWRL, p. 76). This building cost slightly less than $100 per square foot of floor space to build. 'Sample forms and procedures for every stage from defining the appropriate planning principles to scheduling the move-in will also be provided,' the description says (SWRL, p. 76).

SWRL has a system. Its PPBS contains an eight-page document, 'SWRL Documentation Guidelines.' 'If documentation is to be an aid not an aversion, the function and flow of various kinds of documents must be clearly specified' (SWRL Appendix B, p. 1). All forms of documentation from personal correspondence through the technical memorandum to official reporting documents are covered. Every professional paper or article must be reviewed by the division head or director.

SWRL had its inspiration from Systems Development Corporation (SDC) which, like RAND, is a creature of the Pentagon set up as a private corporation to work on Pentagon problems.

At SWRL, R&D activities 'are essentially a sequence of trial-revision interactions with modification after each test to successively approximate the consequence being sought' (SWRL, p. 21). Trial-revision interactions must mean something other than trial and error because who would give $17 million over seven years for trial and error?

Unfortunately the documentation dealing with trial-revision interactions did not clarify the matter. Development of products

at SWRL goes through seven stages: (1) *Formulation*, outcomes
are identified and strategies for producing methods and materials to achieve outcomes are designed. (2) *Prototype*, potential
strategies are tried under contrived but representative conditions. (3) *Component*, a segment is tried in a natural setting.
(4) *Product*, combinations of components are tried out and
revised until acceptable performance levels are attained. (5)
Installation, programs are combined with existing school instruction to become operational. (6) *Manufacturing*. (7) *Marketing*.
These last two bring a commercial corporation into the picture
(SWRL, pp. 22-3). In the case of the kindergarten program,
that corporation is Xerox. Xerox owns Ginn and University
Microfilms and publishes 'My Weekly Reader' and 'The School
Library Journal.'

The long-range product of SWRL, says my boggled mind, is
the school of Vonnegut's 'Player Piano.' In SWRL's new facility
they can modify the 'prevailing school ecology' and become a
developmental bridge from 'the present group-based teacher-
generated system' to an 'individual-based, computer-generated
instructional system' (SWRL, p. 42).

The kindergarten program is the only one of SWRL's products,
after seven years, that has reached the manufacturing or
marketing stages. Those in the installation stage are: Speech
Articulation, Language and Concepts for Spanish Speakers,
and the Learning Mastery Systems for three reading programs.

The installation phase is a 'holding pattern' waiting for
manufacturing.

Like the aerospace industry it emulates, SWRL gets additional
appropriations every year by asserting its system is economical
even when the costs of its products mount higher and higher
and never seem to fly.

Says SWRL, their products differ from 'extant products not
in terms of superficial appearances but in terms of demonstrated
effectiveness. Effectiveness is not veiled in mysticism, it is
gauged in terms of the utility of a given outcome, the reliability
with which the outcome is produced, and the *time* and *cost*
required to produce it' (SWRL, italics theirs, p. 7). In my
befuddled condition I was glad to hear that SWRL would avoid
mysticism. Still it remained a mystery what the cost of any
particular product had been up to the current stage of its
development.

KINDERGARTEN: OFF AND AWAY!

The one product that is flying and for sale is the kindergarten
program. SWRL and Xerox have an interesting new marketing
technique. 'School districts will be assisted in implementation
of new products as part of a federally supported incentive
program' (SWRL, p. 69). School systems are being given federal
funds to install the SWRL program because it is proven 'cost-

effective.' But if that's so why are special funds needed?

The efficiency of SWRL programs is shown in this comment about SWRL's new 'broader area of training systems': 'when teacher training and skill requirements are program specific, training for year-long programs can be accomplished very briefly, often in less than a day' (SWRL, p. 70). Riddle: What is it that a teacher can learn to teach in a day that will last a year? Answer: The SWRL Kindergarten Instructional Concepts and Beginning Reading Program.

Not only teachers but paraprofessionals, parents, and child tutors from older grades are also easily trained to teach the program.

In my vivid hallucination I saw a California kindergarten room where a Distar-like program was being used by a variety of teachers and tutors. Only the fourth-grade tutors were distinguishable from the other instructors. They were smaller. If a pupil failed to respond in the way the program said he should the instructor gave him another chance. Neither teacher, paraprofessional, nor tutor showed any ability to consider why he might not be responding as the program said he should and no instructor chose to vary the sequence or method. The pupils were treated equally, as if they were alike and inter-changeable with the same attention span.

The cost-effectiveness of the program was doubtful unless one visualized replacing expensive college-trained teachers with cheaper paraprofessionals or free parent volunteers.

Concern for superficial behavior stands out in this program. So does a confusion of technology with science. Playing school is equivalent with teaching and the whole is reminiscent of a Rube Goldberg device with great amounts of motion and energy being expended for no useful end. How many PMY's (SWRL's unit of staff is a 'professional man year') and how many dollars has it taken to turn a kindergarten into a Rube Goldberg cartoon? Only SWRL's computer knows.

My paranoia is almost complete. I'm talking as if all this really exists, really was experienced by me.

SWRL has another marketable package, it's Learning Mastery System. This is a manual version of the 'knowledge generated by the laboratory in developing computer-based systems to provide instructional management capability' (SWRL, p. 35).

The LMS has been applied so far to three reading programs on the state adoption list in California. It turns them all into rigidly sequenced skill programs starting with phonics and leading eventually to comprehension though the teacher is advised to stop at the phonics if that's all he has time for. My uncontrollable mind now sees a vision from a Greek myth; the bed of Procrustes appears. If the guest is too short his host stretches him, if too tall he cuts off his feet.

SWRL can eliminate the difference between reading programs making them all alike and providing instant quantitative data about how well the developing reader fits the measurements of the Procrustean bed.

SWRL is not the only system oriented, technology worshipping, dehumanized organization in education today. It is just the epitome, the distillation to a pure form.

ENTER: ACCOUNTABILITY

SWRL is a prototype for NIE (National Institute of Education) which now has been created to manage all federally funded educational research and development.

The design for NIE was done by Roger Levien from RAND Corporation. The director of NIE is Thomas Glennan who spent eight years at RAND Corporation and whose degrees are in electrical engineering, industrial management, and economics. As deputy director of OEO, he sponsored the voucher plan which promised a marketing bonanza to franchise school operations.

In state after state, cost accounting based on legally mandated tests and industrial management systems is being required as the basis for part or all of state funding.

Schools in Michigan getting special state money for low achievers in reading must use a management control system starting with pretesting at school entrance. They must guarantee a month's progress in reading for each month a child is in school as measured by 'criterion' referenced tests.

In Arizona the law now says any pupil graduating from high school must score above the ninth grade norm on a standardized test.

From Florida to California, legislatures are forcing schools to translate curriculum into lists of behavioral objectives and to provide precisely quantified data on pupils' performance on tests of these trivia which are then equated with learning.

Accountability means that Big Brother is getting his systems ready to watch and control us all from birth to death. Even one's dealings with God are not immune. In Brooklyn the Catholic Diocese has set up a system of accountability for priests. The system will furnish the priest and his superiors with information on his performance, improve his effectiveness, and be the basis for transfers, reassignments, and special ministries (George Dogan, 'New York Times,' May 28, 1972, quoted in NCTE, 'Council-Grams,' September 1972).

One could visualize eventually the priest like the teacher being replaced by 'computer generated systems.'

What would you think of a computer terminal confessional? It would certainly eliminate the human variance the priest introduces in dealing with sin. And it could remind a confessant of all his past sins in specific detail.

I've met Big Brother in education. His name is SAM (Student Achievement Monitoring). The state superintendent in Michigan has great hopes for SAM. If all goes well, long before 1984 one may have SAM report exactly what performance criteria any child in Michigan (or even further if other states employ SAM) has mastered in any school subject up to that very day.

To accomplish this the schools in Michigan are being given lists of sequenced skills in each subject which must be mastered each year. Reading, language arts, English, all will be treated the same. Data will be fed into the computer on a continuous basis. SAM will know and because SAM will know all children will master skills or at least that's the way the theory goes.

My paranoia has produced a sense of outrage that I fancy is shared by many. I see an opposition to the military-industrial cabal forming.

I have another dream and in it I see educationists, academicians, teachers, parents, and kids massing for a huge demonstration of resistance. There's a philosopher with a sign which reads, 'Where have all the values gone?'

Here comes a group of parents marching under a banner that says, 'The Child Buyer can't have our children. They're not for sale!'

Following is the whole faculty of a public school whose sign says: 'The Open School Shall Overcome.'

But stretching as far as the eye can see are kids of every size and shape and color. No two are the same. A disadvantaged group stops to burn their Hostess Twinkies sold by ITT as cost-effective and nutritionally balanced to the OEO School Breakfast Program. And still more thousands of kids march along, joyfully out of step, and as they march they shout, 'Power to the Pupils!'

REFERENCES

National Council of Teachers of English (1972), 'Council-Grams,' vol. 33, no. 4, September.
Southwest Regional Laboratory (SWRL) (1972), 'Program Plan: Systems for Comprehensive Educational Programs,' Inglewood, California: The Laboratory, March.

Originally this open letter was the text of Goodman's keynote
address to the National Language Arts Conference of the
National Council of Teachers of English in Indianapolis, March,
1978. It took the form of a response to President Carter's
education program for 1978. The open letter was widely circu-
lated and reprinted. No response has been received from
Mr Carter.

30 THE PRESIDENT'S EDUCATION PROGRAM: A Response

Kenneth Goodman's address to the NCTE-sponsored National Language Arts Conference (Indianapolis, March 10-12, 1978) was a response to President Carter's education program for 1978. Goodman's letter was enthusiastically received by conference participants; it was mailed with the endorsement of the Elementary Section Committee and with some 300 signatures gathered at the conference. The text of the letter is printed below.

Dear Mr President,

Last week as I was preparing to address the Elementary Language Arts Conference of the National Council of Teachers of English, you announced your education program for 1978. The morning after the newspaper and television networks reported your statement, an Australian graduate student came rushing into my office in a state of great agitation. 'I just can't understand it,' he said. 'I thought this morning the papers would be full of angry responses from educators to the President's statement and there's not a word. I'll never understand American politics,' he added.

I must confess that I was a little surprised too that the wire services and networks had regarded the education message as so non-controversial that they hadn't bothered to contact educators for their reactions.

I was even more dismayed when, a few days later at your press conference, all the questions were about the mine strike and your announced intention to reform civil service, and nobody asked you about your endorsement of the back-to-basics movement, nobody questioned your assertion that 'the basics' have been neglected in the schools in recent years, no one asked about your commitment to more testing, and there were no concerns expressed about your view on the purposes of bi-lingual education.

Mr President, these are highly sensitive issues in American education today. Many schools in America are being torn apart over these issues. So I decided to use this public forum to address an open letter to you, Mr President.

I'm an optimist about educational progress. I believe that ultimately educational decisions that hurt children and interfere with progress in improving teaching and learning will be recognized as such and give way to wiser decisions. But I become quite concerned when I see state legislators, state departments of education, the courts, federal agencies, and even the President of the United States entering into these decision-making processes ignorant of the issues and the facts. Progress will come eventually, but more children will suffer before it does.

When a court orders a school system to adopt a specific reading curriculum and assessment plan as happened in Detroit, or a school board announces teachers will be evaluated by their pupils' achievement on an arbitrary sequence of reading skills, or a state department of education mandates that no student may receive a high school diploma who can't read at ninth grade level according to a test as happened in Arizona, or the state legislature requires by law that teachers in early childhood programs must state behavioral objectives and test for them as in California, or a federal agency endorses structured skills programs as happened following the $100 000 000 fiasco in evaluating the follow-through programs, or the Secretary of Health, Education, and Welfare promulgates a research finding that 'even good teachers' spend only 18 per cent of their time on instruction, or you yourself, Mr President, join the 'back-to-basics' bandwagon, then the struggle for progress in teaching and learning becomes a political one and professional educators must shift their attention from educational to political concerns.

I'm concerned about all these issues, Mr President, but as a teacher and educationist involved in research and development of theory on teaching and learning of literacy and other language arts, I'm going to focus on the back-to-basics issue. The central concern of the 1978 NCTE Language Arts Conference is the real basics.

The slogan 'back-to-basics' is no more meaningful in education than it would be in any other field, Mr President. What would it mean in agriculture for instance? Would anyone seriously suggest that there is basic farming: the farmer using hand tools with no newfangled ideas about breeding, hybridizing, disease control, fertilizers, machines? Shall we drop the frills and grow only corn and potatoes? Certainly basics in agriculture must mean meeting the food needs of all people in society with an abundant, affordable, wholesome and complete variety of agricultural products. That's not something one can go back to since it's never quite been achieved.

In education, what's basic is meeting the need for all people in society to learn to the fullest extent of their needs, desires and capabilities. That surely is a lot more than minimal levels of reading, writing, and arithmetic. And as in agriculture, it's a basic we can't go back to since we never have fully achieved it. We need all the new theories, methods, and materials we can get to achieve this basic objective.

The farmer working by hand with a sharpened stick is not basic farming, and the teacher with a slate and a phonics chart is not basic literacy. If back-to-basics in education is the good

old ways of the good old days, then children would be starved
of learning as surely as they would be starved of food through
such regression in farming. I believe, Mr President, that there
is no literacy crisis in America today.

More people at all socio-economic levels in all parts of the
country are reading and writing more and better than ever
before. I have associates in education and particularly in reading who would be upset with me for telling you that there is no
literacy crisis. They believe that federal, state and local funds
will only come if a sense of crisis is created. When I read of the
district in Chicago that cynically failed half its junior high
school students because of poor reading test scores, I must
confess I took it as a dramatic sacrifice of children in an attempt
to extort more money from funding agencies. Must there be a
crisis, Mr President, in order for us to place a high priority
on literacy? Crisis spending means short deadlines, crash programs that use old ideas with more intensity, ill considered
guidelines, quack cures, unrealistic demands and inappropriate
criteria for results. And all of these evils have become characteristic of federal and state funded programs in reading.

Federal programs in particular have tended to employ an
industrial cost accounting model. These treat schools as factor-
ies in which children are measured, treated, manipulated,
modified, and then measured again. Units of achievement test
gains are treated as products and cost effectiveness is judged
on dollars per unit of gain. Teachers are told they are wast-
ing time if they are not instructing children directly in what
the test tests.

Such dehumanizing constraints make the test itself the
educational 'basic.' Reading is the reading test. Much federal
spending, particularly through Right-to-Read and Title I funds,
has been directed at disseminating programs labeled as exemplary, not because they produce greater literacy but because
somewhere, someplace, they produced greater gains on specific
reading tests.

Testing has become the Frankenstein's monster of contemporary American education, largely through federal guidelines.
Millions of American children are being hurt badly, not helped,
by tests. A recent study of the National School Board Association revealed that Board members receive little or no useful
information from the massive testing programs.

Ironically, the state of the art in language testing is such
that it makes bad programs look good and good programs look
ineffective. There's a simple reason for that. There are no
tests that can really measure growth in language effectiveness.
On the other hand it's easy to produce impressive results on
tests by specifically rehearsing students in the things the tests
deal with.

The follow-through evaluation appeared to show that structured skills programs are superior to other follow-through
programs and that one rigid program that provides explicit

scripts for teachers was most successful of all. The contractor that reported this result got $5 million just for analyzing the computer data tape. That's $250 per child in the whole follow-through study. A careful critique of these results showed that only one program teaches traditional grammar formally to the first to third graders in its program. One sub-test on the Metropolitan Achievement Test that the follow-through evaluation employed deals specifically with traditional formal grammar. So it's no surprise that when performance on that sub-test was eliminated from the analysis the advantage of this program disappeared.

Yet the publisher, a subsidiary of IBM, is widely advertising that the federal government has endorsed the effectiveness of this program. Is that what basic education is, Mr President? No, it has to be a lot more than irrelevant test performance. Language is communicating to others in oral and written forms, understanding and being understood. It is not scores on the Metropolitan Achievement Test.

There ought to be a national inquiry into the follow-through evaluation, Mr President; it wasted so much money, $5 million for data analysis and at least $55 million for the whole evaluation, some estimate up to $100 000 000. But it also demonstrated that the test and evaluation establishment in this country has failed, that it cannot deliver on its promises. The federal contracting effort with this huge level of funding should have brought the best minds and best knowledge available for this evaluation. All that money and talent and effort produced nothing more useful than comparisons of performance gains on an achievement test. That could have been accomplished for little more than the cost of the tests. At a time when you are suggesting more testing, Mr President, the evaluation-testing establishment has been exposed as an abysmal failure. They should be held accountable and not rewarded by federal guidelines which require more and more testing.

The alternative to testing is to get back to a basic concern for kids. When testing of all kinds was just beginning to gain respectability, there was a flourishing child study movement in this country. New concepts and tools from developmental psychology, linguistics, psycholinguistics, anthropology and education are available which can make child study even more useful than it was then. We can learn about what kids know and can do in language, as in all fields, through careful observation of natural, functional use. Nothing is more basic than the kids themselves. Statistics and testing lured us away from child study, promising equally useful results at less cost. Now we know that the results aren't useful and costs aren't low. Both teachers and researchers have come to treat direct study of learners as less worthwhile than use of statistically manipulable test results. The faith teachers need in their professional ability to make decisions about the strengths and needs of their pupils from their day-to-day interaction with them must be restored. Nothing is more basic to successful teaching.

No test was ever designed to provide knowledge that teachers intuitively develop six hours a day, 180 or more days a year, through constant interaction with real live pupils.

Fortunately, Mr President, the relentless drive for schools to institute test-based minimal competencies as requirements for promotion and graduation in elementary and secondary schools received a serious set-back when a panel appointed by Secretary Califano recently raised serious doubts about the value of such devices for improving education.

The panel has finally raised to a level of federal awareness the concerns educators and professional organizations of educators have been expressing that such so-called standards exceed the level of the art of testing, distort or destroy educational programs, and will cause far more problems for minority groups than they solve.

I believe, Mr President, that the real crisis in American education today is one not of a lack of concern for the basics but of a conflict over what is basic in American education. In this crisis, science and humanism are on one side while mindless technology and behavior management are on the other.

In language and literacy, science has produced, in recent years, tremendous new knowledge about how language processes work, what their functions are, and how and why they're learned. This scientific knowledge forms the base of new respect and appreciation for human language and for children as language learners. We can put literacy in the context of this new scientific humanism and find strength where we saw only weakness. We can develop curricula and methods that work with language learners rather than at cross purposes to them. A new pedagogy is developing in which children are helped to build pride and confidence in their language, and expansion is the key word.

But arrayed against this tremendous potential for progress is a know-nothing view that combines the outward vestiges of technology - machines, management systems, arbitrary controlled atomistic skills sequences, and constant testing - with a philosophy of behavior management. In behavior management, outcomes are assumed or arbitrarily determined and the behavior of human learners is shaped, conditioned, reinforced, extinguished, rewarded or punished until the learners achieve the target behavior. I refer to this as a know-nothing view because it requires no knowledge, no scientific insights about language or literacy.

The advantage in battle to the scientific humanism side is its potential for long-range and fundamental answers to basic questions. The advantage to the technological behavior management side is its promise of quick remedies and its apparent directness. Those characteristics make it seductively attractive to governmental decision-makers eager for simple answers and quick results. And that's where the basic battle becomes uneven.

I've criticized governmental policies and some of the key points in your education message, Mr President. So I'd like to conclude this letter with some constructive advice. I'd like you to know how I would allocate federal funds and efforts if I controlled the spending.

First, I would eliminate much of the categorical support and instead concentrate on using federal funds to equalize spending across American schools and to reduce classroom size.

Schools with large minority and/or impoverished populations need special attention not to compensate for assumed deficiencies but to make the special efforts possible to design more relevant programs which can build on individual and cultural strengths. That must include bi-lingual programs designed to maintain and expand on the advantage of having two languages and cultures.

Most federal efforts in my view should be focussed on helping teachers become more competent. Reducing classroom size would provide jobs for the many well-educated and eager young teachers who are in touch with new concepts and take strain off present teachers. In-service education helping teachers to understand, evaluate and put new concepts to work should be a major concern. This can be accomplished through teacher education institutions, through teacher centers run by the profession and through professional organizations. Cooperation among all groups concerned for quality of teaching should be fostered.

Federal support for research needs to not only be substantially increased, but it also needs to be redirected. In research there is also controversy over what is basic. The current dichotomy between basic and applied research is nonproductive in education. Useful research as in medicine must both produce knowledge and use it to find solutions to real problems. Educational research, particularly in relation to literacy, must focus on language in real situations in and out of the classroom. It must involve interdisciplinary teams that include teachers and others who know classrooms and kids.

Finally, we must focus on creating physical school facilities and administrative policies that reverse the tendency to make schools like prisons. Schools must be warm environments in which children are respected and in which teaching and learning are truly nurtured.

I believe, Mr President, that your administration could bring American education back to basics, if the basics of education is seen as our basic commitment as a society to the full development of every citizen's potential.

Many of us in the teaching profession applauded your decision to send your daughter to a public school in Washington.

Nowhere in America are the issues in American education more apparent than in our nation's capital.

Your daughter and her classmates are growing up in a highly

complex society; they will inherit all the problems our generation will leave unsolved and some new ones we are creating. A school able to help today's children to build on their potential to be all they might be is the most basic resource of our society in reaching its full potential.

The teacher is the most basic factor in an effective school.

But the child - if we come back to the child, we'll be truly back to basics.

We conclude with this comprehensive discussion of what is basic
to reading. Here Goodman criticizes the preoccupation with
technology that leads us to the so-called 'back-to-basics' movement.

I'm going to attack this back-to-basics movement on two
bases. One is the fundamental humanistic one that schools
really exist for kids and not for a technology of learning.
But I'll also attack it on the scientific basis that it simply
is wrong: that that's not the way people learn to read.

Here Goodman discusses the real basics of reading and concludes that attempts to separate the basics from the rest of
the curriculum short-changes the kids 'in terms of the fullness
and richness of the curriculum, but it very much short-
changes them in terms of the development of literacy too.'

31 WHAT IS BASIC ABOUT READING?

When my middle daughter was in kindergarten, she came home one day and announced that she had learned to draw a house. So I said 'Okay, show me.' She went to the chalk board in her room, and she drew a house. You know the house she drew: the box with a triangle on top and the rectangular chimney and the rectangular door. I said, 'That's nice, can you draw another one?' And she did; and for about two years, that was the only house that Karen would draw. Was she getting instruction in the basics of house drawing?

There's a lesson there. The lesson is that we tend, in school, to build a technology of teaching and the curriculum, and we tend to regard that as if it were more basic than reality. We expand on it, vary it, elaborate on it, pull it apart, and so forth. And pretty soon what we're teaching is not art but the technology of how to draw a house. This also happens in reading. Among the 50 dissertation abstracts submitted to the committee of the International Reading Association that chooses which is the best dissertation in reading each year, there is a dismaying preoccupation with instructional technology: which way is best to introduce letter sequence, letter-sound relationships, consonant blends. There are a few encouraging topics, but there's a depressing equation of the technology of instruction with learning to read and problems in developing literacy.

This preoccupation with technology leads us, particularly in the field of literacy, to a preoccupation with what some people think was successful past practice in the teaching of reading that worked in contrast to what we are doing now that doesn't work; a demand for some kind of reassertion of the good old ways and the good old days.

I'm going to attack this back-to-basics movement on two bases. One is the fundamental humanistic one that schools really exist for kids and not for a technology of learning. But I'll also attack it on the scientific basis that it simply is wrong: that that's not the way people learn to read. We wouldn't have anybody not learning to read, if all that was required was that somebody teach them a few letters and a few letter-sound combinations. 'Back-to-basics' often is getting back to some kind of simplistic phonics system.

Recently I have had pass over my desk a circular from the University of Chicago Press advertising a program that they've published which, they assure us, is a marvelous new breakthrough in reading instruction. Actually it is one more systematized, sequential phonics program, and there isn't anything new about it at all. It isn't even new that it involves the technologizing 'systems-approach' that grabs kids by the back of the neck and shakes them to make them learn to do the things that somebody has arbitrarily decided are necessary.

Another example was in a recent edition of the 'Reading Teacher,' the elementary school journal of the International Reading Association. It was a full page ad by a particular publisher, but it wouldn't surprise me if any publisher had used it. Interestingly, it doesn't matter if it describes their program or not. Ads for school text programs frequently have little to do with what's in the program; what they reflect is what the sales department has decided are the things to say to sell the program. This ad says they are very proud of the fact that they were the publishers of the McGuffey Reader because 'We stuck to the basics with McGuffey's. Today 141 years later, we still stick to the basics.' Their program 'includes the link of supplementary materials that go right to work.' It 'concentrates on basic reading skills you (the teacher) and your kids can trust...carefully sequenced phonics skills...structural skills...all right in the pupil's text. It provides entrance tests and objectives referenced placement tests and ditto masters and consumable, 'no-nonsense' skills books. (Advertisement, American Book Co., 'Reading Teacher,' vol. 30, no. 4, January 1977, p. 445.)

The implication seems to be that entrance and placement tests, ditto masters, and skill books have been basic instruction for at least 141 years.

I believe what's basic in reading and reading instruction and kids learning to read has nothing to do with a particular method of teaching, good or bad. It has nothing to do with a sequence of skills or expensive technological materials packages. What it has to do with is that language is for the purpose of communication and if you're going to help somebody to become literate, that means helping them to be able to use written language to deal with meaning. So, in the case of reading, what's basic is getting meaning from print: interacting with the author through written language. In writing, what's basic is expressing meaning through written language.

In that sense, literacy is very much like oral language. There's a very unfortunate misconception that's current even among some linguistic circles that there's something less natural about written language than oral language. No respectable linguist would argue that you start to teach a kid to talk by saying phonemes at him and then teaching him to blend phonemes and then say syllables and then produce nonsense syllables and then produce words and then put the words together into one and two morpheme-words and then finally put them together to make sentences. But there are lots of linguists who are arguing that writing is something that you do *with* language rather than something that *is* language itself.

Linguists rejected, for good reasons, a preoccupation with written language that had really prevented us from coming to understand how language basically worked as we neglected oral language. So they argued quite correctly that oral language is primary, that it's developed first by cultures and first by individuals. But individuals cut off from oral language such as the deaf have the same capacity to develop language and will reach out for visual language. But I also think study of written language is haunted by a disrespect for education as a profession, for educational research as a field and discipline, so that you get some psychologists, linguists, sociologists, who are quite good scholars and researchers, but who wander into reading and don't do their homework.

We have not always had the best application of scholarship and the best interdisciplinary interaction in reading programs. We get a strange kind of hook-up. On one hand, there is a kind of know-nothing group that says 'What I want is that my kids get a good education, and good education is what I had when I was a kid, at least what I remember it was like; so let's go back to the good old stuff.' On the other hand are the academicians, who are elitists anyway, and who, therefore, think that the reason that we haven't been successful in schools is that people who go into education aren't that bright, anyway. If they could do something else, they would. 'Those that can, do; and those that can't, teach.' I think that's even underscored in art education. If you're an art teacher, it must be that you couldn't be a successful artist. I don't believe that, I hope you understand; some of my best friends are...

What's basic, then, that we have to get back to is what we were trying to do in the first place: to teach literacy, and teach it in the reconceived sense of helping people to comprehend written language.

As we built a skill technology, we incorporated it into more and more elaborate tests. I was once asked by Oscar Boros to write some reviews for his 'Mental Measurements Yearbooks.' He asked me to do that because I wrote a very negative review of 'Reading Tests and Reviews,' which is all the 'Mental Measurements Yearbook' stuff on reading pulled out into a separate volume. Boros, when he published the first 'Mental Measurements Yearbook,' said that he hoped, by reviewing tests, to get good tests to replace bad tests. I was impressed by that original intention and then caught by his own introduction in which he said that most of the tests ever published – and this is particularly true in the field of reading – are still on the market. They still make money. Some of the oldest tests published are still selling.

The tests incorporate the technology. And one characteristic of tests is that no matter how inane they are when you give them to large groups of people, you get beautiful bell-shaped curves. You can always produce a group of people who are deficient in whatever it is the test tests. And if you're willing to accept the fact that that equates with the name on the test, then there are epidemics of children deficient in auditory discrimination or grammatical closure or reading comprehension. Suppose the State of California established a state funded program for children with Problem X. That would give each school district a vested interest in discovering among their school population, Problem X children. So they have to get a Problem X test to screen which kids are afflicted so they can then get the funding from the state. And suddenly, it seems that there has been an epidemic in certain populations and Problem X has reached epidemic proportions among Chicano kids, and it really is a terrible critical thing among black kids, though only moderate numbers of white middle-class kids are afflicted (unless that's all a particular school has).

If you look at reading tests, they tend to focus very much on the skills, and those skills are impressively listed. It doesn't much matter that every time somebody has done a correlational study, they've discovered that there's so high a correlation between the various skill subtests of the reading test that they seem to be testing the same thing over and over again. But you can send to the publishers of the Stanford diagnostic test, and they'll send you back a computer print-out of all the skills that your kids need, according to the things that they missed on the particular test.

That creates an aura of technology that intimidates teachers. The teacher thinks, 'I thought that kid could read; he just finished reading "Charlotte's Web," and I saw him crying in that scene where it gets really touching, so I thought he understood. But according to that test he just took, he's deficient in getting the main idea, and blending C with R, so maybe I am wrong. The machines and computers and all those people with all the initials after their names who wrote those things must know more about it than I do.'

We've developed a profession of people who have a vested interest in remediation and the treatment of all the problems that we've identified through the tests. I've been at meetings where colleagues have half-jokingly said, when we reported that according to our best information from our research, inner-city kids read a lot better than standardized tests show they do, 'We know that, but let's not tell the state legislature because then they won't give us any money for reading programs, and our jobs would be in jeopardy.' The technology of reading has even cropped up in comic strips. A few years ago, Charlie Brown had a reading problem, and every day for two weeks, they explored a different possibility; one day he was dyslexic, the next day he had myopia, another possibility was minimal brain dysfunction; it went on and on until one day Lucy said to him, 'Charlie, have you thought about the fact that you just may be stupid?'

That's not an excuse either. We've known for a long time you rarely ever find a kid who is so retarded that he doesn't

have language. Many mentally retarded kids learn to read
easily and well without any particular difficulty. Maybe it's
because we don't put as much pressure on them to learn. I've
argued in print that you don't have to be smart to read, that
there's no particular reason why it would require any more
intelligence to read than it does to listen and understand at a
level where one can deal with the concepts (Goodman, 1975).

We've moved so far away from the basic purpose of literacy
instruction, that we have this terrible curricular syndrome:
the kids that do satisfy the teachers that they're learning to
read get a richer and richer curriculum; they get to do interesting things; they even have time for things like art and music.
But we take the kid out of music to go to a remedial reading
class. After all we have to take care of the basics. Then we
start keeping him after school so he can get an extra dose of
instruction with some teaching machines or with some paraprofessional tutors drilling him on things that he's already
failed on in the regular school time. And then he gets to junior
high school, and he starts a new remedial English and remedial
reading program while the other kids are learning interesting
social studies and science concepts and expanding their interests
in art, dance, music, or drama. Instead of the kind of things
that will begin to create interest, that will begin to create a
relationship between what's read and some kind of purpose,
relevant to the kids, the instruction gets more and more preoccupied with the abstract technology of literacy. Even if
readers develop some kind of functional literacy, they are convinced that they're a non-reader.

Carol Burke, who has worked in various ways with us for a
long time, has been doing some work with adults and finds a
very interesting syndrome. She'll say to an adult whom she's
beginning to work with, 'What can you read?' and he'll say,
'Nothing.' She says, 'Well, do you take a newspaper?' and he
says 'Yeah.' So she says 'Well, are there any parts that are
interesting to you?' Perhaps he says 'Sports.' So she gets the
sports page, and she shows him a picture that has about a
four-line caption under it, and she says 'Tell me what that
says,' and he struggles and omits, and he substitutes, but
when he finishes, she can then say, 'Now, what was that
about?' And usually the person can say, 'Well, that's about
the guy that was out trying to steal second base.' So she then
says 'See, you can read.' In one case this man said, 'No, I
can't,' and she said, 'But you just did,' and he got very angry,
and he said, 'Lady, either you're putting me on, or you just
don't know your business! I didn't know that word, and I
didn't know that word and I couldn't handle that!'

His preoccupation is with thinking that somehow there are a
set of magic buttons or formulas or things that readers do
that he can't do that makes it possible for a reader never to
have a problem, never to not know a word, always to know the
next word. We've begun to call it the 'next word syndrome';

non-readers always believe that if you don't know a word that it's proof that you're a non-reader. Every time they come to a name or anything that's the least bit difficult, they take it as proof, and of course people have been telling them for a long time in their academic careers that they are non-readers.

Periodically we make a crisis out of the literacy problem. In Washington, DC they hired a new superintendent a few years ago and shackled him with a report written by an outstanding New York psychologist on the literacy crisis in Washington, DC. Unfortunately that academic believed that the reason schools weren't succeeding was that they weren't trying hard enough; so the whole thing was built around, 'How do you get the schools to try harder?' They were going to organize district committees and group committees and section committees and school committees, and they would promise that they would bring every child up to grade level by June of that year. That's a statistical impossibility: you can't make everybody average; average is the mean, and if you bring the low ones up, then the mean goes up; so you're chasing your own tail.

I wonder what would happen if we told the nation's doctors and medical researchers that they were going to be expected to cure cancer by next June 15, and that we would spend no federal money or state money on any research that didn't promise immediate solutions with no frills; none of this 'funny stuff with long names' research that doesn't really have immediate payoff. And we're going to bring in some people with quick cures and technological hardware like cancer curing machines. It sounds absurd to suggest it, but we keep doing it in the field of reading. We keep buying the quick cure, the hard sell, and the lavish promises; it makes it very difficult to deal with getting down to the basic issues of what literacy is all about.

I promised you I wasn't just going to deal with this on a humanistic basis, though I'm often accused of being a humanist, and I don't apologize for that. Sometimes when I'm introduced, I tell people I believed a lot of the things I'm talking about now before I had done any research, before I had read other people's research; I'm happy to report that science has supported my own prejudices.

Science and humanism come together because language is a personal, social, human invention. You can't deal with language without dealing with it as an aspect of both a social and a personal development of human beings. To try to understand language by studying porpoises or chimpanzees or bees, or any other kind of creature that has some kind of communication, doesn't work; because they don't use language as the medium of thought, as the medium of learning, and for the kind of social interaction that's so vital for us as human beings. Human beings can't survive without language.

If you've ever seen a deaf child born into a hearing home cut off from language, you can feel the frustration and rage that he has because he has so much to communicate and such great difficulty doing it. The outstanding achievers among deaf kids are deaf kids who are lucky enough to be born into deaf homes, where there's visual language available to them almost from the beginning.

One of the ironies in language learning that we need to make a kind of key premise of curriculum development in language, is that when language is easy to learn, it's so easy that it seems almost unnecessary to teach it. And when we try to teach it and it's not easy to learn, it's almost impossible to do it. There are kids in New York City who are already able to speak two languages before they come to school. They can speak both to a considerable extent more than the tests show because the tests are constructed by people who often don't understand very much about language. And then they have difficulty becoming literate in either or both of the languages as we try to help them. What we need to say to ourselves is 'Why is it hard?' 'What is it about what we're doing that makes it hard?' It ought to be easy, because language under the right conditions is easy to learn.

What I'm arguing is something that it's taken us longer to come to in the field of language than it took people in the field of art. Maybe I'm venturing out beyond my depth, but it seems to me well recognized in art that function has to precede form. That's true in language, as well. Halliday (1975) has, in his recent writing, been focussing on this. He argues that children develop a series of models of language, each of them relating to a function of language, for instance the function of 'I want something.' When the function is developed, then quickly the form of the language develops to accomplish that. He says they learn what language is because they know what language does. Put literacy into that context, and it isn't that reading and writing are harder to learn or less natural, but it's just that there is a different set of circumstances, a different set of things that govern the functions of the language and that vary from culture to culture or subculture to subculture.

Why is it that when the state of Michigan published their scores every year in Michigan and they listed school districts in rank according to the mean score in the fourth grade for that district, you could as easily have ranked the district according to the percentage of minority children in their population.

Dewey said a long time ago that you can't simply make a kid come to school; you've got to make the school come to the kid. We expect children to adjust to a rigid curriculum, a structured technology, and we simply shunt off those who don't meet the expectation. We should have learned after a couple of decades that equal education opportunity isn't really equal educational opportunity if it means that the schools are not flexible in dealing with what kids bring to school, what strengths they have. Equal opportunity has to imply the obligation to understand the learner and to build on that.

We have to ask ourselves in what sense written language is functional for a child or a group of kids. What does it really do for them? How does it work in their cultures? What evidence do we have that they've already become aware of the function of written language?

People often cite the invention of the printing press by Gutenberg as the thing that made mass literacy possible. I'd like to argue just the opposite of that. It was the need for the mass literacy that caused Gutenberg to invent the printing press, and if he hadn't done it, then somebody else would have. One of the reasons why we have the tremendous explosion of quick, cheap, easy reproducing devices today is because of the need society has for multiple copies of things, for large numbers of people to be able to read the same thing quickly right after it's produced. That's a social development.

Why is it that in China and Cuba mass literacy programs have been amazingly successful that have had virtually no money behind them, that in many cases have used archaic methodology or no methodology at all - just somebody with a book working with somebody who couldn't read. And yet in other situations, for instance in India, such campaigns are almost totally unsuccessful. I think one has to argue that it's the changes in the conditions of the culture and the society that make the people need to read and therefore be receptive to literacy. Without such changes, no amount of technology is going to help them. Simply speaking, we can't take our American reading technology to a developing nation and solve the literacy problem there by bringing them translations of our skill series and our skill hierarchies.

The Chicago school system is very proud that they have now a sequential list of 768 skills - and guess how many you have to go through to get to meaning; how many skills does one have to check off; how many exercises do you have to do in those no-frills workbooks in order to be passed on to the point where it begins to make sense? I believe we ought to step aside, look at what we've learned about the acquisition of language, look at what we've learned about the development of literacy. Perhaps then we can see why some things work and some things don't, why some kids find it so hard and some kids find it easy.

I was at a conference on beginning reading at the University of Pittsburgh, and a very well-known educator reported that sometimes it takes 1500 to 5000 repetitions for a kid to learn a single reading skill. And I said to myself, 'Hooray for the kid that has internal fortitude to resist learning something that he's made to do 5000 times!' And how dense we are that we could sit with the kid over and over again and not get the message. There's something wrong; there's something irrelevant; there's something the kid is saying is disfunctional, doesn't fit, doesn't make sense.

I read recently in the 'American Airlines Magazine' that this

technologizing is coming to the humanities, too - this preoccupation with statistics and quantifying things. The article
was talking about a couple of very successful companies that
test new tunes for music publishers and producers by hooking
up lie detectors to audiences and measuring the amounts of
electrical activities on the skins as they listen to the tunes.
That's supposed to be more reliable than asking the people if
they like the song or not. Can't you see the corporate groups
sitting there and being impressed by the statistical tables that
they get with all that technical language; much more impressive than saying we asked sixteen people and they thought the
record was lousy.

One thing was kind of interesting. You always get into this
with technology; it turns out that regardless of whether you
liked it or not, rock tunes generate more skin electricity than
ballads do just because of the volume of the noise. Think of
what that could do with what we have to listen to all day;
suppose somebody hadn't noticed that, and all the reports had
gone in indicating that all rock tunes are liked better by all
audiences. It could literally blow your mind.

Language and culture and thought and learning are all very
much a part of what curriculum must build on for human beings.
We have the basis for making literacy universal. But it turns
out that it isn't a new sequence of skills; nobody has ever
validated a hierarchy of skills anyway. What we really have to
do is to get it all together. When you're reading, it has to be
because there's a message you need to get, and that has to
relate to what you're interested in, what turns you on, and
what gets you involved.

It can't be separated; you can't first learn the skills you
need so then you can use them. Did it ever happen to you, at
some point in your education, when you complained about all
the grammar corrections on that paper that you'd poured your
heart into, and you said 'But Steinbeck writes that way,' that
the teacher said, 'When you get to be Steinbeck you can write
that way too, but at this time we'll use the rules.'

Language development doesn't work that way. Writing is even
more cut off from meaningful functional use than reading in
school instruction. The things we ask kids to write are often
never read for the purpose that they were written and often
never written for the purpose that was self-generated by the
writer. Can you think of how it would be if kids had to learn
to talk in a situation where nobody ever listened or responded?
Suppose people instead of answering their questions or giving
them what they had asked for, told them what they had done
wrong in the way they had said it. We do it with literacy all
the time in school.

The kind of curriculum I'm arguing for must be rich and
varied; it has to employ all the kinds of things we know a curriculum ought to have. There can't be any excuse that literacy
is so important that it takes precedence over art or music or

math or science or whatever. Language without content isn't language. Literacy skills don't exist in a meaningless vacuum.

I know a lot of people are concerned about the lack of the arts in the curriculum. But I see little social studies in the elementary curriculum. I see little science; maybe the teacher does an experiment once in a while, and lets the kids watch. Social studies just gets shoved off in the background as controversial, anyway; and art becomes an activity you have the kids do when they've finished the workbook. The teacher's not ready to go on to the next thing, so she gives them a crayon and a piece of paper, and they can draw. Of course, there are some kids who never get to do it because they never get done with the important things.

Even reading gets shunted aside for the sake of teaching reading. Isn't that strange? I was in a classroom once to see a student teacher. The kids were sitting at grouped tables, and in the middle of each of the groups of tables was a stack of trade books. I said to the teacher, isn't that great, the kids can just reach out and take a book. She said, 'Yeah, but we're going to take them back to the library because the kids are supposed to read them after they finish their workbook pages, but they rush through the workbooks so that they can get to the books, and they're not really concentrating on their work.' So back go the books, and all day is spent teaching reading. But how much time is really spent reading? And how much of that time is spent reading something that they decided that they themselves wanted to read - that was something that had a message for them, that involved them, that was functional in some kind of sense for them?

Well-meaning attempts to play the devil's game are not an adequate response to the technologist and the systematizers who have the schools and curricula in technological strait-jackets. It isn't a question of smuggling in a little art by having the kids take a letter or word and having them do some kind of creative thing around it. Or using dance to bend the body into funny shapes so you can represent all the letters of the alphabet. Or finding ways of stating in behavioral terms the objectives so that they can be tested, and somehow working in a few aesthetic ones which are going to get thrown out because they're not precisely enough defined and you can't provide five items to test each one that can be fed into the computer.

The game of trying to smuggle in something worthwhile or interesting or cultural, or relevant, or aesthetic, doesn't produce an acceptable curriculum, anyway; it winds up acquiescing to the notion that only basics are the true curriculum.

I think that we have to understand that human beings are whole and they learn language whole as they interact with each other. Literacy works the same way; it has to be part of all the other experiences that are going on.

I want to finish with something Sir Alec Clegg said at the

National Council of Teachers of English in 1978.

He said when he was a small child, he would go to his aunt's house, and there was a motto on the wall burned into wood, something about 'If you have two loaves of bread, sell one and with the money buy hyacinths.' And he made the analogy that in school curricula we seem to fluctuate between bread and hyacinths. The bread is the basics: we've got to teach the kids the things they need; and the hyacinths is the rest of the curriculum. I don't quite agree with him. I think that somehow we've got to find a way of making bread out of hyacinths, or finding beauty in bread. The attempts to separate the basic from the rest not only short-changes the kids in terms of the fullness and richness of the curriculum, but it very much short-changes them in terms of the development of literacy, too.

REFERENCES

Goodman, K.S. (1975), Do You Have to be Smart to Read? Do You Have to Read to be Smart? 'Reading Teacher,' vol. 28, no. 7, April, pp. 625-32. (See Chapter 25 of the present volume.)
Halliday, M.A.K. (1975), Learning How to Mean, in 'Foundations of Language Development,' vol. 2, ed. Eric H. Lenneberg, New York: Academic Press.

AFTERWORD

As an afterword we offer a recent article in which Kenneth Goodman has restated both his theory of reading and his theory of reading development and instruction in the context of two current movements.

The first he calls the 'know-more' movement. This is, he says, an 'explosive seeking of greater knowledge of the reading process.' It has involved a massive incursion of cognitive psychologists into reading research and a strong focus on comprehension of whole texts.

The second movement he calls a 'know-nothing' movement. It is an 'overwhelming systems-oriented...movement...based on tightly structured arbitrarily chosen skill sequences; it is an empty technology so inflexible it can not tolerate new knowledge.'

Thus Goodman has set his own work out against the background of the major movement of the current era.

THE KNOW-MORE AND THE KNOW-NOTHING MOVEMENTS IN READING: A Personal Response

Reading, how it works, how it's learned, how to teach it, has never gotten more attention than it is getting now. Ironically, at the same time that more productive theory and research from a widening range of vantage points is producing new insights and knowledge, developments in reading instruction are dominated by reactionary backward-looking pressures that lock teachers into arbitrary inflexible methods, curricula, and materials and lock-out knowledge and enlightenment.

In this brief presentation I want to respond to both movements: the know-more movement and the know-nothing movement. I can do this best, in the first case, by a restatement of the theory of reading I've been developing over the years, indicating how I see current theory and research directions relating to that theory. I can do it best in the second case by restating a theory of reading development and reading instruction which I feel are solidly supported through application in classrooms. In doing this it will be necessary to react explicitly to current trends and catch-phrases. In a sense, this is a personal progress report on where I am and where I think the field is.

The theory of the reading process I developed is still best summed up in the statement 'Reading is a Psycholinguistic Guessing Game' (Goodman, 1967). I reached the conclusion that tentative information processing, guessing on the basis of minimal actual information is the primary characteristic of reading. The reader interacts with an author through a text to construct meaning. That means that there is an interaction between thought and language, hence a psycholinguistic process is in operation. Most recently, I've realized that the *tentativeness* of the information processing is even more significant than I had thought earlier.

The level of confidence of the reader at any point in time strongly affects the process. If the reader is unsure of the meaning being constructed, finds the text syntactically complex, the concept load heavy, or the concepts strange, then the reader becomes more tentative, more cautious, more careful. The reader uses more cues, monitors more closely, reprocesses frequently, corrects often. If the reader has a high level of confidence then the reading plunges forward with only minimal sampling and self-monitoring.

Reading depends on the use of strategies for comprehending, that is, constructing meaning in interaction with texts. Comprehending is seeking after meaning. Comprehension is what is, in fact, understood. The latter always is the combined result of what the reader understood prior to reading and the effectiveness of comprehending. The two will be related strongly, but even highly effective readers are severely limited in comprehension of texts by what they already know before they read. The author may influence the comprehensibility of a text particularly for specific targeted audiences. But no author can completely compensate in writing for the range of differences among all potential readers of a given text.

At the core of the theory I have developed is the view that language processes must be studied in the context of their use. If they are dissected, stopped or unnaturally constrained then the relative significance of constituents to wholes is altered. Similarly long complete texts have characteristics that short texts, partial texts, or specially contrived texts can't have.

I've described reading as cyclical with optical, perceptual, syntactic and semantic cycles linking into each other. Again tentativeness is important. The reader's main preoccupation is with constructing meaning. While the reader must utilize all cycles, the confident reader moves through to syntactic prediction and semantic construction as quickly and easily as possible. Efficient reading uses the least amount of effort possible.

Schema are used on the basis of minimal perceptual information which make it possible to predict syntactic patterns and leap toward a sense of the text. Effective reading can only be defined in terms of comprehension. Proficient readers are both efficient and effective. Such readers get to meaning with minimal use of cues, minimal monitoring, confident prediction, minimal correction. Of course, proficient readers can shift to more cautious processing as their level of confidence drops. Proficient readers can also become non-proficient readers in coping with some texts.

Readers use the strategies of sampling, predicting, confirming, and correcting. These strategies depend on use of graphophonic, syntactic, and semantic cues as they are found in natural language texts. And again they function always in the context of the readers' striving to make sense of the text. The same cues that are used to confirm prior predictions are used to make subsequent ones. So as proficiency increases readers become highly selective in sampling available cues and highly effective in their predictions.

The difference between readers of different levels of proficiency is not in how this process works but how well it works. Less proficient readers can not construct meaning by a different process. They must use the same cues, cycles, strategies.

To say they read less well does not imply they are either devoid of skills or more careless, in fact they may read less well because they are too cautious, use too many cues, overuse some strategies, or have been taught non-productive strategies that may conflict with their more natural productive strategies.

The terms I've used to describe reading are interactive, psycholinguistic, active, constructive, tentative. Commentators on my view have applied other terms popular at various times.

For a while my model was being referred to as an 'analysis by synthesis' model (Gibson and Levin, 1975). As nearly as I can determine, this term was used originally by Henri Bergson, the philosopher. It has some applicability, particularly since I do believe that no intermediate aspect of reading can be regarded as complete until meaning has been constructed, that we only 'know' the parts when we've created meaning for the whole.

But I have never used the term because it is not explicit enough. Nor are either the terms 'analysis' or 'synthesis' really appropriate for what I see happening in the reading.

My model has also been referred to as a top-down model (Pearson and Kamil, 1978). Again the term is not totally inappropriate. I do believe language is learned from whole to part in full communicative contexts.

I also believe that processing in reading is meaning-seeking so that language parts have no real existence outside the whole.

But this term developed as an alternative to frankly bottom-up views, such as Gough's (1976) or Laberge and Samuels's (1976). They see reading as processing each small part successively and accurately to get to each larger unit. For Gough 'Merlin' puts the parts together into meaningful wholes. For Samuels automaticity does the trick. Learning to read, for bottom-up folks, is also a matter of starting with small units and graduating to larger more real ones.

If the only alternative to a bottom-up view is a top-down view that's where my theory is often put because it surely is not bottom-up. But I've always seen parts in relationship to wholes. I've talked for some years about how use of distinctive features operates in language. I see optical and perceptual cycles preceding syntactic and semantic cycles.

Recent classifications of reading models create a third, interactive category in which processing is simultaneous at many levels all interacting. That's where I've always placed my view. Rumelhart's (1977) work is cited as an example of an interactive model. I find little in his view incompatible with my own except that he is hesitant to integrate fully the aspects he discusses or to expand his view of reading comprehension to a full model of the reading process. Louise Rosenblatt (1978) has been using another term, transactional, taken from Dewey, to apply to the reading process. Like Dewey she prefers transactional because it applies a more complete involvement with each other, of text and reader, than does interaction.

Some psychologists discussing text analysis, such as Bonnie Meyer (1975), have used top-down to apply to the 'story grammar' of the text - placing more significant aspects of a story structure in a kind of pyramid dominating less significant aspects. She argues, in that sense, that the reader's comprehension is top-down, focussing on the dominating features of the structure.

Such a view is more related to how we select and organize what we comprehend from reading than to the reading process. A problem with many recent attempts at reading theory - particularly that involving cognitive psychologists - has been a tendency to avoid macro-theories of the entire reading process. We get, instead, partial theories of text comprehension, of propositional structures of texts, or of schema functioning.

It is very significant that much modern theory focuses around comprehension of meaning and falls broadly within a focus on the writer, the text, or the reader.

But all the findings and theories will eventually need to come together into an inclusive view. Though my theory has not been explicated in complete detail, since it is a macro-theory of the reading process it must accommodate research findings, provide alternate explanations if it cannot, or yield to a new, better theory. But there must be a macro-theory of reading and it must account for all aspects of the process and serve as a base of theories of reading development and reading instruction.

My theory is sometimes also referred to as an inside-out view. Such a view is contrasted with outside-in views. In the outside-in view reading is often called 'text driven.' The reader is seen as relatively passively responding to the text. Conversely, reading is reader-driven in inside-out views with the reader operating actively and without dependence on the text.

Again if there are only two choices I'm at the inside-out pole. But I've never used these terms to describe my view. I believe that what the reader brings to the text is as important as what the author did in understanding the meaning a given reader constructs. I've said above that readers use all three cue systems in interaction with the text but that proficient reading uses minimal cues and minimal effort in reading. It follows that the more proficient the reader is the less constrained the reader is by close attention to text features. So I'd prefer again to call reading an interactive process - one in which the reader interacts with the text.

I've referred above in passing to the reader's schema. The old concept that human interaction with our environment and learning depend on development of complex schema has become popular again in cognitive psychology (Anderson et al., 1977). It has been applied recently to studies of comprehension of oral and written texts.

The schema view fits well with the concepts of sampling, predicting, confirming, and correcting. The reader uses minimal cues to construct schema. These are not selected, I believe, from a mental file cabinet of preformed schema but rather rules are used to generate schema. In a sense the rules are schema for schema formation. The schema must utilize syntactic rules to generate (predict) the clauses and clausal relationships.

They must also use semantic cohesion, semantic structures, sense of story to predict the meaning. The schema are not 'instantiated' as some schema theorists have argued. Rather the details of the schema are predicted and monitored through confirming and disconfirming strategies. The reader, being always tentative to some degree, is always prepared to modify or produce an alternate schema, to correct, seeking new perceptual information if necessary to achieve the constant goal of meaning construction.

Thus the schema concept is one highly compatible with my view of reading and useful in relating the comprehension of any text by any reader to an interaction of what the reader brings to the text, what the text characteristics are, and what the author has brought to it.

The systems of analysis of the semantic structures of text, which are rapidly developing, offer exciting possibilities for our understanding, in considerable detail, the semantic aspects of how readers construct meaning. A problem with many of these analyses is that they do not relate syntactic to semantic structures in any useful way. That again requires a fully articulated macro-theory such as mine. The macro-language theories of Michael Halliday (1973) offer promise as the most solid base for an understanding of how syntax and semantics relate to language processes.

At the beginning, I said there were two concurrent movements in reading. The first, which I described above, is the explosive seeking of greater knowledge of the reading process which I've called the know-more movement. There ought to be great excitement in the schools over the levels of activity in reading theory and research and the potential the knowledge produced has for application to better teaching and learning of reading.

Instead there is an overwhelming systems-oriented know-nothing movement that is based on tightly structured arbitrarily chosen skill sequences; it is an empty technology so inflexible it can not tolerate new knowledge.

I believe that a solidly based whole-language, comprehension-centered theory of reading instruction has emerged and demonstrated its effectiveness. Here, briefly, are some of the major aspects of this theory:

Literacy, reading and writing, is learned in the same way as oral language. If language learning is, as Halliday has said, learning how to mean, then literacy learning is learning how to mean with written language.

Though written language is comprehended in much the same way as oral language, its use to communicate over time and space create conditions that stretch out the development of written language as compared to oral language.

Children growing up in a literate society do begin development of literacy long before school begins. The roots of literacy are growing strongly long before schools begin instruction.

Children learn that print represents meaning. They learn

general and specific meanings of specific print sequences in
situational contexts; stop signs, cereal boxes, toothpaste
cartons. At the same time, children develop some awareness of
the form of print: directionality, letter names, key features.
They distinguish print from pictures. They can handle books
and know the basic function of books, letters, newspapers.

Literacy development in school needs to be built on this base.
It must be seen as an extension of the natural development.
It must always involve whole, real, natural, relevant texts.
That means the classroom must be a literate environment where
the teacher uses great ingenuity to engage children in real
functional written language to label, to chart, to inform, to
stimulate imagination, to develop sense of story, of semantic
text structure.

Language learning, literacy included, is self-motivated if
language is functional.

Early instruction can include a wide range of whole language
activities; language experience stories, shared book experiences,
read along activities with teachers and records, assisted reading. Writing can co-develop with reading if teachers can help to
create a sense of expressive purpose and function. Interest
must be kept high and the teacher must never lose sight of the
fact that both reading and writing require active involvement
of the learner.

People learn the form of language through its functional use.
Nothing contributes so strongly and continuously to language
development as experience in using language.

The three crucial factors in assuring development in reading
and writing are:

> Continuous focus on meaning
> Legitimizing of risk-taking
> Continuous involvement of learners in reading and writing.

Risk-taking is essential to development. We must try to use
language before we know all we need to know to use it pro-
ficiently. Fine control of the processes and their components
develop through gross attempts. We accept that in oral development, 'baby-talk' charms us. But in written development
we've been put off by reading miscues and invented spellings.

Literacy can develop best in a classroom that encourages use
and accepts progress without expecting perfection.

If children are reading whole functional materials they will
develop strategies for using cues efficiently in relation to their
value in getting to meaning.

Literacy learners must be treated with respect. Children bring
their language competence and their ability to learn language
to development of literacy. We must rid ourselves of the pathological preoccupation with weakness in learners and take the
positive view of building on strength.

Language also must be treated with respect. It's neither an

inscrutable mystery nor an unyielding strait-jacket on expression. It's a marvelous tool people are universally equipped to develop and use. Like all language learning, developing literacy should be easy and pleasurable. It can be if it isn't fractionated into arbitrarily sequenced abstract skills.

If reading development is, as I believe, a natural extension of oral language development in the context of developing functions, then remedial reading is a matter of refocussing non-productive readers and getting those readers to revalue the reading process and their own reading ability.

Readers who are non-productive tend to be in conflict with themselves. They are victims of over-skill, trying to remember skill strategies they've been taught while they struggle to make sense.

Getting them to abandon the 'next-word syndrome,' the ingrained belief that every word must be accurately named, is a major step. Each failure to get the next word is a defeat to such readers and proof to themselves that they will never succeed. In most cases they have strengths they can draw on, natural comprehension strategies, but they think of them as cheating since they have been developed independent of instruction. Such revaluing takes time, patience, and skilled support from a teacher.

Successful reading teachers, whether developmental or remedial, must be well informed about the processes of reading and learning to read. They must be proficient 'kid-watchers,' able to monitor the progress of pupils and see their strengths and problems in action. They must be able to stimulate pupils to read and write. Such teachers build the self-reliance of learners in their own strategies and their ability to use them flexibly. They build a love of reading and writing.

Now if we examine the features of this whole-language, comprehension-centered approach I've outlined, we can see that it has little compatibility with the know-nothing movement.

Literacy in this competency-based, highly structured, empty-technology is reduced to a tight sequence of arbitrary skills. The teacher becomes a technician, part of a 'delivery system.' The children become passive interchangeable recipients of technological treatments to be pretested, exercised, and post-tested. The classroom is an industrial assembly line. Learning is reduced to gain scores on paper and pencil tests. There is much in the know-nothing movement I must reject.

I must reject the skill sequences as arbitrary and baseless. I must reject the 'mastery learning' programs as unfounded in learning theory, empty of language content, dull and dehumanizing and subject to the ancient law of diminishing returns.
I must reject 'direct teaching' as contradictory to much of what we know of language learning. I must reject legally mandated minimal competency requirements as irrelevant to the realities of literacy achievement and punitive to the students they are supposed to help. I must reject simplistic phonics programs

and other assorted back-to-basics propositions as reactionary, negative and rooted in ignorance and superstition. I must reject the evaluation establishment that dominates the teaching of literacy through tests. I must reject the federal and state guidelines that mandate tests and technology and lock out knowledge and humanity.

In all this, however, I remain an optimist. I believe in truth, wisdom, teachers and learners. I believe that eventually we shall overcome the know-nothing movement and then indeed we will find the strength in knowledge to build the literacy programs we need.

REFERENCES

Anderson, R.C. Rand Spiro, and M.C. Anderson (1977), 'Schemata as Scaffolding for the Representation of Meaning in Connected Discourse,' Technical Report no. 24, Urbana: Center for the Study of Reading, NIE, March.
Gibson, Evelyn, and Harry Levin (1975), 'The Psychology of Reading,' Cambridge, Mass.: MIT Press.
Goodman, K.S. (1967), Reading: A Psycholinguistic Guessing Game, 'Journal of the Reading Specialist,' May.
Gough, Philip B. (1976), One Second of Reading, 'Theoretical Models and Processes of Reading,' 2nd ed., Singer and Ruddell (eds), Newark: IRA.
Halliday, Michael (1973), 'Explorations in the Functions of Language,' New York: Elsevier North-Holland.
Laberge, David, and Jay Samuels (1976), Toward a Theory of Automatic Information Processing in Reading, 'Theoretical Models and Processes of Reading,' 2nd ed., Singer and Ruddell (eds), Newark: IRA.
Meyer, Bonnie (1975), 'The Organization of Prose and its Effect on Memory,' Amsterdam: North Holland Publishing Co.
Pearson, P. David, and Michael Kamil (1978), 'Basic Processes and Instructional Practices in Teaching Reading,' Reading Education Report no. 7, Urbana: Center for the Study of Reading, NIE, December.
Rosenblatt, Louise (1978), 'The Reader, the Text, the Poem,' Carbondale: Southern Illinois University Press.
Rumelhart, D.E. (1977), Toward an Interactive Model of Reading, in 'Attention and Performance VI,' S. Dornic (ed.), Hillsdale, NJ: Erlbaum.

INDEX